Canada's Courts

Peter McCormick

James Lorimer & Company, Publishers
Toronto

James Lorimer & Company Ltd., acknowledge with thanks the support of the Canada Council, the Ontario Arts Council and the Ontario Publishing Centre in the development of writing and publishing in Canada.

Cover illustration: *The Supremes* by Charles Pachter, 1985. Acrylic on Canvas 42 x 60 in. 105 x 150 cm.

Canadian Cataloguing in Publication Data

McCormick, Peter
  Canada's courts

Includes bibliographical references and index.
ISBN 1-55028-435-5 (bound) ISBN 1-55028-434-7 (pbk.)

1. Courts - Canada. 2. Justice, Administration of - Social aspects - Canada. I. Title.

KE8200.M33 1994   347.71'01   C94-930432-8
KF8700.M33 1994

James Lorimer & Company Ltd., Publishers
117 Peter Street, Suite 304
Toronto, ON, Canada
M5V 0M3
www.lorimer.ca

Printed and bound in Canada

To My Duchess

Contents

Acknowledgements

I am grateful to a number of people who helped with this book in many different ways. High on the list would be Ian Greene, now at York University, who has been an excellent colleague and collaborator and an even better friend; he also deserves a lot of the credit for helping me realize the importance of studying courts and judges, as well as being kind enough to take the time to read over and comment on this manuscript. I also want to thank Prof. Alvin Esau of the Manitoba Legal Research Institute and Mr. Owen Snyder of the Alberta Law Foundation, for providing the funding for various parts of my research and also for providing encouragement and feedback on some of my research ideas. I acknowledge the support of the Social Sciences and Humanities Research Council, which funded the data collection on which chapters 9 and 10 are based.

A number of judges have spent time with me over the last few years, correcting my naïve expectations and helping to make my descriptions of the courts more precise. There are too many of them to allow a complete list, but I would particularly like to indicate my gratitude to Madame Justice Mary Hetherington and Justice Roger Kerans of the Alberta Court of Appeal, Justice David Griffiths of the Ontario Court of Appeal, and Judge Donald McCormick (retired) of the Alberta Provincial Court.

A number of students have helped with the data collection for the projects that culminated in this book, their contribution going beyond the mere recording of data to the refining of the research instruments and of the methodology. They include Alex Kotkas, Judi Hoffman, Lisa Lambert, Michelle Lewicki, Mike Pyne, Tim Moro, Scott McCormick, Sherry Steele, and especially Suzanne Maisey, who compiled the Supreme Court database almost singlehanded. I also appreciate the contributions of the students in my Political Science 2240 classes over the last few years, whose spirited arguments have obliged me to rethink a number of things I had taken for granted.

Some of this material has previously appeared elsewhere: chapter 6 is a heavily revised version of an article that appeared in the *Supreme Court Law Review*; chapter 10 builds on work published in the *Canadian Journal of Political Science* and in the *Canadian Journal of Law and Society*; part of chapter 9 appeared in the *Manitoba Law Journal*; and chapter 5 draws on the paper that I wrote (with the help of Justice Griffiths) for the Canadian Appellate Seminar.

I owe a large debt to Jane Fredeman, whose copy-editing has made sense out of some of my more flamboyant prose, and to Diane Young, my editor at Lorimer, whose forceful FAXes reminded me of pending (and expired) deadlines and whose advice on style and format and content generally made this a better book than it would otherwise have been. I even forgive her for not letting me give the book the sub-title "Hang 'Em High, Eh?"

Finally, I would like to thank my family, who endured far more descriptions of actual or pending research projects and far more discussions of chapter formats than they really wanted to, and who were still willing to read through and comment on some of the draft chapters. I hope they will recognize their contributions.

Peter McCormick

Courts, Law, and Society

If this were an orthodox book on the Canadian court system, written from a legal perspective, then it would be easy to begin. I would start by talking about law as the rational structure that both reflects social life and provides a stable basis for it. I would go on to describe lawyers as self-regulating professionals dedicated to serving the legal interests of their clients. I would talk about judges who resolve formal legal disputes by grounding their decisions on proven facts against a background of statutory interpretation and the precedential weight of prior decisions. I would discuss the way judges work to serve justice within a rigorous process designed to defend the best interests of all litigating parties, but particularly those accused of a criminal offence. I would append a brief, formal description of the legal system with its divided and sometimes overlapping jurisdictions. The whole discussion would be heavily freighted with legal terms and technical jargon and would end by expressing concern and regret about the overloads and backlogs generated by the combination of an active government and an increasingly complex and interdependent society. In a phrase, the content of the discussion would be dominated by legal professionals acting in formal ways appropriately described by the technical language — the jargon — of those legal professionals and those who provide their support services.

But this is not an orthodox book, and I want to begin by setting that approach aside — not on the grounds that it is mistaken, much less that it might be deliberately deceptive, but because it is simply not the most appropriate for the purposes that I have in mind. I want to discuss the judicial system from the perspective of the social sciences. As Lewis has written, the social science study of law "differs from writing by practitioners and most academic lawyers in refusing to take for granted law's own account of its significance" (1988, 29). "Law's own account" is far from irrelevant — it is important to know how lawyers and judges think about their work and define their ideals — but it is not complete.

My shift in focus is twofold. First, I want to translate the descriptions of the context and the operations of the judicial system into more everyday language — or at least into the language of the social sciences. This translation will eliminate some of the mystique of the court system, some of the tendency to assume that its operations are so technical and abstruse that only certified experts can criticize or discuss it. I do not seek to demystify because I have any disregard or disrespect for judges or for the legal profession. Rather, I want to help others recognize that any institution, any formal process, has many faces and "belongs" in different senses and to different degrees to many different sets of actors. I want to make the courts comprehensible to non-lawyers.

Second, I want to put the courts in an overtly social context. Judges come from somewhere; they have families and schools and friends and connections. The cases that come before judges similarly have "real-life" causes and consequences. On the other side of the process, the way judges decide cases (both the process and the outcome) has a real social impact, on the immediate parties, of course, but also on a lot of other people who receive cues from the court about how they are expected to behave and how judges will react if they do not. The judicial process is not self-contained; it is embedded in a social and political reality with which it constantly interacts. Judges are not ignorant of this fact, but the whole point of the legal process is to work through a process of deliberate abstraction that creates considerable distance from this reality; that this distance is functionally important does not mean that it is optimal or even useful for a broader understanding of the courts. The judicial mountain has many sides, and the legal professional's is only one of them.

The reason for studying the courts and for thinking that a broader public awareness of them is necessary is quite simply that the courts are an important part of the way that public and private affairs are handled in Canada. At a time when a Charter of Rights-wielding Supreme Court appears regularly on the front pages of our newspapers, this comment is not particularly radical. Yet, it is a mistake to assume that the only courts that have an impact on Canadian society are the multi-judge panels of appeal courts in general and/or the Supreme Court in particular that sit at the apex of the judicial pyramid. Quite the contrary: most people have no experience with the judicial process except through the lower trial courts, and, therefore, the cumulative impact of the decisions made in them is very great. By contrast, appeal rates are very low — hard figures are difficult to come by, but notionally we are probably safe in assuming that fewer than 1 per cent of the decisions of any court are appealed to the next and "higher" court in the judicial hierarchy. Because of the way judges make and justify their decisions, the cases in higher courts are normally presumed to have an influence that can extend far beyond the immediate case, but in practice the process is much more complex than it appears to be at first glance.

It is also a mistake to think that judicial influence began with the Charter or that it is only since 1982 that enquiring into the nature of this influence has become appropriate. Instead, we should recognize that judges have always had power, have always affected our society by the decisions they make (and by the way they decide *what* to decide and *how* to decide). The Charter has simply made a longstanding reality more immediately visible and directed us belatedly to an assessment of the implications of judicial power. Whether its use is intentional or incidental, whether the purposes that direct it are benign or indifferent, whether it is genuinely impartial or masks a deeper set of influences that disadvantage some sets of actors that appear before it, the power of judges necessarily has a significant effect on the Canadian political and legal process as it is experienced by the "person on the street." This book is about the framework within which that influence can be understood and discussed.

In rather loose terms, we can think about power as the joint product of impact and discretion. *Impact* — the extent to which an action or circumstance intrudes upon the lives of others and obliges them to take a particular course of action they would not otherwise have taken — is the most obvious dimension, but it is not sufficient in itself. The second dimension, *discretion*, is the extent to which the actor who had the impact on the lives of others had any choice, any alternative that would have had a different impact. The impact of the courts is obvious to anyone who has ever been sued or accused of an offence; the discretion judges exercise individually and collectively is neither as extensive as it sometimes looks when we stand in front of them nor as restricted as they suggest in their own formal descriptions of what they do, and a good part of this book will be spent in trying to come to terms with what has been described as "the unacknowledged side of law" (Wexler 1975). The combination of the two is judicial power, and as Posner (1990, 21) points out, this idea "is, no matter how fancied up, a source of unease to the legal profession."

The power of the courts may seem remote from most of us, because most Canadians seldom or never have direct contact with the courts and the judicial power that operates within them. However, we all live in the shadow of that power, and we structure our calculations of the range of possible behaviours available to us, and the probable behaviour of those who associate with us, in the light of our understanding (accurate or inaccurate) of what would happen if our interactions came under judicial scrutiny. "The law is real, but it is also a figment of our imaginations. Like all fundamental social institutions it casts a shadow of popular belief that may ultimately be more significant, albeit more difficult to comprehend than the authorities, rules and penalties that we ordinarily associate with law. What we believe reflects our values; it also colors our perceptions" (Scheingold 1974, 3). Courts and judges have an impact upon our lives, not just because of what they really do but also because of how we believe they operate.

Basic Elements of the Western Conception of Law

Any discussion of the legal and judicial system must first make clear that lawyers — and also judges, who in our system are drawn from the ranks of lawyers — "have a distinct way of thinking, which nonlawyers do not share" (Abel and Lewis 1988, 506). This observation may sound exaggerated, either as grandiloquent praise of legal intellect or as a casual cheap shot against an entire profession, but it is entirely serious. The legal process in modern Western nations is grounded upon a distinctive way of thinking about the world and of reaching decisions about things that are in it. Much of the point of legal training (more so than for any of the other professions) is to instil this cognitive and logical mode; recruitment (that is, the fact that "only people of a certain mind-set enter legal careers" [Friedman 1988, 11]) and the social situations in which lawyers and judges work are also contributing factors. This special way of thinking is a critically important part of the way that the legal process works. As Vilhelm Aubert (1983, 78) pithily observes, "The reason why law can answer all questions, albeit in a specific and restricted way, is that it creates its own reality. It does not permit any problems to be legitimately raised other than those it can answer. All other questions are legally irrelevant, even if lawyers have to admit that they are far from insignificant."

We can identify at least four major elements of the way that our legal system orients itself toward the rules. The first is *abstraction*. In the words of Ethan Katsch (1989, 248):

> One of the secrets of the legal profession is the knowledge that law is less concerned with the real world we live in than with another world, a world that bears some similarity to our real world but also differs in substantial ways. The power of the law is to place into this legal world entities that are intangible and that do not exist in our world. The process of law requires that before law can affect the real life of any person, it is necessary to determine how the law would apply in the special abstract world that exists only in the minds of lawyers and the books of law.

To put the point in different terms: the essence of law is not *command*, but *definition* — the creation of legal categories to which specific consequences are attached. The way that lawyers argue, and that courts work their way toward a decision, is to take a specific set of individuals with a dispute arising out of a specific and allegedly factual situation and to argue about the appropriate category or categories to which the individuals and the situation should be assimilated. This assimilation accomplished, there is a specific set of legally mandated consequences that follow: if the will is valid, then the money goes to Ms. X; if the actions are correctly described as negligent, then Mr. Y is liable for damages; if the taking of the property constitutes theft, then Mr. Z will receive one of a specified range of punishments; and so on. The process has three stages: *first*, we translate the specific case into the appropriate general categories; *then* we read out the formal consequences attached to that category; *finally*, we translate those consequences back into the specific form that applies to the immediate case.

This translation process requires a progressive stripping away of idiosyncratic detail to transform the situation into one that can be described in increasingly abstract and general terms. As Scheingold points out, "the key to understanding is, of course, simplification. The legal approach simplifies complex situations by stripping away all those elements which do not pertain." At its best, this stripping away of irrelevant detail to reveal the basic elements of the dispute is the proudest achievement of our legal order: it does not matter whether the person's skin is black or white or whatever, if they are male or female, if they are popular leaders of the community or shunned outsiders; the only concern is how the facts direct their assimilation to a particular legal category. This legal logic defines the ideal that actual processes may or may not approximate.

However, there are ironic overtones to this process. As Abel and Lewis say (1988, 492), "Although laypeople perceive the law as incredibly complex — a perception lawyers encourage — the translation of lived experience into legal language often is a process of simplification." We live in an age suffering from what is often called an "information explosion" and frequently find that too much information is just as large an impediment to effective decision-making as too little. We can therefore appreciate the tactic that the courts have long taken to avoid this problem — the rigorous, even ruthless, control of the amount and type of information that will be accepted as relevant and allowed to affect the outcome. Exaggerated television programs that spin off the drama of the courtroom often catch (but never explain) this phenomenon; a witness will make a common-sense observation that we could all see ourselves making in the same circumstance, only to have the lawyer object and the judge sternly warn the witness to avoid speculation.

This rigorous pruning of irrelevant detail is the great methodological achievement of Western legal systems. It also represents a blind side of potentially overwhelming dimensions because it makes lawyers and judges the slaves of whatever the previously defined legal categories happen to be. If the categories are benign, logical, and principled, then this is asset rather than liability. However, if those categories are morally objectionable (for example, Nazi Germany's Nuremberg decrees singling out the Jews or South Africa's apartheid laws organized around skin colour), then the rigorous logic of the legal process is the servant, not the opponent, of the morally objectionable principles embedded in the law. There is no easy solution to this problem — no convenient middle ground between, on the one hand, judges as the banal instrument of evil and, on the other, judges as super-legislators imposing their own values on society — although classic movies, such as *Judgment at Nuremberg*, have explored some of its dimensions.

The second feature of the legal mind-set is the focus on general *rules*. "The dislike of vague generalities, the preference for case-by-case treatment of all social issues, the structuring of all possible human relations into the form of claims and counterclaims under established rules, and the belief that the rules are 'there' — these combine to make up legalism as a social outlook" (Shklar 1986, 10). This narrowness is the flip side of the stress on abstracted generalization; your case is turned into an example of a broader category precisely so that it can be dealt with in exactly the same way as other examples of the same category — that is, so that it can be resolved in terms of a rule. But just as the process of abstraction strips away the human and idiosyncratic elements from the situation to be resolved, so the general rule precludes a response uniquely fashioned to respond to the specific features of the parties; it guarantees that some cases will be dealt with more generously, and some more harshly, than would be the case if every situation were dealt with from first principles. In our system, we do not seek "to make the punishment fit the crime" but rather to make it fit the rule, which is not at all the same thing and not always intuitively satisfying.

Shklar's final point, about the "given" nature of rules, is more opaque, but it is extremely important; both the objective existence of rules as the way to resolve disputes and the specific contents of those rules are built into the legal mind-set. Friedman (1988, 19) believes that this attitude represents an attempt "to cleanse the image of law from the dirty business of politics ... to blur the idea that law is connected to a particular social and economic structure." However, it is always important to remember that the interpretation and application of general rules can never be truly mechanical operations but always presuppose a degree of discretion and creativity on the part of the person who does the interpreting and applying. Indeed, the quest for mechanical precision is both self-defeating and expensive. As Neely (1983, 92) sharply notes, "The more we attempt to protect society from the vagaries of the idiot judge, the less discretion there is for the imaginative, creative and intelligent judge."

The third element of the legal orientation is its stress on arguments from *analogy* as a way of filling the gaps between existing rules.

Stare decisis refers to adjudicating particular cases by means of precedent, that is, by trying to show an analogy with previously decided cases. The motivation for doing so is to insure that the same principles used to resolve prior cases are also applied to a current case. Of course, new cases are never exactly the same as prior ones ... Two lawyers representing opposite sides of a dispute may thus cite two different lines of precedent. A judge then evaluates the two proposed lines of analogy to arrive at a final decision. (Heiner 1986, 228)

The predilection for arguments from analogy allows the legal system the flexibility to accommodate unforeseen circumstances and new development and contributes to consistency in the development of new rules. However, for all its attractiveness, the power of analogy as a mode of argument is still suspect. If you let me pick all the examples, I can win any argument, as I continually caution my students. Analogy provides a focused spotlight not a broad overview; for example, Biblical parables provide splendid examples of the use of analogy, but try retelling the story of the prodigal son from the point of view of his loyal brother.

The fourth characteristic of the legal system is an emphasis on *procedure*. "The law as an enterprise is characterized by a distinctive way of doing things and, in particular, by a preoccupation with procedure" (Scheingold 1974, 45). This emphasis is implied in the familiar image of justice, the woman with the scales and the blindfold; it is critical that the image is "Justitia blindfolded" not "Justitia blind" because the blindfold suggests an act of choice, of deliberate self-restraint. "Procedure is the blindfold of justice" (Curtis and Resnik 1987, 1728).

There are, of course, real advantages to the process. When we implicitly rejected alternative approaches by developing the Western style of justice, we were certainly not getting nothing for something. The legal project is a powerful mechanism for guiding and framing choices and decision-making. As Scheingold observes:

> Like all world views, the legal paradigm is basically a focusing device. Rather like a complex of roads through the wilderness, it provides both guidance at a particular point along the way and a sense of confidence and understanding about the entire area. But like a road map the law game simplifies as it explains. The sense of mastery conveyed by the paradigm is at least partially an illusion, built as much on what is excluded from the analysis as upon the rigor and logic of the method. (1974, 160)

But the very strengths of our legal system are, in a necessarily imperfect world, at the same time its weakness; legal process is a two-edged sword, and so is each of its elements.

The process of abstraction often means that we strip away the human overtones and the social context that is a part of what goes on around us. To translate a concrete situation into its legal generalities is to turn technicolour into monochrome and sometimes to make the outcome unrecognizable and emotionally unsatisfying. "The legal process does not ask: What are all the rights and wrongs of this situation — on both sides? Rather it asks: Is John Doe guilty as charged? John Doe may be utterly depraved — may be shown to have treated Richard Roe abominably — but if he cannot be shown to have violated the rule as charged, he (as far as the legal process is concerned) goes as free as if he were a saint" (Fallers 1969, 13).

The use of rules as a guide to behaviour is so pervasive that it appears unproblematic. However, by definition, rules provide a general course of action that is the optimal outcome most of the time but the suboptimal outcome some of the time. The advantage of rules is that they simplify the job of the decision-maker by precluding the necessity of responding to the idiosyncratic details of the particular case, and to say the rule is a good one is to say that usually it yields a fair result even in the light of those details. But "usually" is not "always," and sometimes the general rule results in the sort of intuitively unsatisfactory outcome that journalists love because it sells newspapers. It is a necessary characteristic of operating under a system of general rules that "although in no case can we make a decision that is better than optimal for that case taken in isolation, in some cases we will make decisions that are worse than optimal for that case taken in isolation" (Schauer 1987, 590). Therefore, the Western notion of justice is recurrently subject to criticism on the basis of comparisons with systems that focus more directly and sympathetically on the immediate case in its full human detail, such as the "*khadi*" justice of traditional Islam (see e.g., Shapiro 1981, ch. 5) or the more consensual and persuasive processes of the aboriginal peoples (see e.g., Littlebear 1991, Monture 1991). The point is not that these alternative systems are on all counts preferable, or that they would be easily implemented in a complex society, or that they do not lend themselves to similar "worst case" critiques, but simply that the approaches that characterize Western law have their inherent limitations.

The focus on analogy presents certain problems. Because any given unusual situation can be seen as analogous to several different sets of rules and because plausible arguments can be made to support each and every alternative, arguments from analogy can only be illustrative, never conclusive. We know only that before a certain judge, as argued by a specific set of lawyers, and against the background of a specific factual situation that may or may not be typical or representative of a larger social universe, a particular argument from analogy was more persuasive; but this description itself raises the possibility that before a different judge, or with different lawyers, or with a different factual situation (a less attractive defendant or a more pitiable victim), some other outcome might have prevailed. This is a fundamental difference between the legal method and that of the social sciences: in the end, law rests on the tentativeness of persuasive analogy, not on the finality of conclusive refutation (see e.g., Haney 1980, passim).

The problems that flow from a heavy focus on procedure are pervasive: first, the dragging delays that dog the judicial process; second, the heavy consequences that follow from procedural error or omission; and, third, the incentives for parties to take advantage of the opportunities for delay or error. Every time an apparently guilty party gets off on a technicality, we pay the price for a process-based system. But any shift away from procedural to substantive justice undermines the legal profession (and its judicial counterpart) and its claims to neutral expertise in the service of its clients (Szelenyi and Martin 1987, passim). The essence of our legal system is its focus on technicalities; it cannot dodge the consequences without ceasing to be itself.

The purpose of the social scientific study of law is to see the legal system "warts and all." This perspective requires a different vocabulary and a different frame of reference from those used by the legal professionals, and it means treating as problematic or controversial many things the legal framework tends to take as givens, as premises to be assumed rather than propositions to be proven.

For example, it is characteristic of legal discourse to assume that there is a single correct answer that is achieved by the final disposition of the highest court whose intervention has been invoked; any different perspectives suggested by the contending lawyers or by lower courts whose decisions have been reversed upon appeal are brushed aside as at best speculation or at worst error. Our judicial system builds upon the adversary system, which involves two contending parties trying to persuade the Court to accept their description and categorization of the contentious events. It seems to follow that the normal outcome is success ("victory") for one side and failure ("defeat") for the other. I do not believe the successful party does something conceptually akin to guessing the content of a sealed envelope; rather, I think we should take "persuasion" at its face value and think of lawyers and judges as shaping, not simply discovering, the best and most appropriate outcome.

The best response to the assumption that objectively correct answers exist is demonstrated by a story that Justice Roger Kerans of the Alberta Court of Appeal likes to tell in this context. The story is about an argument between three baseball umpires. The first solemnly declares, "I calls 'em like I sees 'em"; the second vigorously disagrees, insisting, "I calls 'em like they was"; and the third candidly shifts the ground by announcing, "They ain't nothin' until I calls 'em." The point is that there is something to all three views but that we would be foolish to try to deny the third.

Similarly, from the legal point of view any case can fairly be presented as a quest for justice, a consideration of such pre-emptive importance that it is fully appropriate to deploy the resources that will allow it to be pursued as far up the judicial hierarchy as either party thinks necessary. When I joined several colleagues to do a study of the Ontario Court of Appeal and we wondered whether the hundreds of sentence appeals every year were not contributing to the growing backlog of that court's caseload (Baar et al. 1992), a lawyer assessor took violent exception. His argument was that every person convicted of a crime but having doubts about the appropriateness of the sentence was fully entitled to ask a higher court to review it, and the success rate for appeals demonstrated that such concerns were frequently justified. Our position was, and is, that it is expensive and inefficient to have a panel of three appeal court judges reading the files and listening to oral arguments on whether a sentence should be reduced by a few weeks when these same resources could be turned to answering other appeals whose decisions would resolve broader legal issues and guide the outcome of future trials. More generally, since the judicial system is "a realm in which exalted symbols are wedded to limited resources" (Galanter 1985, 544), we must look for the appropriate balance between high-sounding slogans and gritty budget-conscious realities.

Which point of view is correct? I believe that they both are. Like the story of the blind men arguing over the true nature of the elephant, these points of view represent different perspectives on a single complex reality. To switch metaphors, we are looking at different sides of the same mountain and not really suggesting that either view, either language, either set of concepts is exclusive and perfect for all purposes.

In general, I see our legal and judicial system as a serious attempt, administered in the main by conscientious individuals, to deal with intractable problems. My gentle criticism may well annoy both serious radicals, who will see it as legitimizing a flawed and imperfect system, and true believers, who will see it as using unfair conceptual models to condemn the system for not doing things it could not hope to do. More generally, this book is simply a part of a larger process whereby the law becomes more accessible and familiar to wider circles of the public. In the process, it loses its remote and transcendent character and "its ability to bedazzle us with symbols of legitimacy and with Potemkin Villages of enforcement" (Galanter 1985, 551). Some worry that law will falter without its mystique; this book is based on the assumption that common sense and realism contain their own antidote and that the legitimacy of the courts rests on foundations much stronger than the black robes and the Latin phrases and the bewildering technicalities. The everyday knowledge of law is a first step to an everyday law explicitly and consciously connected to the everyday world it serves.

The Courts and the Public

The social importance of the courts is often simply assumed, considered so obvious that neither elaboration or justification is required. However, both the nature of this importance and the way it is experienced and perceived by the general public must be examined more closely because the judicial system is obviously not important in quite the same way as the postal system or the telephone system or the road system. That is, it is not something that most people personally and directly use every day as part of the normal routine of their lives. At any time, only a minority of Canadians will be directly involved in a criminal or civil court action as litigants or witnesses. A few more will take advice from a lawyer on the action or behaviour they should follow to accomplish their purposes or the action or behaviour they should avoid to stay out of trouble with the law. Most people will do neither. For them, the influence of the courts is more indirect, filtered through the selective, simplified, and possibly sensationalized reports in the news media about crimes, arrests, trials, and lawsuits and through the anecdotal penetration of these events into conversations with those around them.

Consuming Judicial Services: Criminal Cases
The most obvious and certainly the most newsworthy judicial activities involve the resolution of criminal cases. Without question, a large number of criminal offences are committed in our society: about three million per year (1989 figures), or more than one for every ten Canadians. About one-twelfth of these — a quarter of a million in 1989 — are violent crimes (*Canada Year Book 1992*). It is also true that both the total numbers of crimes and the crime rates per 100,000 of population generally seem to be increasing, although these are not "hard" figures and are necessarily subject to differences in perception by victims, differences in readiness to contact police, and differences in police reporting practices. Generally, the crime

rate (overall, and for property and violent crimes separately) rises as
one moves from east to west, the major exception being unusually
high rates for armed robbery in Quebec. However, such conclusions
must be made carefully because the same factors that make it difficult
to compare crime rates from one time period to another also make it
difficult to compare communities and regions (Griffiths and Verdun-
Jones 1989, 17). Curiously, Canadian crime rates generally display
more similarity to those of France than to either the United States or
Great Britain (Brantingham and Brantingham 1984, 192).

Table 2.1:

Criminal Offences in Canada, 1989

Type of Offence	Number
Federal Statute Offences:	
Violent Offences	248,992
Property Offences	1,445,748
Other Criminal Offences	736,688
Total Criminal Code Offences	2,431,428
Other Federal Statute Offences	108,215
Provincial Statute Offences	361,467
Municipal Bylaws	98,973
TOTAL OFFENCES:	3,000,123

Source: *Canada Year Book 1992*

The number of criminal cases that reach the courts is smaller,
although not as much so as one might expect. In 1979, for example,
the criminal division of the British Columbia provincial court handled a total of 114,354 cases, including a small number of preliminary hearings for trials in higher courts (Griffiths, Klein, and
Verdun-Jones 1980, 147). If we think of British Columbia as having
roughly one-eighth of the population of Canada, this implies a national total of roughly one million cases, although local practices
vary to such an extent that extrapolations have to be made cautiously
and the numbers must be treated as indicative rather than definitive.
It is a mistake, however, to assume that this lower number necessarily
represents police inefficiency or means that the vast majority of
crimes and criminals go unpunished. Such a conclusion "presumes

that each crime is committed by a separate criminal, that every report of a crime is valid, and that there is no overlap or duplication in crimes reported by police. On each of these points, evidence suggests the contrary" (Brannigan 1984, 94). The first point is the most important: many criminals are responsible for more than one crime, although they may not be called to account for each and every one of them.

The normal outcome of a criminal proceeding is prosecutorial success in the form either of a guilty plea (50 to 70 per cent of all cases) that may or may not have been preceded by explicit bargaining or of a judicial finding after a trial (75 per cent or more of all cases that go to trial). Those raised on a steady diet of the exploits of television lawyers might find those numbers startling, but they reflect the reality of the criminal justice system, which involves the routine processing of tens of thousands of minor offences occasionally interrupted by lengthy trials for major offences. Like the Mounties of movie lore, Crown prosecutors usually get their man — or, much more rarely, their woman. The low proportion of women among criminals and especially among the perpetrators of major crimes may seem obvious, but is in fact a relatively modern development. It was only in the nineteenth century that the female share of indictments for major offences fell to the current level (Feeley and Little 1991).

Most admissions or findings of guilt do not result in terms in provincial jails or federal penitentiaries. Although Canada sentences a higher proportion of offenders to jail than any other comparable country except the United States and Switzerland, the most common sentence is a fine. Such penalties are assessed in more than 90 per cent of summary offences (minor crimes), and in one-third of the indictable offences (major crimes) that make up about one-thirtieth of the criminal caseload (Griffiths, Klein, and Verdun-Jones 1984, 173). Failure to pay a fine may itself result in serving time, although this is not automatic and calls for judicial investigation of the reasons for nonpayment. Only about 1.5 per cent of all fines result in imprisonment, typically brief, for nonpayment (Griffiths and Verdun-Jones 1989, 289). In 1988-89, a total of 120,103 persons received custodial sentences, more than 95 per cent of them to provincial correctional institutions where the median term was 30 days (*Canada Year Book 1992*). On any given date, the total number of offenders in custody is closer to 80,000. Clearly, neither criminals nor imprisoned offenders constitute a random cross-section of the general population. They tend to be young (about 15 years younger than the average Canadian adult), to be male (about 95 per cent), and to be disproportionately drawn from the ranks of ethnic minorities or other socially marginalized groups. In particular, the aboriginal peoples in many provinces make up a proportion of the prison population that is eight to ten times larger than their share of the provincial population.

Logically, given that some criminals commit many offences, there is a statistically better chance that any given Canadian will be a victim rather than a perpetrator of a crime. However, it is still the case that only a minority of Canadians are touched by crime in any direct way and even fewer by violent crime. A 1985 study, for example, found that only one-seventh of respondents in Montreal, Toronto, and Winnipeg said that they or another person in their household had within the past year been the victim of a crime, with property crimes — usually theft, breaking and entering, vandalism, or trespassing — outnumbering violent crimes by more than fifty to one. This compares with the 3 per cent of respondents who indicated that they had been charged with some offence other than a minor traffic infraction during the previous year. A much larger proportion — more than three-quarters — indicated that they were concerned about falling victim to crime.

One reason for this low number is quite simple: just as three million crimes does not mean three million different criminals, neither does it mean three million different victims. Both sides of the relationship are overrepresented by some groups and underrepresented by others, and the same type of people tend to be overrepresented as both victims and perpetrators — young males who are members of ethnic minorities or otherwise disadvantaged groups. At first glance it seems curious that the wealthier groups should not be the most frequent victims of (for example) property crimes at least, but the explanation is very simple — crime tends to occur where the criminals are, which means that their victims tend, by and large, to be very much like themselves.

Civil Cases

The caseload for civil cases is comparable although — based on extrapolations from limited data — possibly slightly lower than the criminal caseload. This implies a similar breadth of direct impact for the civil courts: just as criminal cases usually involve a perpetrator and a victim, so civil cases involve a plaintiff and a defendant, either of which may be either an individual (a "natural person") or a company (a "legal" or "artificial" person). Moores (1985, 80) found that

13.0 per cent of respondents had at any time in their life been in a courtroom because of involvement in a civil case, compared with 3.3 per cent who had ever been present in court because they were the accused person in a criminal case. (The number jumps significantly if one includes minor traffic offences.) Just as much of the criminal caseload is concentrated at the lower end, in minor crimes rapidly processed by provincial court judges, so much of the civil caseload consists of disputes over relatively small points or relatively small amounts of money rapidly processed by small claims courts — although, of course, "small" is a relative term, and any specific case may well carry considerable significance for either or both of the parties.

As Russell (1985, 237) has suggested, designing the appropriate mode of adjudication for disputes involving small amounts of money is "one of the most difficult challenges confronting contemporary justice systems," and the style and the calibre of the response varies from one side of the country to another. This level of courts is caught in something of a double squeeze. On the one hand, the monetary jurisdiction of small claims courts is generally rising much faster than the rate of inflation (in Quebec, it is now $15,000), which means that these courts are handling significant legal cases with the formal representation this involves. On the other hand, in many cases the amount at stake is so small that it is hardly worth retaining a lawyer (and some provinces encourage this absence of lawyers by making no allowance for the winning party to recover any legal expenses). At its best, such a tendency offers more accessible justice although it enormously complicates the role of the judge, who must explain the law to both parties, give legal advice to both parties, and reach a judicial decision as well — a blending of responsibilities that cannot easily be optimized (Axworthy 1978). At its worst, "it may be that in many jurisdictions in Canada we have the worst of all possible worlds: small claims judges trying to adhere to the adversary system without professional adversaries" (Russell 1985, 242). And encouraging the exclusion of lawyers carries its own disadvantages. Whatever the emotional attractiveness of Shakespeare's famous advice ("The first thing we do, let's kill all the lawyers"), for any save the most routine of situations legal representation helps identify the opportunities and to avoid the pitfalls.

Small claims courts tend to accomplish a variety of functions, the most important of which is often that of a collection agency. One of the most common types of action involves a corporate entity suing a natural person for nonpayment of some obligation (Galanter 1975). Companies are the plaintiff — initiate the legal action — more often than individuals; they usually take action against individuals; and they tend to be successful more often than individuals, although Vidmar (1984, 545) points out that this success rate is significantly lower if we exclude cases where the defendant simply fails to appear to present a case and that these successes are often partial rather than total. He therefore questions criticisms of the court "as anti-defendant, anti-consumer, anti-little guy" and argues that they perform in a rather more even-handed and balanced ways than these accusations suggest.

Mention should also be made of another type of court — namely, family court — which has a much smaller caseload than the ordinary criminal and civil courts but whose impact is arguably out of all proportion to those numbers. It is symptomatic of the impact of modern society on the traditional family that very large numbers of people should be involved in the business of family court. Moores (1985, 81) found that almost 20 per cent of respondents had been in a courtroom as party, witness, or spectator at least once in their lives because of divorce or separation or custody matters. Family court is a court unlike any other; the demands on its personnel are great. If criminal division judges suffer burnout because of the sheer volume of cases and small claims judges because of the mind-numbing repetitiveness of the caseload, the problem with family court judges is the intense emotional overload.

Nevertheless, the general point remains. In any given period, only a minority of Canadians have any direct contact with the courts. Moore found (1985, 53) "the vast majority of respondents indicated they had a very limited experience of courts and court procedures. Those who had been in court had attended either as a spectator or a witness, or because they had been charged with a traffic offence." It follows that for most Canadians the impact of the law is more indirect, mediated through a variety of sources.

Consulting Lawyers

It is also possible to get some idea of another relevant population, namely those who have consulted lawyers. This population and the population directly involved in trials is partially overlapping for two reasons. The first is that not all persons accused of criminal offences are represented by lawyers. Most but not all persons accused of indictable offences are represented by counsel, and some but by no means all persons accused of summary conviction offences or offences against provincial statutes are represented. Similarly, in civil cases, most people who bring action in small claims court are unrepresented. Therefore, on the one side, many people who appear in court do so without the benefit of legal representation and advice, either because they cannot afford it or because the matter is not serious enough to justify the expenditure.

On the other hand, many people who visit lawyers for advice do so without any direct anticipation of a court appearance. Only a small percentage of the people who flow through the offices of Canada's lawyers are asking questions that are directly related to trials, actual or anticipated. Conversely, only a fraction of the average lawyer's working day — possibly one-sixth — is spent preparing for or taking part in criminal or civil trials or appeals, and many lawyers never appear in a courtroom on a regular basis (Stager and Arthurs 1990, 57).

Nonetheless, lawyers must be considered as a critically important part of the process whereby the courts have an impact on the general public. As a general principle, law "usually works not by exercise of force but by information transfer, by communication of what's expected, what forbidden, what allowable, what are the consequences of acting in certain ways" (Galanter 1985, 545). Lawyers are an important part of this transfer of information; what people are often seeking from their lawyers is advice about how best to arrange their affairs to render them "court-proof." "In a vast number of instances the application of law is, so to speak, self-administered — people regulate their conduct (and judge the conduct of others) on the basis of their knowledge about legal standards, possibilities and constraints" (Galanter 1985, 545). But this knowledge is second hand, partly transmitted by the legal profession. For one set of purposes, what many Canadians know about courts and their future actions is what lawyers have told them, and they have no independent way of verifying this information.

Of the adults involved in a three-city survey in 1985, just over two-thirds (67.4 per cent) had ever used a lawyer's services; more than five of every seven of these indicated that they had consulted a lawyer only once or twice (Moore 1985, 78). The most common reason for seeing a lawyer is property transactions (39.6 per cent) and drafting a will (21.6 per cent); in Quebec, the drafting of a marriage contract is an even more frequent motive (43.8 per cent of respondents). Business or employment problems, accidents involving property damage and family matters accounted for about 10 per cent of respondents. Only 2.8 per cent were seeking advice on criminal charges; another 7.3 per cent were seeing advice for traffic offences. This breakdown of reasons for consulting lawyers suggests the reason why only a minority of Canada's 40,000 or so practising lawyers are criminal lawyers and why the work of many lawyers seldom or never involves appearing in court (Stager and Arthurs 1990).

Generally, the respondents in the three-city study were well satisfied with the services they had received from their lawyers, and most felt that the fee was reasonable (Moore 1985, 79). Indeed, those individuals who used lawyers more frequently had a higher opinion of them, while non-users were more critical in their assessments. However, both groups felt that lawyers worked harder for richer clients, that people have to use lawyers more often than is really necessary, and that lawyers are more concerned with making money than with helping their clients. This same pattern — general satisfaction in personal dealings with lawyers combined with low or ambivalent feelings about the profession as a whole — emerges in U.S. studies as well (e.g., Sarat 1977).

Public Opinion about the Courts

Canadians exhibit the same ambivalence about their courts. By and large, Canadians think that their judges are capable and conscientious and that they are appointed as much or more on the basis of merit as on political considerations (Moore 1985, 54). In a similar vein, a 1992 Gallup poll revealed that half again as many Canadians have "quite a lot" or "some" confidence in the Supreme Court as in their provincial or federal government. Admittedly, it would probably be unrealistic to project the same level of support of the lower levels of the court system, but the figures suggest a strong degree of public confidence in the courts and the judges and a general support for the role that they play.

At the same time, a majority of the participants in the three-city survey, and an overwhelming majority of the respondents to the 1992 Gallup poll, thought that criminal sentences should be tougher than they are now, and they blamed the courts for not dealing harshly enough with criminals. General satisfaction with the judges and general confidence in the court system is not incompatible with serious reservations about the general course of outcome.

But the concerns go deeper. Most people agreed that a person could arrange almost anything in court if he had enough money, that individuals do not have a chance against big business, that taking someone to court is too expensive for most people, that the courts take far too long to deal with cases, and that the system would work better without the stilted formalities and strict procedure (Moore 1985, 81). These are very pointed complaints. "Respondents had serious questions about the efficacy of the courts. They believed that expense and time rule out access to the system for a large number of individuals, and although believing that the courts are administered by competent people, many viewed them as dispensing a questionable brand of justice, one seemingly influenced by money and power" (Moore 1985, 58). Most see the court process (either the system itself, or the judges within it, or both) as being biased against low-income Canadians and in favour of wealthy Canadians (Gallup 1992), a perception that varies remarkably little from one region to another and survives age, education, and class controls. In the same survey, a clear majority thought the system was biased against women who are the victims of sexual assault, and just short of a majority thought it was biased against Canada's native peoples.

These are rather serious reservations for a broad cross-section of Canadians to have about their court system in general — it is slow, expensive, and biased — and about the way that the system affects specific groups within the population. Such concerns have been explored and generally confirmed by public enquiries in Alberta and Manitoba examining the impact of the justice system on native peoples and by former Supreme Court justice Bertha Wilson's massive 1992 report to the Canadian Bar Association on discrimination against women within the law schools, the legal profession, and the ranks of the judiciary.

It is intriguing and important, however, that the general confidence of Canadians in their courts survives these realistic appreciations of the problems in the courts. Procedural and structural difficulties may call for changes in the way that the courts do things, but in the general patterns of public opinion, they do not call for a dismantling of the courts or for a transfer to other forums of much of what the courts do. For the Canadian public, the courts are flawed but redeemable, imperfect but useful.

Canada's Court System

In describing the Canadian court system, it is easy to fall into technical detail and thereby simply reinforce the confusion the average citizen feels about the maze of courts with bewildering names. But the modern Canadian court system can be built up logically from a few basic principles, something that is increasingly appropriate because the court system is being consolidated. The first four of the five principles listed below establish the basic hierarchy of the Canadian courts and provide an outline for the rest of this chapter. The last principle modifies the hierarchy for a range of more specialized concerns and is included here to supply background and context.

The basic building principles are:

First: Identify the more routine cases and those that involve less serious possible outcomes and assign them to an accessible high-volume, low-delay court, preferably one that sits in many different centres.

Second: Assign the less routine and more serious cases to a lower-volume court that can devote more time and more focused attention to each individual case.

Third: Establish a court of appeal to correct simple errors and to promote uniformity in the application of the law within each province.

Fourth: Establish a "general court of appeal" to promote uniformity in the application of law within the country as a whole and to provide judicial leadership.

Fifth: Create a system of federal courts for cases directly involving the federal government as a party or raising issues concerning the administrative law applied by federal departments.

One striking feature of these principles is how little they reflect any federal dimension. In the United States, there are two parallel court systems, each with a full repertoire of trial and appeal courts. State courts deal with matters of state law, and federal courts (such

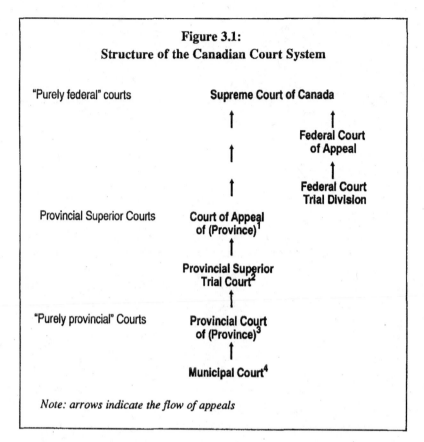

Figure 3.1:
Structure of the Canadian Court System

"Purely federal" courts

Supreme Court of Canada

Federal Court
of Appeal

Federal Court
Trial Division

Provincial Superior Courts

Court of Appeal
of (Province)[1]

Provincial Superior
Trial Court[2]

"Purely provincial" Courts

Provincial Court
of (Province)[3]

Municipal Court[4]

Note: arrows indicate the flow of appeals

as the district courts or the U.S. courts of appeal) deal with matters of national law. Cases begin and end within one or the other of these systems and cross from state to federal court jurisdiction only if they raise a significant constitutional issue. By contrast, the Canadian system is a single pyramid (possibly best conceptualized with a large lump on one smooth side representing the federal courts), with pronounced provincial input at the lowest levels. That input diminishes as we move up the hierarchy and disappears altogether for the Supreme Court at the apex. This single pyramid deals with all provincial laws and almost all federal laws, and any case may rise to any appropriate level.

In outline, these are the basic principles of the Canadian court system. What remains is to put some flesh on the bones in terms of the specific courts and personnel and procedures that make the basic logic operational.

First Principle: The Purely Provincial Courts

The court system distinguishes "major" from "minor" cases by the complexity of the issues raised and the seriousness of the possible outcome (in objective rather than subjective terms). Minor cases are referred to trial courts that have enough judges to deal with the enormous volume of such cases. To serve public needs, these courts are geographically dispersed, so that as many parties as possible will find the relevant court close at hand. This is the provincial court, typically divided into functional divisions (criminal division, civil or small claims division,[5] youth and family division — the first named is the workhorse with most of the caseload). Its judges are appointed and paid by the various provincial governments to serve in courts established and maintained by the province. Although I will discuss the issues of judicial appointment in general, and the implications of the Canadian process in particular, in more detail in a later chapter, it is important to point out that provincial appointment tends to ensure a high degree of responsiveness to local issues and priorities in the staffing and procedures of the courts.

This court used to be called "magistrate's court" in most provinces, but the new terminology is more than a new label for an ongoing reality. It reflects the extensive reforms in the judicial system since the 1960s, when the professional qualifications of this bench were increased (only lawyers are now appointed) and its internal organization was formalized. It is now usually the case (as it was not before) that the individuals who preside are screened before appointment by a neutral body of judges and lawyers, protected from casual removal from office, and answerable to their own chief judge and associate chief judges rather than directly to the office of the provincial attorney-general. More than half of all the judges in Canada serve on these courts (McCormick and Green 1991, 21), and they conduct trials and hearings in more than eight hundred centres (Millar and Baar 1981, 80). The recent entrenchment of the Canadian Charter of Rights and Freedoms in the constitution and cases (such as *R. v. Valente*) arising from it have reinforced these structural and institutional changes and made the judges far more independent and autonomous. Moreover, the increasing professionalization improves the quality of justice dispensed, and improvements at the bottom end of the judicial system constitute an almost invisible but extremely important transformation of the Canadian justice system.

Much of the jurisdiction of these courts is mundane; the stakes are low, and the procedures, brief and perfunctory, as the routine repetitiveness of traffic court clearly exemplifies. Silbey (1981) has estimated that the average proceeding in the lower courts takes less than two minutes, which may startle those whose expectations derive from the television exploits of Perry Mason and Ben Matlock. But the lower jurisdiction of provincial courts does not make them insignificant. Although it is true that "lesser" matters are dealt with by the lower courts, it is not correct to assume that the more important matters are excluded. Three major considerations affect the weight of the deliberations.

First, provincial courts have original jurisdiction (which means that they conduct the trial and give the first judicial determination, subject to appeal) over all offences created by provincial legislation. Given the recent expansion of provincial legislative activity, especially in provinces such as Quebec, which has established its own provincial income tax system, the maximum consequences that can follow from the court's decision are very serious.

Second, the cut-off point at which lawsuits become too large for provincial court to consider has been moving upward at rates far in excess of the rate of inflation. "Monetary limits were originally set at well under $100, [and] in most jurisdictions they had risen to a few hundred dollars by the 1970s" (Russell 1987, 238). Today, however, the "civil division" of the provincial court can hear very large cases — as high as $15,000 in Quebec (Lachapelle et al. 1993, 282), although in other provinces the upper limits are typically in the low thousands.

Third, under the Criminal Code serious crimes called "indictable offences" (the Canadian equivalent of American "felonies") are defined as offences for which the maximum penalty is greater than six months in prison and/or a fine of two thousand dollars. Persons accused of such crimes (except for murder and a short list of exotic crimes like piracy, which must be tried in the provincial superior court) have the right to "elect" the method of their trial — by provincial court judge, provincial superior judge, or provincial superior judge and jury. The consequence of this opportunity to choose is that these lower courts "exercise a vast criminal jurisdiction which appears to be unmatched by the lower criminal courts of any other liberal democracy" (Russell 1987, 204).

To these objective considerations we should add the fact that, subjectively, the stuff of provincial court may well be overwhelmingly important to the people involved. A lawsuit for a few thousand dollars looms larger in the lives of average citizens than a million-dollar case does in the balance sheets of a major corporation, and for many people even a minor (summary conviction) criminal appearance is a devastating experience. The provincial courts are the workhorses of the system, resolving about 95 per cent of all the cases that enter the judicial process, and they are the only courts with which most Canadians are ever likely to have any contact.

Second Principle: The Provincial Superior Trial Courts

While "minor" cases are streamed to a high-volume bench, "major" cases are dealt with by a separate court, staffed by a smaller number of judges sitting in a smaller number of centres but structured to provide the longer and more focused attention that these less routine cases require. These courts are the provincial superior trial courts, variously named in the different provinces: Superior Court in Quebec, Court of Queen's Bench in the prairie provinces, Ontario Court of Justice (General Division) in that province. Because they are established by provincial legislation, the precise details of their jurisdiction and their procedure vary from one province to another, but the core of their powers derives from sections 96 through 99 of the Constitution Act 1867.

At one time, there was another level of trial court, the county or district court, between the "purely provincial" courts and the provincial superior courts in every province except Quebec. Over the last fifteen years, in every province except Nova Scotia, the consolidation movement has fused this court with the trial court above it (using "fusion" in the most literal sense; all judges of the county/district courts simply became judges of the provincial superior court). Although Canadian society may be becoming more complex and court caseloads may be steadily growing, the court system has been streamlined and simplified and may well become more so in future.

Provincial superior court judges are federally appointed and paid, but the province maintains the courts and administers court services — a longstanding and remarkably successful experiment in co-operative federalism that has no counterpart in any other country. Hogg (1992, 165) suggests that federal appointment has become something of an anachronism because there is no indication that the provinces would not be appointing from the same set of senior lawyers on much the same criteria. The obvious and telling counterargument is Quebec. Not surprisingly, federally appointed judges in Quebec tend to be staunch federalists, and several of them (Mr. Justice Jacques being one of the more outspoken examples) often read the Parti Québécois stern and unappreciated lectures on federalism in the course of their decisions. The attitude of these judges is hardly enough to stem a nationalist tide on its own, but it does indicate the ongoing significance of what is otherwise a curious historic anomaly.

Kerwin, Henderson, and Baar (1986) (see also Baar and Baar 1986) have suggested that we can characterize court cases as "decisional" (involving the straightforward application of general principles to specific factual circumstances), "procedural" (involving adversary proceedings to resolve more complex legal issues), or "diagnostic" (involving more flexible processes to deal with a broad range of causal circumstances rather than a single specific event or action). Using this classification scheme, we can say that procedural cases comprise the bulk of the provincial superior trial court caseload. They typically involve two or more parties represented by legal counsel (many parties appearing in provincial court are unrepresented), presenting extended legal arguments (many cases in provincial court hinge on narrow findings of fact), in cases that may take days, weeks, or even months to resolve (most cases in provincial court take less, often much less, than a day), and sometimes involving a jury (provincial court judges never sit with juries).

Tentatively, we might hypothesize that provincial superior judges are recruited more carefully and exhibit a higher average level of ability. It is an underlying principle that the hierarchy of courts should be at the same time a hierarchy of ability. There are some indications that support this contention: for example, judges are sometimes elevated from provincial court to these courts, but they never move down, and there are many lawyers who would turn down an appointment to provincial court but accept one to a higher court. However, the fact that judges on these two benches are appointed by different levels of government suggests that political connections may often matter at least as much as objective ability in determining which court a specific lawyer is appointed to. A second way of looking at the relationship between the levels of trial court is in terms of specialization. It may be helpful to distinguish superior court judges from provincial judges by saying that they do different things in distinctively different ways. A survey of court professionals in Ontario and Alberta suggested that judges and lawyers in these provinces are less likely than those in others, and Ontarians less

likely than Albertans, to think of the court system in terms of specialization rather than a hierarchy of ability (McCormick and Greene
1984).

The overlapping jurisdiction of the two trial benches gives a possible basis for a direct comparison of ability. If provincial superior
judges are of higher quality, then they should be reversed less often
on appeal. A study of the Laycraft Court in Alberta (1985–92) suggests that this is indeed the case — success rates for both criminal
and sentence appeals are about a third higher for provincial court
than for provincial superior court — although the comparison is
complicated by the frequency with which provincial superior trial
judges sit as ad hoc members of appeal panels and qualified by the
fact that there is almost no difference in the success rate of crown
appeals (presumably screened more rigorously and focused on questions of law) (McCormick 1993).

Third Principle: Provincial Superior Appeal Courts

The apex of the court system of each province is the provincial court
of appeal (in P.E.I. the Appeal Division of the Supreme Court),
although this has only been true since 1987, when P.E.I. acquired a
full-time appeal bench. Ontario and Quebec had specialized provincial courts of appeal at Confederation; Manitoba established such a
court in 1906, and British Columbia in 1909; Alberta and Saskatchewan followed suit in the 1920s, Nova Scotia and New Brunswick
in 1967, and Newfoundland in 1975 (Russell 1987).

The major function of the appeal courts, as their name implies, is
to review the decisions of the "lower" courts within the province. (In
all provinces, they also have a limited original jurisdiction, significant but infrequently invoked, in the form of the reference process,
which allows the provincial attorney general to refer an abstract
question of law directly to the highest provincial court [McEvoy
1988]). As a general rule of thumb, all parties are entitled to appeal
the first trial determination of a case. Further and subsequent appeals
usually require the leave of the court, although this leave is frequently
granted. Nevertheless, appeals are rare (notwithstanding the tendency of news reports of dramatic trials invariably to state that an
appeal is pending); a reasonable estimate is probably on the order of
1 per cent or lower. Trial court caseloads in most provinces are
measured in the tens of thousands; appeal court caseloads, in the
hundreds. Damaska has suggested that one of the important charac-

teristics of the judicial systems of continental Europe is the frequency and routineness of higher court review of lower court decisions; in contrast, he characterizes as "embryonic" the judicial hierarchy of the Anglo-American systems because "lower court judges retain vast 'discretionary' or virtually unreviewable powers" (Damaska 1986, 45).

The most obvious function of an appeal court is the correction of error. If the trial judge has "goofed" — in stating the law, in applying the rules of evidence, in instructing a jury — then the lawyer for the wronged party can bring the matter before the appeal panel, demonstrate the error, and receive the appropriate remedy. However, error-correction is not the only — and arguably not even the most important — appeal court function. Because there is an unavoidable element of discretion within many judicial decisions (different judges can, without error, give somewhat different outcomes for generally similar cases), review by appeal panels can also contribute to judicial uniformity in the exercise of this discretion. The clearest example is sentence appeals. The Criminal Code lays down a fairly wide range of possible sentences for specific offences, leaving it to the judiciary to decide where in the continuum any specific defendant should be placed. The element of discretion makes it more or less inevitable that different judges will arrive at different answers. From time to time, the provincial court of appeal therefore delivers "benchmark" decisions that establish the basic "tariff" for a specific offence and the additional features that justify something above or below that standard. (Strictly speaking, these standards apply only within the individual province, although in practice appeal and trial courts in other provinces will often take them into account, thereby contributing to — but hardly guaranteeing — national uniformity.) As well, the appeal court is called upon to provide judicial leadership in dealing with new legal problems or issues, such as the changing status of women within matrimonial relationships, that take new forms with evolving social expectations.

Basically, an appeal court has four options in resolving an appeal. First, it can dismiss the appeal and uphold the trial decision. Second, it can allow the appeal and reverse the trial decision (substituting a finding of "not guilty" for one of "guilty," or whatever). Third, it can uphold the decision but vary the results (increasing or decreasing a sentence in a criminal case or an award of damages in a civil case). Fourth, it can "quash" the trial decision — that is, reject the outcome and send the case back for retrial as if the first trial had never occurred. The first option is the most common result; the fourth, the least.

Fourth Principle: Supreme Court of Canada

The Supreme Court was established by federal legislation in 1875 during the political opportunity created when suspicion of a federally appointed court in Quebec was briefly balanced by extreme annoyance in Ottawa with an unpopular decision by the Judicial Committee of the Privy Council in Britain (Bushnell 1992). Despite the implicit claim of its name, the Court was not in fact "supreme" until well into this century; it was instead, in Bora Laskin's pithy phrase, a "captive court." Not only could its decisions be appealed to the Judicial Committee, but also the decisions of provincial appeal courts could be, and often were, appealed directly to Britain without any reference at all to the Supreme Court (Snell and Vaughan 1985). Only in 1949, when an amendment to the Supreme Court Act abolished appeal to Britain, did the Court begin slowly to carve out its own distinctive jurisprudence, and only with the appointment of Bora Laskin in the 1970s did it begin to acquire the profile and the prestige of its American counterpart.

Unlike the United States Supreme Court, which is barred from hearing appeals from decisions on matters of state or local law, the Canadian Supreme Court is, in the words of the constitutional section that authorized its creation, "a General Court of Appeal" for all legal matters, local, provincial, or national. Even parking tickets can theoretically be appealed all the way to the Supreme Court. (The example is not altogether frivolous; it was a parking ticket that started the trail of litigation in the 1980s dealing with the issue of language rights in Manitoba.) However, too wide a jurisdiction can be just as frustrating to effective influence as one that is too narrow, and for much of its history the Supreme Court caseload was clogged with "appeals by right" (capital criminal cases and civil cases over $10,000 that it was obliged to hear regardless of the significance of the legal issues they raised). Finally, in 1974, the Supreme Court Act was amended to give the Court more effective control over its own docket. Although the category of appeals by right has not completely vanished, 85 per cent or more of the Supreme Court caseload is now drawn from its discretionary jurisdiction, which means that would-be appellants apply for leave to appeal and the Court decides whether or not to grant leave. Seventy-five per cent of the time, it does not (see Bushnell 1982).

The annual Supreme Court caseload is about one hundred cases (plus or minus 20%), and about 85 per cent of these are appeals from the provincial courts of appeal. (The remaining 15% comprise appeals from the Federal Court of Appeal, rehearings of Supreme Court decisions, references from the federal government, and *per saltum* appeals from provincial trial courts [McCormick, 1993].) Since the combined annual caseload of the provincial courts of appeal in recent years has been around six thousand cases, it appears that just over 1 per cent of all such decisions are reviewed by the Supreme Court — a caseload-to-appeal ratio comparable to that of the trial court decisions appealed to the provincial appeal courts. Some commentators have worried about the implications of this restricted caseload, particularly when it is combined with a growing public law component dominated by Charter cases. One result seems to be the virtual disappearance of private law appeals to the Supreme Court (Gibson 1989, 4).

Fifth Principle: The Purely Federal Courts

In addition to empowering Parliament to create a general court of appeal, Section 101 of the Constitution Act 1867 also permits the establishment of other courts "for the better administration of the laws of Canada." At the same time that Parliament passed the Supreme Court Act, it also created the Exchequer Court of Canada. Indeed, it was created by the same piece of legislation and for over a decade used the same judges, who sat as single judges in admiralty matters and in cases between a subject and the Crown in right of Canada. In 1887 the Exchequer Court was established as a separate court with its own judges — initially, a single judge, gradually increasing to seven judges by 1964 (McConnell 1977, 326 ff.). It lasted until the major reorganization of 1970 saw the creation of the current Federal Court. (There is another federal court — the Tax Court of Canada, established in 1983 — with a much more restricted jurisdiction [Appleby and Greenspoon 1978].)

The Federal Court has both a trial and an appeal division. Essentially, its jurisdiction originally comprised three elements. The first, and least problematic, is a simple continuation of the jurisdiction of its predecessor, the Exchequer Court. The second, accounting for the majority of its cases, is an extensive administrative law jurisdiction, which essentially provides a judicial backstop for federal boards and tribunals and for the federal administrative process, "to provide a basis for developing federal administrative law in a more unified and cohesive fashion" (Russell 1987, 313). The third, and most controversial, was jurisdiction over private suits in certain areas of federal legislative competence, but subsequent rulings of the Supreme Court of Canada have thoroughly undermined this element. The Federal Court has become a significant in the Canadian court system, and it has a large and growing caseload (and an expanding contingent of judges to deal with it), but it would be completely inappropriate to equate it with the hierarchy of U.S. federal courts.

This account of the court system would be misleading without any mention of the administrative tribunals that have proliferated in this age of proactive government (Ratushny 1987). Built into the governmental bureaucracy are a wide variety of mechanisms for the review of "ground level" decisions. If people think that a policy has been wrongly applied or that they have been unfairly excluded from a program to which they are entitled, then there is a process whereby that decision can be referred to, and possibly reversed by, a "higher" body. Sometimes this process is embedded within the government department; sometimes it enjoys a more distinct and independent status.

There are two reasons for the proliferation of such structures. The first is simply numbers. Bourgeois has suggested (1990) that the total caseload of the quasi-judicial administrative tribunals may exceed that of the formal court system. The volume would overwhelm the courts, the more so because the rigour and meticulous procedural rules of the courts consume great amounts of time. Wexler felt that there is a basic distinction between "bureaucratic" and "judicial" decision-making and that each is appropriate to and functions in specific circumstances (1975). The second is the nature of the decisions that are needed; frequently, they call for specialized expertise in the subject matter at hand rather than the abstract expertise of the lawyer. As well, the performance of the Anglo-American courts has over time suggested that they are more sympathetic to some interests (such as business) than they are to others (such as labour), and so a wide range of responsibilities have been handled over to differently constituted authorities, such as labour relations boards and workers' compensation boards. These quasi-judicial bodies have substantial ongoing importance, but their relationship to the formal court structures is frequently problematic (Mullan 1982).

The Constitutional Basis of Judicial Authority

Given the longstanding solidity of the Canadian judicial system, it comes as a surprise to discover how brief, casual, and permissive its constitutional underpinnings are. Because the Constitution Act 1867 did not create any courts, it could hardly establish clear boundaries between their respective jurisdictions. Section 92.14 gives the provinces authority over "the Constitution, Maintenance and Organization of Provincial Courts, both of Civil and of Criminal Jurisdiction, and including Procedure in Civil Matters in those Courts." Section 101 gives the Parliament of Canada the power "to provide for the Constitution, Maintenance and Organization of a General Court of Appeal for Canada, and for the Establishment of any additional Courts for the better Administration of the Laws of Canada." Both simply give constitutional permission for such courts to be created.

Even more curious is the status of the provincial superior courts, which are dealt with by Sections 96 through 100. These sections do not create any courts either; they simply assume their continuing existence as artefacts of the earlier practice of the colonies that were united to form Canada. All these sections indicate is how the judges of these courts are to be appointed and paid (by the federal government), what qualifications they must possess (membership of the respective bars of the various provinces — that is, they must be lawyers admitted by the province to the practice of law), and how they are removed (by joint address of the Senate and the House of Commons). But the courts themselves are *provincial* courts, even though the judges that preside over them are federally appointed. When the structure of provincial superior courts is altered — for example, when Alberta fused its district courts with its supreme court (trial division) to create the new Court of Queen's Bench in 1979 — the change is accomplished by provincial legislation, although the co-operation of the national government is necessary because only the federal government can appoint judges to serve in the new court.

What can be done when a constitution provides for courts without clear delineation of their respective jurisdictions? The courts have done the only thing that they could do: they have made the rules up as they have gone along. Whenever a dispute arises that revolves around the question of which court has which jurisdiction, the court system is obliged to give some kind of a response. If the answer is not specified within the constitution, then the courts must read between the lines. The doctrine of precedent means that each answer that the courts give becomes the logical foundation for the way that they respond to the next question. Since the courts described in Section 96 through 100 already existed when the Constitution Act 1867 was passed, "Section 96 doctrine" became the solid core of the constitutional foundations of Canadian judicial authority, to be defended from erosion from "beneath" (the provincially controlled "purely provincial" courts), from "beside" (federal and provincial administrative tribunals), and from "above" (in the form of the "purely federal" courts). Nor are the lines to be defended only from provincial legislative creations: *McEvoy v. A-G New Brunswick* (SCC, 1983) explicitly extends the same restrictions to the federal Parliament as well. These are not abstract questions remote from the daily concerns of citizens: there was, for example, considerable doubt about the constitutionality of the whole youth court scheme envisaged by the federal Young Offenders Act until a surprisingly flexible reading of the doctrine by the Supreme Court settled the issue in its favour (McEvoy 1986).

The core of Section 96 doctrine is the proposition that any matter decided by a provincial superior court in 1867 must be handled by the same kind of court today. It was, of course, logically possible that this historical investigation might yield different results in different provinces, which is precisely what happened. Essentially similar statutes were found to be unconstitutional in Ontario (*Re Residential Tenancies Act,* 1981) but valid in Quebec (*A-G Quebec v. Grondin,* 1983). The Supreme Court's solution, in *Sobeys Stores v. Yeomans* (1989), was to fall back on an examination of "the general historical conditions in all four original confederating provinces" — i.e. a fictional composite. With regard to the administrative tribunals that have recently crowded the decision-review process, there are two additional escape hatches. The first is that the Section 96 monopoly applies only to bodies exercising a "judicial function," which is defined for these purposes as involving adversary proceedings adjudicated through the application of a recognized body of rules in a manner consistent with fairness and impartiality. Leaving to one side a certain "loading" of the descriptive categories, this definition seems to match Wexler's distinction between bureaucratic and judicial decisions. The second escape route is that a board's power can be more extensively legitimized if it is an integral part of a broader regulatory scheme rather than solely and narrowly a mechanism for rule-based resolution of disputes between parties, which seems to respond to the specialization argument.

The Section 96 courts that lie at the constitutional core of the judicial system constitute a double-edged sword. On the one hand, they are a permanent guarantee that for a wide range of major issues, legal disputes will be resolved by a legal professional operating with the independence guaranteed by the secure tenure assured by Section 100. On the other hand, they are a standing roadblock to any major restructuring of the Canadian court system (such as the consolidated trial courts contemplated by Ontario's recent reforms [see e.g., Baar 1988, Greene 1988]), all the more difficult to overcome because so much is in the form of judicial doctrine rather than in the specific (and therefore directly amendable) words of the formal constitution. There is room for disagreement on how serious this problem is; where some say an evaluation is overdue (McEvoy 1987) and worry about its "chilling effect" on dispute resolution (Hatherly 1988), others wonder if it is "really necessary to amend it" at all (Lyon 1987).

Conclusion

But logic is only a test for the internal consistency of ideas, not a test for truth. This chapter has suggested that if the Canadian court system did not already exist, we could build it up from first principles that were themselves defensible. Nevertheless, there are other approaches, equally logical, that have guided the construction of the court systems of other countries, such as those of continental Europe, and they seem at least as functional as our own. That is to say, their general acceptance by society is accompanied by widespread awareness of significant problems.

To design a judicial system is to be impaled on the horns of several different dilemmas, none of which have easy answers. One is the dilemma of specialization, the question of whether court procedures and court personnel should be generalized or focused on specific types of case. The court systems of continental Europe, for example, are characterized by separate hierarchies of specialized courts dealing with commercial contract cases or landlord and tenant cases or whatever. The price is such a bewildering maze of courts that citizens find it difficult to know where to go. The trend in our court system is toward consolidation, toward "one-stop" judicial shopping and the "one-size-fits-all" court system, the implicit cost contained in the fact that no judge can be an expert in everything. There is some specialization at the lowest (provincial court) level but none higher in the system, creating the conceptually curious situation where the decisions of specialized judges are reviewed by generalist judges.

Another is the user-friendly dilemma: those who go to court are a mixture of professionals and regulars, on the one hand, and amateurs and outsiders, on the other. If one set needs to have procedures, requirements, deadlines, and the meaning of technical phrases carefully spelled out to them, the other finds such explanations an unnecessary waste of time. Our system generally presumes knowledge ("ignorance of the law is no excuse"), softening the harsh edges with formal provisions like duty counsel or informal provisions like a friendly judge. Such an approach can generate both success stories and horror stories, not necessarily in equal measure.

A third is the "big-small" dilemma. Neely (1983, 291) has suggested that "because the minor courts are structured as 'baby' major courts, litigants with human problems are usually saddled with rules developed when one multi-billion dollar company sues another." In one sense, everyone who comes before the justice system is entitled to the fairest possible outcome of their dispute, regardless of how large the necessary expenditure of resources might be. In another sense, there are times when the answer is not worth the time and expense of the full judicial machinery and a cheaper, quicker, and possibly less perfect answer would be more useful. This is another example of what Galanter (1985, 544) referred to as the problem of "exalted symbols wedded to limited resources."

Easy answers to any of these dilemmas do not exist. In an imperfect world, only imperfect solutions are possible, and the first (and for most of us the only relevant) component of Canada's imperfect solution is the trial courts, to which I will now turn.

Trial Courts

If trial judges collectively possess power in the form of a capacity to influence the fortunes and prospects of those who appear before them, this power is reactive rather than proactive. They are limited to answering the questions that people bring to them, and their power consists in the extent to which they exercise some discretion, some degree of choice, in answering those questions. The questions that individuals bring to the trial courts have to do with legal rights and claims, and the reason they bring them to this forum is that two or more parties disagree on their precise nature and limits. That is, these parties come to court because they have a dispute about the kind of question that courts are created to resolve.

The basic social function of courts is the resolution of disputes against the background of settled law, although both elements of this short answer are more problematic than they appear at first glance. For one thing, "disputes" are not simple natural phenomena; they are "cultural events, evolving within a framework of rules about what is worth fighting for, what is the normal or moral way to fight, what kinds of wrongs warrant action, and what kinds of remedies are acceptable" (Merry and Silbey 1984, 157). The notion of a "dispute" is influenced by the subjective perceptions of the individuals directly involved and by the "gate-keeping" role of the courts in accepting certain types of disagreement for resolution and refusing others. Attitudes of both disputants and courts are subject to change over time.

Moreover, although the background of law does in one sense provide an objective set of standards for the resolution of disputes, in another sense the law itself is the product of the patterns of social, economic, and political advantage so pervasive in any society, including our own, and the judges themselves are an important part of the process whereby that background is developed and clarified. The formulaic definition — "the resolution of disputes against the background of settled law" — is therefore less a solid and final definition than an indication of where and how to look. Indeed, "there has been considerable criticism of the concept of dispute in the past few years, leading some to suggest that the concept be abandoned altogether," one of the critical problems being the embedded assumptions "about the nature of disputing as rational, self-interested, choice-making and fundamentally instrumental behavior" (Merry and Silbey 1984, 156).

At the same time, "dispute-resolving mechanism" does not exhaust the meaning of "court mechanisms." Such an assumption badly blurs important elements. Function and definition are not the same thing, and it is a serious logical error to treat them as if they were (Galloway 1991). Nor do courts exist simply to impose financial penalties. First, although there is an extensive literature that describes litigant behaviour in terms of rational economic behaviour, optimizing strategies, and anticipated pay-outs discounted for probabilities and time delays, it does not catch what the courts mean for all actors. Many litigants seek vindication as much as compensation, official recognition of rights and status as much as material advantage. A purely economic approach reduces such behaviour to irrational distractions, which will not do for an understanding of the courts. Second, too strong an emphasis on "dispute resolution" implies that what matters is the disputes and their accommodation; but since courts are only one component of such a process, and not necessarily the preponderant one, we risk overlooking the fact that courts make a difference, that there are specific and important ways in which courts and judges and lawyers shape and package the disputes that are referred to their attention (see Friedman 1988). Third, dispute resolution is only one of the many functions of courts. As Millar and Baar point out (1981, 27), courts also serve both grander tasks, such as "doing justice" and "protecting citizens against tyranny," and more routine ones, such as providing formal acknowledgment of legal facts that are not in themselves contentious.

Despite all these qualifications, it is a useful starting point to point out that a central function of courts in Canadian society is resolving certain kinds of disputes in a certain manner. This description is not complete, and it should not be allowed to impose blinders that keep us from noting the other things that courts do, but it is a useful simplification.

The Notion of Dispute

Researchers have begun to shed some light on the psychological and behavioural aspects of the dispute process and the factors that bring some disagreements, but not others, into the judicial process. Felstiner, Abel, and Sarat, for example, have identified, and aptly labelled, the three critical early stages in the process (1980, passim). First, there is "naming" — the identification of a problem in the form of an injurious experience. Second, there is "blaming" — externalizing the responsibility for the problem by identifying another party whose fault the experience was. And, third, there is "claiming" — using some formal or informal procedure to seek some form of redress from those perceived to be responsible. Clearly all three stages are influenced by a wide variety of factors. What some identify as an injurious situation others will see as the unpleasant lower edge of normal human experience; some will accept as their own what others see as the fault of external parties; some will suffer in silence (in Marc Galanter's phrase [1983], "lumping it") rather than approach the offending party to ask for some remedy. "Ideas about how to respond to grievances are linked with socially constructed definitions of normal behaviour, respectability, responsibility and the good person," and these in turn "derive from habits and customs embedded in social groups and cultures" (Merry and Silbey 1984, 157).

But these considerations are only the prehistory of disputes, the early stages of the developmental process. A dispute occurs when the claim for redress is rejected because the initial situation is not admitted to be injurious, because responsibility is denied, or because the suggested remedy is rejected as inappropriate. "Those claims not granted become *disputes*" (Galanter 1983, 13). Even here, further evolution and maturation of the disagreement is required. Some disputes are simply abandoned; Ladkinsky and Susmilch (cited in Galanter, 1983) have coined the awkward but useful term "clumping it" to describe those who make a claim but go no further when it is rejected. Only a small minority of disputes — the important tip of the iceberg — go beyond the manager or school principal or shop steward to the lawyers' offices, and even fewer make it into the courts.

Kritzer, Bogart, and Vidmar (1991) suggest that we should see the "legal mobilization" of disputes in terms of crossing a series of thresholds or "barriers." The first is the *recognition barrier*, corresponding to the "naming" stage indicated above, just as the second, the *attribution barrier*, corresponds to the "blaming" stage. The crossing of the *confrontation barrier* escalates the disagreement to the status of a claim; we might want to add a further notion of a *"third-party barrier"* when the argument expands to include some other party in addition to the blamer and the blamed; and the final hurdle to clear is the *litigation barrier*.

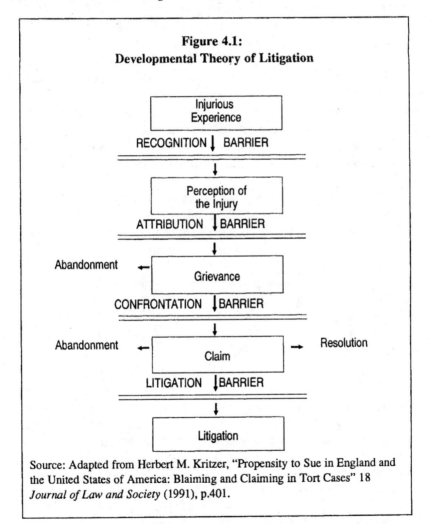

Figure 4.1:
Developmental Theory of Litigation

Source: Adapted from Herbert M. Kritzer, "Propensity to Sue in England and the United States of America: Blaiming and Claiming in Tort Cases" 18 *Journal of Law and Society* (1991), p.401.

Obviously, a large variety of factors will influence whether or not a particular grievance clears any or all of these barriers. For example, on the basis of an Ontario study, Kritzer, Bogart, and Vidmar suggest that Protestants are more likely to pursue a problem to the level of a claim or a lawsuit than are Catholics; they also find that higher levels of education and higher levels of income correlate with a greater readiness to pursue complaints. This finding might seem obvious, but similar studies in the United States have not found any correlation with religion, education, or income.

We must not imagine that all disputes result from rational calculations of optimal benefit — "dispute behaviour, as is true of much human behaviour, is affective and habitual and is not entirely a matter of rational calculation" (Merry and Silbey 1984, 158). Many "disputants pursue grievances not only in terms of material interests, but also in terms of norms about integrity, self-image, self-respect, and duties to others which are neither calculated nor subjects of individual choice. An adequate analysis of conflict behaviour must include both normative rules and pragmatic strategies" (Merry and Silbey 1984, 160). As any trial lawyer or judge will confirm, some lawsuits are pragmatic and coldly logical, but many others arrive at the court still wrapped in bad feelings, barely constrained by the formal civility and strict procedural rules of the court system. In some types of court cases, judges and lawyers would be naive not to realize the calculating self-interest that drives the parties; in others, they would be even more naive to ignore the emotional imperatives that cloud or even overwhelm pragmatic self-interest.

A final point to bear in mind is the way that the legal process brings about the "transformation of disputes": before they can be resolved by the system, they must be translated into the language appropriate for the forum (Mather and Yngvesson 1980). Sometimes doing so means broadening the issue; sometimes, narrowing it. Sometimes it escalates the scale of the dispute and the scope of the outcome; other times it limits them. If your initial purpose is to get someone put into prison or to make them pay some dollar sum of damages, you may or may not succeed, but at least you are talking a language that the court can understand. If you want someone to apologize or to acknowledge your status, or if you just want someone to say that you were right, then you will inevitably frustrate your lawyer, the judge, and in the end yourself.

Disputes and Thresholds

Since the courts cannot deal with all disputes that arise in society, or even with all the disputes that people might want to refer to them, access is limited in several ways. The first is legal practices dealing with such questions as "standing," "mootness," and "remedy." *Stand-*

ing requires that a party demonstrate a real connection with the legal issue rather than a remote or abstract interest. Recently, with the advent of the Charter, standing rules have become extremely flexible and (sometimes) generous, but historically they have served to limit what kinds of parties may raise what kinds of questions. *Mootness* refers to the need for a real ongoing issue rather than one whose practical relevance has, in the eyes of the court, vanished. (For example, Joseph Borowski's appeal to the Supreme Court on the issue of whether the rights of the fetus were violated by the Criminal Code sections on permissible abortions was rendered moot because the Court had, in the Morgentaler case, already declared those sections to be unconstitutional.) Finally, the courts limit themselves to hearing cases that have a remedy that is within the court's power — the barrier is not just, "What is your problem?" but also, "What can we do about it?" All three considerations ignore the fact that disputants often want vindication or acknowledgment as much as a practical outcome.

A second threshold is imposed by the financial costs of pursuing judicial remedies. As Friedman (1988, 14) drily observes, "Modern legal systems are typically rather expensive to their users." Lawyers charge a high tariff for their professional services and work hard to protect their monopoly by excluding lower-priced outsiders. The result is that even a brief and minor brush with the law (a dismissed charge for a summary conviction offence or a minor lawsuit) can put a serious dent in the average person's budget. Costs are all the more important when we remember that all courts cast some precedential shadow over subsequent similar cases, and higher (and more expensive) courts cast longer shadows. There is an American solution to this problem in the form of the contingency fee — if the case succeeds, the lawyer gets a percentage; if it fails, the lawyer gets nothing. Although such a system does not discourage worthy cases by poor clients, it has been criticized for going too far in the other direction and encouraging frivolous and opportunistic litigation (Olson 1991). Although contingency fees are permitted in every Canadian province except Ontario and are common in Quebec (Baudoin 1993), the normal Canadian practice involves "fee-shifting," which means that the loser pays part of the winner's legal fees (Kritzer 1984). Clearly, this makes a real difference to the litigant; just as important, it makes a real difference to how much effort lawyers apply to which cases (Kritzer et al. 1985).

A third way to limit, and thereby to manage, the access of disputes to the courts is through caseload limitations and the delays that are their inevitable consequence. Delay carries costs — in the form of ongoing legal expenses, the anxieties generated by uncertainties about the final outcome, and the possible attrition of a case as witnesses forget or become unavailable. These costs create a pressure on parties to find some other acceptable outcome. "The basic price mechanism for access to courts has proven to be queuing (which implies waiting time) ... Expansion of public capacity lowers costs and brings more cases; contraction tends to deflate the number of cases" (Krislove 1983). Put simply: the courts are prepared to give authoritative resolutions to those disputes whose parties are willing to wait in line long enough for their turn in the courtroom, and the backlog constitutes the waiting list of those to whom the dispute is important enough to make the wait worthwhile. Increasing the capacity of the courts — adding more judges and courtrooms or creating more streamlined procedures — will process the backlog more quickly, but it will also call forth a certain number of cases deterred by the old time-lag but attracted by the new. As Neely (1983, 58) puts it: "Building a court system is like building a road. The better the road, the more the traffic."

The Notion of Decision

Logically, the trial judge's decision comprises three distinct but interrelated elements. First, the relevant facts must be determined. Usually the facts are obvious, or else the contested factors are few in number, easily identified, and resolved in terms of the balance of evidence or the credibility of witnesses although sometimes determining the facts can be protracted and difficult. Second, the relevant law must be determined. Again, doing so is usually straightforward, a simple matter of identifying the right section of the Criminal Code or the basic principle of contract or whatever. On occasion, however, it can raise constitutional questions about the scope of authority of legislative bodies. Third, the facts and the law must be put together to generate the appropriate result (guilty or not, liable or not), and if the former is the case, the appropriate penalty must be assessed. It is characteristic of judicial decisions that they almost always take the form of a written argument, tracing the findings of fact and the logical sequence that leads up to the outcome — not only "you lose," but also "here is why." Depending on the case and the judge, these legal essays can be extremely short or very, very long, but they typically answer three logical questions: *What happened? What are the appropriate legal categories in which to describe what happened? What legal consequences follow?* But these questions raise two more — first, what are "facts"? and, second, what do judges do with them?

Courts and facts

Historically, the notion of the trial grew from the circuits travelled by the king's official, who would arrive in a centre and summon a number of respected elders (the *juratores*, so called because they were sworn to tell the truth) to provide the factual background against which disputes could be fairly resolved. In a simple agrarian society, doing so was usually not difficult. Where the critical facts could not be established with sufficient clarity, the question could be put to trial (by ordeal or by combat), which was basically understood as calling upon God to make a choice where secular means had failed. Eventually, the trial moved into the courtroom and was held before the *juratores* (later, the jury). There the issue was resolved by logical and rational processes rather than by reference to the supernatural (Baker 1979; Shapiro 1981). The basic logic of the trial, however, remains the same: to move from uncertainty (the two contending versions that provide the core of the dispute) to certainty. As Shapiro observes, "The central problem of judicial fact-finding is the problem of certainty" (Shapiro 1981, 46), although the goal necessarily remains relative, not absolute, certainty.

But the search for certainty requires the limitation of information. The court deals with the facts, but the relevant facts are those that have been established by the court's procedures and standards. Some commentators suggest that we should view the trial process and the rigorous rules on evidence as a way of limiting information to permit a rational conclusion; the general problem in reaching decisions is often less the absence of information than a surfeit of information of varying degrees of relevance. "Social institutions are concerned with the *meaning* of information and can be quite rigorous in enforcing standards of admission ... In even the simplest law case, thousands of events may have had a bearing on the dispute, and it is well understood that, if they were all permitted entry, there could be no theory of due process, trials would have no end, law itself would be reduced to meaninglessness. In short, the rule of law is concerned with the 'destruction of information'" (Postman 1992, 72). Indeed, patrolling this gateway between the complex uncontrollable realm of social facts and the artificially narrowed and therefore manageable realm of legal facts is an ongoing problem for the courts. If the doors open too wide, the courts risk being overwhelmed, but if they are not open wide enough, the courts risk *either* disadvantaging some categories of potential litigant *or* making themselves absurdly marginal to the very social interaction they help to regulate.

As anyone who has ever observed or participated in a trial knows, the rules of evidence are strict and, to a lay person, confusing. There are severe limits on hearsay or on personal conclusions except by experts. If you were limited to conducting your daily life on the basis of the courts' rules of evidence, you would have very poor conversations indeed. You couldn't even discuss the sports scores unless you had seen the game yourself or the weather unless you had recently been outside. We all "know" lots of things that we cannot "prove," and this distinction is both the strength and the weakness of the court system: the strength, because it prevents the court from being swept away by misleading appearances or half-truths; but the weakness, because it often operates at some distance from simple everyday common sense.

There is a real emphasis in our system on the trial itself and on having individuals give evidence in person and subject to direct cross-examination. Innovations such as taping the testimony of child witnesses, for whom court appearances can be terrifying ordeals, work at the margins of this preference, too much so for some purist defenders of the adversary system. By contrast, the continental European systems deliberately fragment the information-gathering process and lean more heavily on the creation of dossiers than on in-person confrontations with witnesses. The focused dramatic event of the trial itself is far less important than in Anglo-American systems. Although it may seem surprising, many cases can be decided simply on the basis of the written submissions without any courtroom trial (Damaska 1986, VanKoppen and TenKate 1984).

The basic legal principle of the Anglo-American process is that everything must be proven at trial — indeed, criminal cases can be dismissed if the Crown fails to establish that the town where the offence took place was within the province over which the judge has jurisdiction. However, there is an important (and therefore problematic) exception: the court can take "judicial notice" of facts that are so obvious as not to require proof — "facts which are (a) so notorious as not to be the subject of dispute among reasonable persons, or (b) capable of immediate and accurate demonstration by resorting to readily accessible sources of indisputable accuracy" (Sopinka, Lederman, and Bryan 1992). The alternative is the absurd prospect of requiring presentation of evidence and opportunity of cross-examination for every single factual element, however trivial or obvious. The problem is that not all of us draw the line of self-evident truth in the same place. It is simple common sense to take judicial notice without requiring evidence that Christmas falls on December 25, or that Toronto is the capital of Ontario, or that the normal period of human gestation is such that a pregnancy cannot last 360 days; but it is less so to dismiss divorce proceedings by taking judicial notice of the fact that it was physically impossible to commit adultery in the cab of a certain kind of truck — although it is intriguing to think about what evidence might be useful in resolving this issue. (For these and other examples of judicial notice — such as the fact that there was an economic depression in Saskatchewan in 1933 — see Schiff 1978 and Carter 1988). More recently, in *RWDSU (Retail, Wholesale and Department Store Union) v. Saskatchewan,* Chief Justice Dickson took judicial notice of the fact that cows continue to produce milk even if striking dairy workers do not milk them. On the other hand, the Supreme Court has refused (in *Moysa v. Alberta*) to take notice of the fact that giving public testimony would hinder a journalist's ability to gather news or (in *Mackay v. Manitoba*) that only candidates from the major parties are likely to be elected. As a result, the process whereby certain types of facts enter the realm of judicial notice is of necessity haphazard and sporadic (Davis 1987).

Still, judicial notice can, and historically often has been, the conduit through which pervasive stereotypes and systemic prejudice have entered the courtroom and structured the outcomes. Chief Justice Dickson was without doubt one of our great judges, but his decision in the Morgentaler abortion case contains a paragraph on woman's great calling as the bearer of future life that is already jarring in the 1990s and will probably be even more so in the future. As feminist legal literature makes abundantly clear, not all judicial recognition of the role and the nature of women has been so benign.

The problem becomes more complicated as we move from "physical facts" to "social facts." One person's common sense is another person's prejudice; what you think of as a realistic assessment of the circumstances and prospects of individuals in a specific segment of society, someone else might bitterly repudiate as an insulting belittlement of their capacity and potential. Because they are obliged by the nature of their duties to apply common sense to the evaluation of evidence (above all, to the assessment of credibility), judges must continually make unproven assumptions about social facts. To take only one example: in Western cultures, the normal response to an accusation of guilt is a forthright denial, yet in aboriginal North American cultures more passive and accommodative responses are normal; for people who have fled oppressive regimes, silence is more appropriate than denial; and for still others, such as Mediterranean and Middle Eastern peoples, an angry, even violent, response is normal. (For these and other examples, see Salhaney 1993.) The problem runs deep: all of us act on the basis of a specific worldview containing a set of assumptions about social roles and expectations, and normal societal interchange is impossible without it. Yet embedded in that worldview are assumptions of facts and values that may be more limiting than we realize and that change more slowly than they should. We are all the prisoners of our own assumptions and preconceptions, most of which are less often subjected to the light of public scrutiny than is the case for judges who write controversial opinions.

Another aspect of the same problem is the fact that our system draws its judges from the ranks of successful and respected lawyers. We are far from atypical; "study after study has confirmed that lawyers in most countries are not recruited from the ranks of the underdogs" (Friedman 1988, 20). As one judge rather plaintively put it to me, "I spend all my time enforcing middle class values on people who will never know what a middle class existence is" (McCormick and Greene 1991). Gender issues raise comparable problems (see e.g., Mary Eberts 1991); as Madame Justice Wilson wrote in Morgentaler (speaking specifically of abortion, although the idea is more broadly applicable):

> It is probably impossible for a man to respond, even imaginatively, to such a dilemma not just because it is outside the realm of his personal experience (although this is, of course, the case) but because he can relate to it only by objectifying it, thereby eliminating the subjective elements of the female psyche which are at the heart of the dilemma.

Models of Decision-Making

But it is also relevant to ask what it is that judges do with the facts and the law as they are presented to them. At first glance, the question seems too obvious to be worth answering, but there are inscrutable dimensions to it. To what other human activities can we compare the judicial decision — is it artistic or scientific or bureaucratic or technical or intuitive? Can it be taught discursively, or learned through experience, or reduced to a formula that lends itself to computer algorithms (D'Amato 1977, Mefford 1990)? Is it perfectly replicable, or are there elements of performance that are intrinsically situation-specific? One of the more intriguing aspects of the interviews that I conducted with several dozen judges was their invariably apologetic beginning ("I'm sure I'm just telling you what everyone else did"), which was then followed by accounts of unique and idiosyncratic models and processes.

It is possible to do a great deal of work with judicial decision-making without trying to penetrate this intellectual process. For example, you can correlate case outcomes with fact patterns that go beyond the formal legally relevant criteria (Goldman and Jahnige 1976), or with the socioeconomic and political backgrounds of individual judges (Goldman and Sarat 1976; Tate 1981), or with perceptions of role (Howard 1977), or with environmental factors (Canon and Jaros 1970; Hall and Brace 1989; Brace and Hall 1990). What I am concerned with here, however, is the question of how to think about or describe the process.

Blackshield (1974) identified five types of judicial decision. The labels he suggested were proverbial, prescriptive, principial, pragmatic, and pronormless. The first two refer to earlier stages in the evolution of Western legal practices, and the third is more a pathology than an alternative. Weiler's "Two Models" (1968) spoke of the problem of choosing between legal positivism (the formal legal formulas drives the result) and legal realism (the formal legal formulas are at least partly a screen for the preferences of individual judges). McCormick and Greene (1991) derived a "two by two" table based on the extent to which the self-descriptions of judges indicated high or low degrees of *formalism* (decision-making "could be articulated as a specific and discrete rational process") and *discretion* ("requiring a significant degree of personal choice or judgment, as opposed to a mechanical process") and found that a plurality of judges located themselves on the high end of both factors.

Alternately, we can discuss judicial decision-making in terms of five different "models" (loosely based on, and expanded from, Shapiro 1981). By a "model" I mean a conceptual map of the decision-making process on which we can track what is going on. The question is of more than idle or intellectual interest. How we conceptualize what judges do is critical to the way we structure the courts and the services provided to courts and to the way we identify what personal or professional qualities are relevant to selecting the most appropriate people to be judges.

First model: the judge as computer

On this model, the function of the judge is largely mechanical, analogous to that of a clerk punching codes into a computer and the best answer popping out of a slot. To a certain extent, it is useful for the judiciary to promote some aspects of this model because it implicitly plays down the significance of the individual judge and plays up the importance of technical expertise. That is, it contributes to a situation in which the judicial decision is generated by the system, not created by the individual who happens to be sitting on the bench. But the utility of this model is in fact extremely limited. As D'Amato (1977) suggests, computers could indeed replace judges but only for disputes that are either very routine or very technical in nature — and of course the system would simply process the cases without being able to identify whether or not they were properly assimilated to either category. Furthermore, mechanical processes are those most likely to generate the cases that the media and public find so outrageous: the ones where the headlines read "welfare grandmother sent to jail." "Punching a code into a computer" makes the process sound simple. Knowing which code to punch in for a particular entry is the problem, precisely the point at which discretion enters. The mechanical model is the one that laypeople tend to take for granted but that legal scholars find of limited utility.

Second model: the judge as umpire/referee

A fairly common metaphor likens the judge to the umpire or referee in a game — the person with the striped shirt and the whistle. The metaphor identifies two important features: that the judge is apart from the game and, therefore, presumably impartial and that there is a body of rules independent of the judge's will. Otherwise, the utility of the metaphor is limited. For one thing, the referee does (but the judge does not) respond proactively to the flow of the play without waiting for one of the players to invoke authority. For a second, the referee's rulings are secondary to the point of the game (which is to score enough goals or touchdowns or baskets), while the judge's rulings in some sense *are* the game. For a third, the umpire's ruling is immediate and unappealable, whereas courts are ponderous and reflective and all parties have the right to appeal. And, finally, the sphere in which the metaphor is invoked most routinely (the Supreme Court as the umpire of federalism) is perhaps the most problematic, raising the question of why "Team National" gets to name all the referees and "Team Provincial" none.

Third model: the judge as resolver of specific disputes

This is the most obvious model, and it seems almost to be forced upon us. What triggers judicial involvement is a dispute between two parties, at least one of whom invokes the authority of the court; and what the two parties are asking for is a resolution according to law. On this model, the judicial function is case-specific and backward looking. What does the law have to say about this individual case in the unique circumstances in which it occurred? And the dispute belongs to the parties who are seeking resolution; within extremely broad limits, if one party or both want to state their claim strangely or mishandle the argument supporting it, risking loss in the process, that is their own business.

But an important feature of some court decisions (not of all or even of most) is that they send signals to broader classes of actors — although the judge is looking backward, the effect of the case ripples forward. Suppose the legislature passes a new Landlords and Tenants Act and Smith v. Jones is the first case that invokes a particularly ambiguous section. The dispute is only partly between the two particular individuals; in an equally important sense, it is between *all* the landlords and *all* the tenants who will live in its shadow. Neither group can afford to stand idly by while its champion botches the play. In such a situation, it is less than obvious that the judge's focus should be exclusively on the specific dispute and the idiosyncratic way that its owners choose to present it.

Fourth model: the judge as policy maker

The fourth model grows out of the limitations of the third: if some individual cases are really important primarily for the long-term policy issues that they raise, then the judges should resolve them in these terms — not single-case, backward-looking, but general-category, future-oriented. Although purists may be uncomfortable with this sort of poaching on legislative preserves, there are circumstances under which it is clearly functional. For example, Richard Neely (1981) argues that there are some issues (such as prison reform) that are so low on the legislative agenda that they will never be considered without judicial prompting, just as there are some groups and interests in society so disadvantaged politically that only the courts can be their champion.

One of the major devices that allow the courts to transcend the limitations of the immediate parties is the intervention — a procedure whereby third parties can make presentations to the court to ensure that their legitimate arguments, legal or otherwise, are not overlooked. Until recently, such interventions have been rare and limited to the appeal courts, especially the Supreme Court of Canada (Brodie 1992, Sopinka 1988, Welch 1985). They involve an application (typically to a single judge, sometimes to the Chief Justice) for intervener status, which is usually but not invariably granted. Intervention involves a written brief and sometimes the opportunity for oral argument as well. On occasion, the courts can be more proactive about seeking wider input. When the Ontario government submitted the issue of separate school funding in a reference case, the Ontario Court of Appeal took out newspaper ads inviting the public to submit briefs, but this sort of action is highly unusual.

The problem with such overt recognition of the policy role of the courts is twofold. First, courts build on the adversary system — one side will win and the other lose — yet it is not clear that this is the best way to handle the trade-offs and compromises that public policy typically involves or that the cases that come before them and the interest groups that intervene are necessarily representative of the broader world to which that policy will apply. Second, it is not clear that the narrow professional training and experience of judges makes them the best people to deal with such choices. Intervener briefs often move away from "black letter" law to deal with issues of sociology and economics and political science and psychology. A very good judge may be a poor economist and at best an amateur psychologist. If the role of the courts (or of some portion of the courts) is truly to set certain types of public policy, then perhaps we need to rethink not just the appointment process but also the criteria on which we have traditionally evaluated judges.

Fifth model: the judge as Solomon

A fifth model, which I have never seen articulated in such terms in the literature but which was urged upon me by my students, sees the judge as an intuitive seeker of justice. The reference, of course, is to the Biblical King Solomon and the story about two women who each argued that the same child was hers; Solomon's solution was to order the child cut in half, with the result that the true mother identified herself by being willing to surrender her child to the other rather than see it harmed. But the story itself hints at the difficulties of operationalizing such a concept. What would King Solomon have done had his bluff been called? And how would he deal with the second such case, when both women might well know in advance about that particular little trick? There are individuals who are on occasion capable of these abrupt departures from normal routines and who can use them to good advantage. These departures make marvellous anecdotes, but one's approval is always conditional on agreeing with the outcome. One person's intuitive King Solomon is another person's arbitrary kangaroo court. Rigorous procedure and logic spelled out in written decisions are our protection against being caught on the wrong side of this dichotomy.

To be sure, some judges describe the decision-making process in intuitive terms, of reaching a "feeling" for how things should turn out. Most judges, however, use more prosaic language to describe what they do. Moreover, many judges are aware of a recurrent tension between perfect "justice" and "resolution of disputes according to established rules," a distinction that this model finesses altogether.

The point of this catalogue is not to single out one model as the "real" and legitimate process but rather to identify the range of roles within which judges oscillate depending on the case, the level of court, and their personal styles. Different models better approximate the role of different courts — the assembly line of traffic court calls forth the model of the mechanical judge, the tangled causal webs that lead into family or youth court require judges to attempt the wisdom of Solomon, the typical civil or criminal case of provincial or superior court evokes the judge as the resolver of specific disputes, and the more academic overtones of appeal courts trigger a higher proportion of forward-looking policy concerns. If there is a centre of gravity to the Canadian judicial system, it is somewhere between the third (dispute-resolver) and fourth (policy-maker) models, with the Charter tilting things toward the fourth.

Conclusion

The core idea for understanding the functions and operations of trial courts is the concept of dispute resolution. As this chapter has demonstrated, however, the transparency of such a simple formula is deceptive. For one thing, it obscures the extent to which courts resolve not all disputes but only certain kinds of disputes and resolve them in characteristic ways that have significant implications. For another, both "dispute" and "resolution" are far more complex ideas than they appear to be at first glance. That said, however, it is important to remember that courts exist primarily to answer in an official and authoritative way certain kinds of questions and that these questions are brought to the court by parties who are unable to find satisfactory answers in other places or other ways. The reactive nature of the judicial function is one of its important features, and it is one of the reasons why fears about democracy being supplanted by a "judge-ocracy" are inherently farfetched. Judges in trial courts do not "seek justice" in any proactive way, and they have little opportunity to pursue personal agendas. Rather, they seek to approximate justice through the resolution of a disjointed stream of specific disputes, a more modest but by no means unworthy ideal. They also face the very real limitation that everything they do is theoretically subject to review by their colleagues on the country's appeal courts, to which I will now turn.

Appeal Judges

Above the trial courts stand the courts of appeal. One frequently used definition of an appeal is "a request to a competent tribunal to reconsider a decision arrived at by another body" (Blom-Cooper and Drewry 1972, 44). Such a "competent" tribunal is always a "higher court"; saying that Court A is higher than Court B is simply another way of saying that the decisions of Court B can be appealed to Court A. This relationship allows us to speak of a "hierarchy" of courts — to establish the formal pyramid diagrammed in Chapter 3 — with the various courts linked by the upward arrows of appeals and the downward arrows of binding precedent.

The focus of this chapter is on the provincial courts of appeal, although there are also appeals (on summary conviction offences and on small claims cases) from provincial court judges to single judges of the provincial superior trial bench, from the Trial Division of the Federal Court to the Appeal Division, and from the provincial appeal courts to the Supreme Court of Canada.

Historically, the courts of appeal in Ontario and Quebec preceded the Supreme Court, and the high reputation of those courts, especially that of Ontario, was at the time an argument against creating the Supreme Court; it was also a source of difficulty in recruiting good judges to the new Supreme Court and a cause of recurrent indignant outrage when the upstart court had the temerity to reverse a strong appeal panel (see Bushnell 1992). These concerns gradually faded, and for about half a century (and certainly since the abolition of appeals to the Judicial Committee of the Privy Council in 1949), the Supreme Court has drawn the bulk of academic and public attention.

The study of the provincial courts of appeal is particularly important in view of the Supreme Court of Canada's restricted caseload and tight focus on public law matters; by default, extensive responsibilities for law-making functions and legal uniformity issues on a wide range of other matters now fall to the provincial courts of appeal. Such considerations make it all the more important that we be aware of the context in which these courts operate and the general parameters of their decisional tendencies. The provincial courts of appeal are no longer (if they ever were) simply way stations along the road linking initial trial court decisions with final Supreme Court of Canada determinations; instead, they are increasingly important and increasingly deserving of study in their own right.

Appeal: The Exception Not the Rule

The pyramid of Canadian courts, with "lower" trial courts at the bottom and "superior" appeal courts above reviewing their decisions, is usually accepted as implying a fully developed structural hierarchy, but such an inference is a mistake. In fact, it is an important characteristic of the Anglo-American court systems that this hierarchy is imperfectly developed compared to the judicial processes of continental Europe (Damaska, 1986). In a fully developed judicial hierarchy, review by a judicial superior would be both more frequent (more appeals) and more routine (built into normal procedures rather than triggered by litigant dissatisfaction). The double result is that there would be relatively more superior judges (a taller, slimmer pyramid) and that the distinction between trial judges of first instance and appeal judges would be harder to make because both original decisions and review of the decisions of "lower" judges would permeate the pyramid. As well, the results of such review are enforced both by a formal hierarchy with internal sanctions and by an immediate impact on the prospects of judicial advancement, neither of which is the case in Canada.

For example, in a decision handed down in July 1993, the Alberta Court of Appeal not only reversed the decision of a trial judge but also accused him of "judicial mischief" for ignoring the guidelines previously laid down by the Court of Appeal and of thinking that the law that applied in his court need not be the same law that was applied in the other courts of Alberta. This is pretty stern talk for an appeal court decision, but the loudness of the bark is directly connected to the weakness of the bite — the frustrated appeal court could only correct the immediate decision and thereby implicitly encourage more appeals from the decisions of this particular judge. In terms of hierarchical discipline, this criticism is small stuff. There is no blighted career, no threat of dismissal, no posting to the remote north, no docking of pay, no loss of secretarial services — nothing but the personal and professional embarrassment of being singled out for a stern reprimand. And if a trial judge feels strongly about the issue and about the rightness of principled disagreement with the court of appeal, she may wear this martyrdom with pride rather than shame. The inevitable flip side of judicial independence is a weak hierarchy riddled with individual initiative, a glorious thing if we value flexibility but far from the "first glance" implications of those bold arrows on the diagrams of the judicial system.

In American studies of judicial behaviour, the pure hierarchical model represents the "first generation" approach, and the assumption of top-down control is now generally rejected as an example of the "upper-court myth" — that is, "the myth that upper courts are the heart of courthouse government" (Frank 1949). This approach was replaced by a "bureaucratic model" (Murphy 1959, Shapiro 1968), which stressed the bureaucratic constraints, such as inefficiency and recalcitrance, that are imposed upon higher courts by lower courts. More recently, other scholars (Vines 1963, Howard 1973) have suggested an "interaction model," a "bottom-up" view that stresses the possibility for limited and focused upper-court control combined with a considerable lower-court capacity for both innovation and evasion.

But the notion of appeal, of a right to seek a judicial "second opinion" from a higher judge or panel of judges, is a very modern addition to the English-style judicial system that we inherited. As Van Caenegem (1987) says, "What is understood by 'appeal' nowadays, i.e. bringing a case before a higher judge in the hope of obtaining a better outcome, was unknown in classical times and was, in fact, introduced [in England] in the nineteenth century." More bluntly, Justice Roger Kerans (1993, 10) of the Alberta Court of Appeal has written that "It is no part of our tradition that the just resolution of a dispute necessarily includes a review of the trial decision. If it were otherwise, we should have automatic appeals." Instead, we seek "to produce a just result at trial," which necessarily makes the appeal unusual — the exception rather than the rule. At that, Canadian rules are even more permissive of criminal appeals by both defendant and Crown than are American practices (Russell 1987, 293).

There are three different indications of the exceptional nature of appeal in the Canadian judicial process. The first is simply the fact that the volume of appeals from any given court is small relative to the total volume of cases handled by that court. Although hard numbers are difficult to come by, a reasonable estimate is something in the neighbourhood of 1 per cent, probably lower for many courts. From the news reports of major trials, it sometimes seems that a failure to appeal is tantamount to an admission of being in the wrong, but this assumption completely falsifies the way the system operates. The average trial judge in Canada handles hundreds of cases a year, fewer than five of which are appealed. From a behavioural stand-point, this fact has a curious implication: if the behavioural approach asks us to think about any social institution or practice in terms of the average member of society, then it follows that the average Canadian will never have anything to do with any appeal court.

Table 5.1

The Canadian Provincial Courts of Appeal: Date of Establishment, Size, and Comparison to Trial Bench

Jurisdiction	Appeal Court Established	Appeal Judges 1993	Trial Judges 1990	Ratio, Trial to Appeal
Newfoundland	1975	6	47	7.8
P.E.I.	1987	3	7	2.3
Nova Scotia	1967	8	61	7.6
New Brunswick	1967	6	47	7.8
Quebec	1867	18	428	23.8
Ontario	1867	16	455	28.4
Manitoba	1906	7	70	10.0
Saskatchewan	1915	9	75	8.3
Alberta	1919	11	167	15.2
B.C.	1907	13	205	15.8
All provinces		97	1362	14.0

The second indication is the relatively recent establishment of the provincial courts of appeal. At the time of Confederation, only two of the four original provinces had full-time specialized courts of appeal;[1] Manitoba and British Columbia created theirs in the first decade of this century, Saskatchewan and Alberta in the second decade; New Brunswick and Nova Scotia followed suit only in 1967, Newfoundland in 1975, and Prince Edward Island in 1987. Before appeal courts were established, appeals were heard by superior trial judges sitting *en banc* as an ad hoc appeal panel, a process that was infrequent but not exceptional. (Indeed, in the nineteenth century it was not infrequent for this panel to include the judge who had rendered the decision that was being appealed, a practice that seems curious now but that had numerous English precedents [see Banks 1991, ch. 15]. This practice is no longer permitted in any Canadian jurisdiction.) Since a specialized appeal court sitting "above" the trial courts is, in modern eyes, such a logical feature of an established judicial system, it is striking how recent this development is.

The third indication of the unusual nature of an appeal is the fourteen-to-one ratio of trial judges to appeal judges. In 1990, there were 1,703 full-time federal and provincial judges in Canada, 1,590 (or 93.4%) of whom were trial judges (see McCormick and Green 1991, 21). Narrowing the focus a little more, there were 93 provincial superior appeal judges and 1,362 provincial trial judges ("purely provincial" and provincial superior combined), and the trial-to-appeal ratio is significantly higher for the larger provinces (see Table 5.1). The practical impact of this ratio is, of course, even greater because appeal judges sit in panels, and so every review of a trial decision takes several appeal judges. Quite unlike the elegant diagrams that are used to represent it, the Canadian judicial pyramid is extremely wide and not very tall — the appeal judges represent the tiny tip of a squat and stubby pyramid of trial judges. The two factors — the small numbers of appeals and the small numbers of appeal judges — are simply different sides of the same coin, the general principle again being that the "transaction costs" of queuing constitute an invisible but highly effective form of rationing.

Canada's Provincial Appeal Courts: Caseloads

The table below is a rough comparison of the 1989 caseload of the ten provincial courts of appeal. There are serious methodological problems in deciding how to count numbers of appeals,[2] and procedures differ from one province to another, so these numbers should be taken as indicative rather than definitive. The table approximates the number of panel decisions by each court of appeal in a single calendar year, excluding both chambers actions by single judges and appeals filed but abandoned or settled.

Table 5.2

Caseload, Canadian Provincial Courts of Appeal 1989

Province	Criminal	Civil	Total
Alberta	746	275	1021
British Columbia	265	399	664
Manitoba	261	184	445
New Brunswick	58	106	164
Newfoundland	65	35	100
Nova Scotia	195	165	360
Ontario	837	492	1329
Prince Edward I.	31	34	65
Quebec	321	830	1151
Saskatchewan	304	194	498
Total:	3083	2714	5797

Source: Report from a judge of each court; except B.C. from
Registrar. All figures 1989 except B.C., 1987.

These overall totals represent the culmination of a twenty-five-year period during which "a remarkable growth in the volume of appeals appear[ed] to be a general North American phenomenon" (Russell 1987, 294). More recent figures (McCormick and Griffiths 1993) suggest that this growth may have peaked toward the end of the 1980s, and some but not all provinces have seen a modest decline in the early 1990s. It may therefore also be the end of a dramatic increase in the size of the courts of appeal in the same period.

The most obvious feature of the table is the absence of a clear pattern. On purely logical grounds, one would expect that the number of appeals generated in any single province would be some function of population (more people mean more disputes), filtered through the number of trial judges operating within the province and the number of appeal judges available (invoking the notions of transaction costs and queuing theory). That this is not the case is shown by the high caseload of Alberta — much higher than that of neighbouring and larger British Columbia, almost as large as that of Quebec. On any per capita basis, the two large central provinces are surprisingly quiet, while the people of the prairie provinces litigate much more enthusiastically. Similarly, each trial judge in Alberta generates almost seven appeals, her counterpart in Manitoba 6.5; the figures for Ontario and Quebec are less than half as large. In some provinces, such as Alberta, appeal judges sit on panels that hear several hundred appeals each year, each judge delivering and explaining the decision in about one-third of them. In others, such as the Atlantic provinces, the per-judge workload is about one-fifth as large.

Nor do the vagaries of the appeal process operate similarly on civil and criminal appeals. Some provinces, such as Alberta, hear almost three criminal appeals for every civil appeal; in others, such as Quebec, that ratio is reversed. Six provincial courts of appeal confront a caseload that is primarily criminal, three have a workload dominated by civil appeals, and in P.E.I. the numbers are almost equal. If there were an average provincial court of appeal, it would have Saskatchewan's nine judges, B.C.'s total caseload (about 600-650), and Nova Scotia's criminal/civil balance. These ratios are not single-year accidents; generalizing from a tracking of the caseloads of Alberta and Manitoba over most of the last decade, they persist in remarkably similar form from one year to the next.

These variations confirm the observation (Blom-Cooper and Drewry 1972, 45) that the apparently straightforward phenomenon of appeal is actually far more complex. It depends on the local legal culture, on the relative reputations of trial and appeal judges, on the formal and informal processes that surround the appeals process, on calculated or impressionistic perceptions of the prospects of success, and so on — the relationships are so complex, they drily suggest, that we might as well attribute them to "'historical accident,' a term whose use excuses the scholar from seeking more sophisticated answers."

Canada's Provincial Appeal Courts: Procedures

As a general principle, litigants have a right to the appellate review of a trial decision.[3] This statement would be too direct for a legal textbook, which would insist that appeal courts will review findings of law but not findings of fact (leaving mixed questions of fact and law to a problematic middle ground). Such a textbook would rightly point out that there is an important distinction between "appeals by right" (which must be heard on the merits) and "appeals by leave" (in which an appeal judge or panel will decide whether or not the case deserves a hearing on the merits). However, the fact/law distinction is easier to utter than to carry through in practice (one appeal judge has written, "I see no clear line in law between matters of law and matters of fact" [Kerans 1993, 72]) and may very well be technologically obsolete. To accept the trial judge's intuition with regard to such things as witness credibility was one thing fifty years ago, but it is another today when the testimony may well have been videotaped. And the leave procedure itself involves one or several judges hearing the arguments and reviewing the material (to such an extent that the application for leave and the substantive decision virtually collapse into a single process for many appeals, which in itself is some kind of review of the trial judge's performance).

Virtually all appeals in Canada are appeals "on the record." (The alternative, once common in this country, is appeal by trial *de novo* — that is, when the loser appeals, the trial is held all over again before a higher judge or judges. As Kerans [1993, 71] says, "If we lacked confidence in magistrates' courts, the proper course, we belatedly realized, was to reform that institution rather than repeat the trial process before a tribunal we trusted.") An appellate hearing does not involve the examination of witnesses or the physical presentation of evidence; rather, it centres on an argument based on the written transcript of the original trial, focusing on the passage or passages that the appellant believes demonstrate error — and not just any error but one that is large and serious enough to suggest that the result may not have been fair.

The volume of written material that flows past an appeal judge is staggering — in some cases, the stack of files for a single month's cases is as tall as the judge who has to work through them. The list includes trial transcripts (usually of the entire trial, because only some provinces permit, and not all lawyers offer, partial transcripts of the problematic portion of the trial), appellants' factums (containing the legal argument that is the basis of the appeal, usually several dozen pages and sometimes much longer), respondents' factums (trying to refute the appellants' arguments), and lists of authorities cited in both factums. In most provinces, all members of the panel are expected to prepare for every single appeal; in Quebec (and from time to time in Saskatchewan), the practice is to assign each member of the panel (the "designated" or the "circled" judge) the responsibility for preparing to take the lead in the courtroom consideration and the conference room discussion of a share of the caseload.

Different judges have evolved different strategies for deciding how much of this material, and in what order, it is necessary to read.

It is misleading (not to say unrealistic) to assume that every page of any file is read by any judge, let alone by all three or more members of the panel. Most Canadian appeal judges (there are a few outspoken exceptions) are committed to the principle of a "hot bench," by which they mean that the judges arrive in the courtroom having already read through the material and prepared to respond to it. Counsel do not have to present the entire material but only the central issues and responses to critical questions. The alternative model, the "cold bench," implies that judges will rely on the lawyers in the courtroom to identify and clarify issues — but what this method saves the judges in preparation time is more than made up in the lengthier oral arguments that may be necessary to clarify issues and fill in the background.

Despite the importance of the written documentation, all Canadian jurisdictions are still committed to the oral hearing; that is, an appeal involves an appearance by the litigants' lawyers in person before the judges of the appeal panel. This practice differs from that in the U.S., where "some state supreme courts have essentially done away with oral arguments." Even in the states where it remains, many justices feel "it is questionable whether it has a marked impact on the outcome of cases" (McConkie 1976). Canadian judges, when confronted by these observations, are not impressed. Oral argument remains an important part of the process, and most judges say that they often change their minds in the course of oral argument by well-prepared and competent counsel.

However, it would be wrong to think of oral argument as lengthy prepared oratory: quite the contrary. Lawyers are frequently interrupted by questions from the bench (and would think it an ominous sign if they were not), and the preferred style is very quiet and low key. The histrionics of television lawyers are completely out of place. Nor do lawyers have huge unlimited sweeps of time in which to develop their persuasive points at length. In most provinces, they are asked how much time they will need and argued down to a lower limit if the request seems excessive. In Ontario (which keeps detailed minute books that allow the matter to be measured with precision), the average criminal appellant takes about half an hour to present the argument, the average civil appellant about an hour, although in both cases a very large number of appeals take less than fifteen minutes. All these measurements include the time taken by interruptions from the bench (Baar et al. 1992, 272). The respondent's lawyer is only called on if the appellant has persuaded the court that there is a case to be answered. Much of the time this hurdle has not been cleared ("We will not need to call on you, Ms. Smith" tells the respondent that she has already prevailed). Even when respondents' lawyers are called on, they are typically given only about half as long as the appellants'. Although the observation may seem counterintuitive at first glance, appeals do not usually last anything like as long as trials, and appeal decisions are typically much shorter. The average criminal appeal in Ontario (appellant time plus respondent time plus judge conference and decision delivery time) takes about sixty minutes; the average civil appeal, ninety minutes.

The practice of not calling on the respondent's lawyer if the appellant has failed to make a solid case may seem both rude (to the appellant's lawyer) and inefficient (because the respondent's lawyer has in effect wasted both preparation time and court appearance time). However, it establishes an important principle of the appellate process, namely, the question of who carries the burden of proof. In criminal trials, the presumption of innocence means that the prosecution carries the burden of proof. In civil trials, the standard of proof is the preponderance of the evidence. In appeals, however, "our system asserts a presumption of correctness in favour of the first court, and imposes a burden on an appellant to show error" (Kerans 1993, 73). An Alberta appeal judge I interviewed spoke of a "rule of three" — "one-third of the time, we allow the appeal; one-third of the time, we dismiss it; and one-third of the time we wonder why they are wasting our time." These casual estimates are in fact close to the mark. For those courts and years for which complete figures are available, the overall percentage of successful appeals hovers in the high 30s.

Appeal Court Decision-Making: Panels

The number of members of provincial courts of appeal across Canada varies from the three of Prince Edward Island to the nineteen of Quebec, with ten being an average. P.E.I. aside, they never sit as a single complete body. Unlike the U.S. state supreme courts, almost all of which always sit as a single panel including every single judge, the Canadian provincial courts of appeal sit in smaller panels, with the three-judge appeal panel becoming all but universal in recent decades. Larger panels (of five or even seven judges) are possible and can be specifically requested by the litigants, but they are rarely granted and now seem to be limited to cases of unusual importance (major Charter decisions or reference questions from the provincial government) or to cases in which the court of appeal is being asked to overturn an earlier precedent from the same court. (It has not been the case for many years, as Zimmer [1988] incorrectly suggests, that appeals from certain serious crimes, such as murder, are automatically or even normally referred to a larger panel.) This has been a fairly recent trend in Canadian judicial practices; during the 1920s and 1930s, for example, almost half of all reported decisions by the provincial courts of appeal were handled by panels of five or more judges, but by the 1980s this number had fallen to fewer than 2 per cent. The panels are not permanent; judges rotate between panels from one month to the next. In the Western provinces the rotation process is close to perfectly random (literally so in Manitoba); in Ontario, there is some attempt to put both experienced and "new" judges on panels, in Quebec, to mix the judges resident in Montreal and Quebec, and in the Atlantic provinces, the chief justice assigns panels with an eye to experience and (possibly) expertise (McCormick and Griffiths 1993).

But the increasing size of the courts of appeal, coupled with an (until recently) increasing caseload, creates the serious problem of how to co-ordinate the decision-making of the various panels. This was not a major problem in 1933 when there were only thirty-seven full-time appeal judges on six different courts; or even in 1953 when the number had grown to forty-three; but it began to loom larger in 1973 when eight provinces had a total of sixty-two appeal judges; and it is even more evident now that ninety-six appeal judges (and twenty-eight supernumeraries) sit in the ten provinces. In many provinces, there may be four or more panels sitting at the same time, which means that one panel may be ruling one way on a question of law while down the hall another panel is ruling the other way. Many provinces try to circulate drafts of all decisions to all members of the court, not just to those on the panel, although this material has to compete for reading and research time with the cases already assigned to other panels. Others limit circulation to drafts of significant questions, which begs the question of how judges become aware that their own decision may be taking a different direction from that of another panel. Some courts have periodic or occasional formal meetings of the entire court to discuss how to handle emerging issues; others leave the issue to informal exchanges at meals or at coffee breaks.

Nor is it clear what happens if the formal circulation of drafts or the informal exchange of views reveals major disagreements on matters of law within the court — if, for example, a three-judge panel finds that its members are the odd ones out in a larger court. On the one hand, if the three defer to their colleagues, the decision is effectively being made by judges who did not hear the oral arguments or give counsel a chance to respond to their concerns, which offends the basic premises of appellate decision-making. On the other hand, if they do not, the panel is establishing a precedent that will be resented, or even cheerfully overturned, by their colleagues at the very first opportunity, which offends the principles of legal continuity. Neither alternative is particularly attractive. On one occasion in the 1960s, the Quebec Court of Queen's Bench (as it was called before 1973) called counsel back to re-argue a case before a much larger panel when the depths of disagreement within the court emerged from informal exchanges, but doing so is hardly practical on a regular basis. The problem is structural — every court has its "hawks" and "doves," its "deference to the legislature" judges and its "Charter enthusiasts," and it is inevitable that a minority of the full court will from time to time be a majority of a panel. It is for this reason that most U.S. states have been reluctant to divide their supreme courts into smaller panels to deal with the problems of burgeoning caseload and have tended to prefer other solutions, such as intermediate appeal courts (Stern 1988).

Appeal Judgments

The appeal panel has several basic options in any case that it hears. The first, and by the far the most common, is to uphold the decision of the trial judge by dismissing the appeal. Alternatively, the panel may substitute its own collective judgment for that of the trial judge, either by reversing the original finding (not guilty instead of guilty, liable instead of not liable) or by altering the outcome (increasing or decreasing a sentence or an award of damages). Finally, and least often, it may quash the decision and send the case back for a new trial.

Often, the appeal decision is delivered the same day as the presentation of oral argument, usually after the appeal panel has adjourned for a brief conference. In most provinces, a majority of these decisions are delivered orally from the bench, although they may be accompanied by an endorsement (short reasons handwritten on the back of the file, frequently used in Ontario for criminal appeals) or be followed by a bench memorandum (brief written reasons, possibly edited from a transcription of the oral decision itself, a method often used in Alberta). Alternatively, for a minority of more important or more difficult appeals, judgment may be "reserved," which means that full written reasons will be delivered days (or possibly months) later. The proportion of cases reserved for such treatment varies from one province to another; in some provinces with a modest caseload, it may be the practice to give written reasons for every single appeal, while in others only a tenth or fewer of cases will be reserved.

Appellate decisions are usually not very long. In recent years, about one-sixth of appeal court decisions have been reported (that is, selected as being important enough to be published in one or more of the law reports, the choice being made by the editors of the report and not by the court), and they average half a dozen pages or less. The decisions usually cite a handful of earlier cases to justify the outcome, often ground the findings in one or more federal or provincial statutes, and rarely make any reference to academic literature or legal or legislative reports. The implications of the citation practices of Canadian appeal judges will be considered in Chapter 9.

There is a growing tendency towards having a single unanimous opinion from appeal panels. (In Ontario, more than in any other province, this takes the form of a unanimous anonymous "By the Court" decision; in other provinces, decisions are typically authored by an identified judge with the others simply and silently concurring.) In the 1920s and 1930s, for example, there were dissents in 32.8 per cent of all reported appeal court decisions and separate concurring judgments (agreeing with the outcome but not with the reasons) in 63.0 per cent; the same figure for the 1980s is 10.6 per cent for dissents, 11.4 per cent for separate concurrences, although these overall figures disguise a high dissent rate for provinces like Manitoba and Quebec and a very low one for Ontario and Nova Scotia. The decline in these figures clearly reflects the emergence of a new concept of the appellate role, a role that involves not a set of individuals each responding to a legal issue but rather an institution that provides clear and focused answers (Kornhauser and Sager 1986-87). However, the result is an informal ethic that discourages dissent and thereby overstates the unanimity on any given court (Atkins and Green 1976, Dubois 1988).

Appeal Court Decision-Making: Who Appeals?
If we were trying to compare one store or business enterprise with another, a logical starting point would be to look at the type of customers they tend to attract — yuppies or teens or the working

class or whatever. By the same token, if we think of the appeal courts as providing a service, the logical question is to ask who takes advantage of them. Table 5.3 is based on all the reported and unreported appeals of the Manitoba Court of Appeal that were decided during the thirty-six months between 1 January 1989 and 31 December 1991. The selection of Manitoba is convenient (in that the complete data happens to be available) rather than logical; that is to say, there is no reason to think that the same patterns prevail in any detail for the other provinces and some reason (given the caseload diversities demonstrated in earlier tables) to think that they might well vary, so these numbers should simply be taken as a useful starting point.

The largest single litigant category is comprised of "natural persons" — that is ordinary individuals. Their numbers are not really surprising, given that one side of every criminal appeal is almost invariably an individual (criminal appeals involving corporate entities are extremely rare) and that family disputes (custody, access, division of marital property) often pitch one individual against another. Over half of the litigants appearing in the court of appeal were individuals, making up over two-thirds of the appellants and almost one-third of the respondents.

The second most frequent litigant is the Crown, which appears as appellant in one-twelfth of the cases and as respondent in almost half. These data reflect the fact that criminal appeals loom large in the Manitoba caseload and that most criminal appeals are lodged by the accused. Half of these represent substantive appeals (against conviction or against both conviction and sentence), while the other half are sentence appeals, but again the ratio between these two types cannot be generalized, and the patterns are different in other provinces.

The third most common litigant category is business corporations, which make up about one-twelfth of the caseload for appellants and respondents alike. About one-seventh of the business litigants have been listed separately as "big" businesses, a category comprising chartered banks, insurance companies, and the Canadian Pacific Railway.

Table 5.3:

**Appearances and Successes, by Litigant Category,
Manitoba Court of Appeal Decisions 1989-1991**

Litigant Type	Appellant	Respondent	Total
Individual	684 (69.6%)	326 (33.2%)	1010 (51.4%)
Crown	119 (12.1%)	444 (45.2%)	563 (28.6%)
Business	128 (13.0%)	113 (11.5%)	241 (12.3%)
Provincial gov't	26 (2.6%)	44 (4.5%)	70 (3.6%)
Big business	12 (1.2%)	26 (2.6%)	38 (1.9%)
Municipal gov't	5 (0.5%)	13 (4.5%)	18 (0.9%)
Unions	3 (0.5%)	3 (1.3%)	6 (0.3%)
Federal gov't	3 (0.3%)	2 (0.2%)	5 (0.3%)
Other litigants	3 (0.3%)	12 (0.3%)	15 (0.8%)

Governments (excluding criminal cases) make up the fourth largest litigant category with about 5 per cent of the total. Most of these litigants represent departments or agencies of the provincial government, with only a small number of appearances by municipal governments and even fewer by instrumentalities of the federal government. Trade unions average only two cases a year (one each as appellant and respondent) and are therefore marginal to the activities of appeal courts. The small number of trade union cases may seem curious in a time that has been characterized by a retrenchment of the powers of trade unions, but it may also reflect the longstanding union suspicion of courts as a genuinely neutral arbiter in labour disputes.

There were also a handful of litigants (such as universities, governments of other countries, and church congregations) who could not be fitted conveniently into any of these categories, and they have therefore been left to a miscellaneous and residual "other" category.

The mix of these litigant types is less skewed toward the big businesses and the large lawsuits than we might have anticipated. There are some very important battles fought in the provincial appellate courtrooms, but these major cases take their turn in line with a wide range of much more mundane concerns. Following the reported cases of any court of appeal for any length of time makes the point — there are major Charter issues, important questions of public law, and interpretations of difficult sections of important new legislation, but mixed in with them are decisions that take few pages of text to resolve, that do not involve large sums of money, and that seem to carry little precedential impact. To put this same point somewhat differently: the appellate function is much more preoccupied with routine cases and straightforward results than one might expect (Wold 1978; Wold and Caldeira 1980-81).

Nevertheless, it is not true that all these categories of litigant enjoy roughly similar rates of success as either appellants or respondents. The patterns of advantage, and the implications that they carry for the system, are considered further in Chapter 10.

Conclusion

A provincial appeal court performs two functions that, to some extent, pull in two different directions. The first function implies a supervisory role, accomplished in the primary sense of the correction of error by trial judges and in the secondary sense of visibly reminding judges that there is a statistically small chance of review in which error will result in professional embarrassment. Even an unsuccessful appeal, resulting in an affirmation of the trial decision, may perform a valuable cathartic role by giving the losing litigant the honour of a second opinion and by reducing the "luck of the draw" overtones of a single decision by a specific trial judge. The second function implies a uniformity and leadership role. Without any implication of error, it may be the case that different trial judges have responded to ambiguity or discretion in significantly different ways and that the administration of justice is served by declaring the single optimal response. There may be occasions in which the court finds the opportunity to provide judicial leadership in the accommodation of changing social circumstances and emerging problems.

But these dual functions result in the appeal courts being caught between two fires. On the one hand, to the extent that the court exists to correct error, the general principle of accessibility suggests the desirability of making it easier for disappointed parties to appeal and of providing for the more expeditious resolution of those appeals. The problem is that the resulting high caseload can be accommodated only by more summary processes (oral decisions or endorsements), the general impact being that larger number of cases inevitably reduce the amount of time and attention that can be devoted to any single case. The all-but-inevitable tendency would be for the court to decide specific cases on the narrowest relevant terms rather than to create the general guidelines and the overarching principles that judicial leadership implies. As a U.S. federal appeal judge bluntly suggests, "the bigger the dockets, the less time we spend on the difficult cases and the more mistakes we make." (Edwards 1983, 403).

Beyond a certain point, higher caseload calls for expanding the size of the appellate bench as well, with the inevitable result of co-ordination problems between the panels. The larger the court, the greater the problem. As more panels operate, it becomes harder for appeal judges to know what their colleagues are doing, and the diverging practices of individual panels can make "luck of the draw" considerations increasingly relevant to appeal court deliberations as well as to trial court outcomes (Heard 1991). An appeal court that always meets in fragments is a different kettle of fish altogether from a stable panel of nine or so individuals who collectively respond to the same caseload.

On the other hand, if the court of appeal exists to provide judicial uniformity and leadership, then the caseload should be restricted (for example, by hearing only those cases that the judges agree raise legal issues of general significance), the per-case time for personal re- search and for conference deliberation should be increased, and the size of the court should be restricted to maximize both collegiality and consistency. All of these imply a court that hears dozens rather than hundreds (let alone thousands) of cases per year. Of course, conflict between the two roles is not just a question of caseloads and volumes but also of the types of cases which are considered. Uni- formity and leadership issues could be raised by a case where the trial judge made no error and the court may just wish to add the weight of its own words to the way the case was handled, while an appeal correctly identifying an error might be turned away if it failed to raise legal issues of more general concern.

Obviously, the Canadian provincial courts of appeal try to do both jobs at the same time — by giving each panel a mixture of the routine and the significant, by trying to schedule regular "decision weeks" to free up research time, by collapsing the application for leave into the substantive consideration — but it is surely not unfair to suggest that this means they do neither job as well as they could if they were more single-minded. The U.S. solution has typically been to inter- pose an intermediate court of appeal between the trial courts and the state supreme court, dealing with the routine appeals and thereby reserving the docket of the state supreme court for a smaller number of critical cases to which the court can devote focused time and attention (Fair 1971). This has not been the Canadian practice except for Ontario's Divisional Court, discontinued in the recent amalgamation, which reduced the caseload of the Ontario Court of Appeal by dealing with specific categories of appeal. Indeed, the creation of a further level of court runs counter to the current tendency toward a simplified and streamlined court system. The consolidation movement is giving us fewer and more generalized courts, not an increasing number of functionally specialized courts.

The same general logic of function and procedure applies to the Supreme Court of Canada as well, although, as the next chapter will indicate, it has in recent decades organized itself more single-mindedly around the second of the appellate roles.

The Supreme Court of Canada

The apex of the Canadian judicial system is the Supreme Court of Canada, from which there is no further legal appeal. The decisions of its nine judges constitute binding precedent for all other courts and judges. But it was not always so, not even within the comparatively short span of time that marks Canada's existence as a nation. The emergence of the modern Supreme Court can be outlined by describing three major dates in its history and filled in by identifying three minor ones.

The Establishment and Evolution of the Supreme Court

The first key date is 1875. One of the anomalies of the Supreme Court is that it was not created by the document that united the British North American colonies to form the Dominion of Canada. Section 101 of the Constitution Act 1867 does not create a court but only empowers the Parliament of Canada to establish a "General Court of Appeal," something that was not attempted until half a dozen years after Confederation and not achieved until 1875. The Supreme Court that serves from time to time as the great "referee of federalism" was itself unilaterally created, and its six judges (after 1927, seven judges) were unilaterally appointed by the national government.

Although the empowering legislation was entitled The Supreme Court Act, the new court was not truly supreme. Confusion about compromise amendments and unfulfilled expectations for reforms to the English judicial system clouded the issue, but when Parliament created the Supreme Court, it did not abolish appeals "to the foot of the throne" in the form of the Judicial Committee of the Privy Council — a body established in 1833, technically advisory to the monarch but staffed with respected judges and law lords, which served as a final court of appeal for the British Empire (Strayer 1988). Not only could the Supreme Court's decisions themselves be appealed to the Judicial Committee, but if both parties agreed, it was often possible for appeals to go directly from the highest court of a province to London, bypassing the Supreme Court entirely. These *per saltum* appeals happened fairly frequently; in fact, until after the First World War, most Canadian cases before the Judicial Committee followed this route.

Table 6.1:

Appeals from Canada to JCPC, by decade and source

Appeal From	1870s	1880s	1890s	1900s	1910s	1920s	1930s	1940s	1950s
SCC	2	21	16	35	48	52	41	24	14
NS	3	5	5	2	1	4	2	0	0
NB	2	1	1	0	0	3	0	0	0
PQ	48	22	21	27	12	22	9	1	0
ONT	1	4	10	26	31	18	16	7	0
MAN	0	1	3	1	7	4	1	0	0
SASK				0	3	3	0	1	0
ALTA				0	5	4	4	2	2
BC	0	0	6	7	26	13	9	1	3
Other						2	2		
*per saltum	54	33	46	63	85	73	43	12	5
TOTAL	56	54	62	98	133	125	84	36	19

Total JCPC appeals	667
Total from SCC	253
Total *per saltum* appeals	414

* Appeals that bypassed (leapt over) the Supreme Court.
from Snell and Vaughan, *The Supreme Court of Canada*, p.180

As Table 6.1 demonstrates, most *per saltum* appeals before 1900 came from Quebec; afterwards, most came from Ontario (and, to a lesser but still striking extent, B.C.). This is an interesting display of the ambivalence at the core of Canadian nationhood. The national court that could symbolize national unity and the maturity of judicial supremacy for many Canadians represented for Quebeckers the threat of English-Canadian dominance and possibly put in jeopardy Quebec's unique civil law heritage. Only the cause célèbre of an unpopular Judicial Committee decision on a church-related appeal from Quebec broke the impasse in Parliament long enough to permit the Supreme Court Act to slip through (Bushnell 1992). The same ambivalence continued to dog its steps for many decades. An assertive and confident Supreme Court provoked Quebec fears and avoidance, sometimes to the point where proposals were made to abolish it. But a fragmented and hesitant court, trapped in the Judicial Committee's shadow, provoked unfavourable comparisons with the status and reputation of Ontario's own Court of Appeal and triggered Ontario-based complaints and end-runs. As a proportion of the Supreme Court's total decisions, appeals to the Judicial Committee do not loom very large and did not always result in reversal, but they created, in Bora Laskin's words, a "captive court" that was reluctant to display initiative or judicial leadership and to which it was frequently difficult to recruit the most able lawyers and judges (Russell 1987, 337).

Whether the Judicial Committee of the Privy Council provided Canada with useful and effective constitutional guidance, valuably insulated from local pressures, or whether it derailed the constitutional designs of the Fathers of Confederation on the basis of uneven and possibly obtuse motivations is a debate that continues to rage (recently revived by Cairns 1971 and Vaughan 1986). It is certainly the case that it jostled the elbows of the nascent Supreme Court of Canada and made more difficult the emergence of a distinctly Canadian jurisprudence. Bushnell (1992) tells the tale of the Supreme Court's frustrations; and Snell and Vaughan (1986) capture its spirit when they recount an episode in which the Supreme Court declined to give written reasons for a decision on the grounds that the matter would be appealed to the Judicial Committee and that committee never seemed to read the reasons.

If 1875 is the first significant date in the history of the Supreme Court, 1949 is the second. That year marked the abolition (by an amendment to the Supreme Court Act, following a 1947 reference case taken to the Judicial Committee itself) of appeals to the Privy Council. What Russell has aptly called its "long adolescence" was finally over. Because the effect was not retroactive, it did not apply

to cases already before Canadian courts, and cases — some, like
A.-G. Ontario v. Winner, with important constitutional implications
— continued to wend their way through the system for almost another decade, the last one being decided in 1957 (Morrow 1978). The
amendment also increased the court to its present size of nine, and
the number of appointments required from the bar of the province of
Quebec rose from two to three.

The heavy hand of precedent — that is, the doctrine that older
decisions should be followed in new cases — undercut the possibility
that the patriation of judicial authority would be marked by dramatic
changes. However, there were several indications that the Supreme
Court was now prepared to blaze its own trail. The first indication
was that it began to adopt more of an "institutional" approach to
making decisions. Its judgments in earlier decades often looked as if
each judge approached the matter on his own, resolving the question
not just in different ways but also at different levels of generality
with different sets of reasons. Indeed, early in the century it was not
even clear whether the court conducted conferences after hearing
arguments or scattered to write their own first drafts independently.
After 1949, however, the ratio of written opinions to decided cases
began a sharp and permanent decrease, and unanimous judgments —
in which a single judge delivered a single opinion speaking for the
entire Court — became more frequent. The second indication was a
higher calibre of appointment, characterized by such individuals as
Rand and Laskin. These changes allowed the court to play a stronger
leadership role for the lower courts. The third indication was a
willingness gradually to build up its own jurisprudence, its own
constitutional direction — breathing life into the "peace order and
good government" clause of Section 91; tilting the balance toward
the federal trade and commerce power and away from the provincial
powers over property and civil rights; striking down popular Quebec
statutes in a string of bold civil rights decisions in the 1950s. To be
sure, the Court retreated from the opportunity presented by the Die-
fenbaker government's quasi-constitutional Bill of Rights, but its
general performance over the first decades of true supremacy was
mildly encouraging.

The third date, fittingly occurring near the Supreme Court's one
hundredth birthday, was 1975. At this time, Parliament made major
amendments to its jurisdiction and procedure. There are essentially
two different kinds of appeals: appeals by right, which the Court must
hear if the parties request review, and appeals by leave, which the

Court can decide to hear or not to hear at its discretion. The 1975 amendments accomplished a major expansion of the Court's discretionary jurisdiction, constituting something of an "invisible revolution" in the Supreme Court's operations that could hardly have loomed large in the eyes of the average citizen but was of enormous importance. Essentially, discretionary jurisdiction allows the Supreme Court to focus its limited resources of hearing and research and writing time to cases that raise important questions rather than to the consideration of routine questions elevated to the Supreme Court docket by virtue of the amount of money at issue. It also allows the Court (as the U.S. Supreme Court has transparently done on a number of occasions) to wait until it is ready to hear a case — until a string of appeal court decisions have clarified a range of related issues, until a background of Supreme Court jurisprudence has developed, until the judges have sorted out with a reasonable degree of unity how they want to deal with it. Although courts are by definition reactive institutions, unable to set their own agenda and obliged to respond to the initiatives of the parties who bring cases before them, a generous discretionary jurisdiction gives the Court a more effective role.

However, the 1975 amendments did not establish complete discretionary control. Bushnell (1987) indicates that further amendments to the Supreme Court Act, which would have further extended discretionary leave, were twice introduced but never passed by the Commons. He suggests that this fact must be interpreted as a vote of non-confidence in the Supreme Court's performance. The incompleteness of the revolution is reflected in the fact that after a sharp drop (from about 85% of total caseload in the early 1970s to about 15% in the late 1970s), "appeals by right" are again increasing in the Supreme Court caseload (Supreme Court Bulletin, 1992). On a continuum between the near-total discretion of the U.S. Supreme Court and the large number of appeals by right to the provincial courts of appeal, the Supreme Court of Canada falls in between, but rather closer to the provincial courts. This limitation on its capacity to choose the substance and the timing of important decisions leaves it in some sense still a "captive court" — a captive of the litigants who determine its caseload.

The evolution of the Supreme Court must be filled out by three other dates, more minor but still important. The first is the appointment of the brilliant and controversial Bora Laskin, first as associate justice in 1970 and then as Chief Justice in 1973. More transparently than most of those appointed earlier, Laskin brought to the court not only a reputation as an expert in constitutional law and a provocatively outspoken appeal court judge but also a clear agenda in the form of a stronger vision of the federal government's role and a commitment to civil liberties. But he also carried an expanded notion of the Court's own role, and he played a part in bringing the Court to declare both a more relaxed attitude toward "binding" precedent and a stricter reading of the extent to which its pronouncements bound lower courts. Under Laskin's prodding in the form of frequent dissents in his early years and under his leadership, the Supreme Court established itself as a force to be reckoned with rather than a sideshow in national politics.

The second of these minor dates was the patriation reference of 1981, which stalled the Trudeau government's unilateral initiatives for the patriation of the constitution and an entrenched Charter of Rights and thereby created the conditions that allowed a compromise consensus to emerge that excluded only Quebec. Although the substance is open to criticism on jurisprudential grounds (Russell 1983) and the precedent-setting live broadcast of the decision was botched, the event clearly demonstrated the new centrality of the Supreme Court in national life.

The third date was 1982, the entrenchment of the Charter. The Charter is a declaration of the fundamental principles of citizens' rights, but it is up to the courts — and above all up to the Supreme Court — to interpret the practical meaning of the general phrases and to apply them to specific social circumstances. In the process, the Supreme Court becomes, at least potentially, the final word on all public policy, federal or provincial, examining the actions of elected representatives and appointed officials to see if they measure up to constitutional standards. The fact that the Supreme Court has been so often prepared to uphold Charter claims (Morton, Russell, and Witley, 1992) makes the new prominence of the judicial system in general and Supreme Court in particular much more than hypothetical. Every time it rules on the constitutionality of abortion legislation, or the validity of compulsory retirement rules, or voting rights for prisoners, or any other issue, the Supreme Court demonstrates the importance that it has finally achieved and seems unlikely to relinquish.

The culmination of all these developments is the modern Supreme Court of Canada, far more of a major actor in ongoing public affairs than it has ever been before. A few decades ago, it was a rare month that saw a front-page story on a Supreme Court decision; today, it is a rare month that does not.

The Supreme Court Caseload

Three basic components comprise the Supreme Court caseload. The first, and by far the largest, is appeals from the various provincial and territorial courts of appeal (or, earlier in the period surveyed, before the last of the provinces acquired a full-time specialized appeal court, the provincial superior trial court of the province sitting *en banc*). These cases are the focus of this analysis. The second component is appeals from the Federal Court of Canada (before 1971, the Exchequer Court of Canada), which account for about one case in seven. The third, and smallest, is a miscellaneous category including reference cases from the federal government, *per saltum* appeals from provincial superior trial courts, appeals from federal boards and tribunals, and rehearings of various kinds.

Table 6.2:

**Proportions of Appeals from Provincial CAs
Reported Decisions, September 1949 to June 1990**

Chief Justice SCC	BC	AB	Ssk	Mn	Ont	Que	Atl
Rinfret	15.3%	11.2%	4.6%	5.1%	26.5%	29.1%	8.2%
Kerwin	15.2%	7.9%	5.8%	3.7%	32.5%	30.7%	4.2%
Taschereau	14.9%	10.8%	6.3%	8.2%	32.1%	23.9%	3.7%
Cartwright	14.6%	11.7%	4.9%	5.3%	34.0%	26.7%	2.9%
Fauteux	15.2%	10.7%	7.4%	5.9%	31.5%	23.0%	6.3%
Laskin	12.8%	9.6%	4.4%	6.3%	27.5%	28.6%	10.7%
Dickson	17.2%	11.7%	6.1%	9.2%	25.0%	21.6%	9.2%
TOTAL:	14.7%	10.1%	5.5%	6.3%	29.2%	26.7%	7.5%

Between September 1949 and June 1990, there were 2,976 reported decisions on appeals from the provincial courts of appeal. The long-term breakdown between the various provinces is roughly 25 per cent Quebec, 30 per cent Ontario, 35 per cent West, 7.5 per cent Atlantic. However, as shown in Table 6.2, these figures obscure a two-decade swing away from central provinces (whose share of total SCC caseload has never been lower, falling below 50% for the first time during the 1980s) to the Western and Atlantic provinces. A typical recent "package" of appeals would include four or five from Quebec, five from Ontario, eight from the West, and two from the Atlantic provinces. In the case of the Atlantic provinces, these changes may well be connected to the more recent creation of specialized full-time appeal courts (1967 for Nova Scotia and New Brunswick; 1975 for Newfoundland; 1987 for Prince Edward Island), but it is harder to see an obvious causal factor for changes in the proportions of appeals from the other regions.

The most obvious a priori explanations — success rates, population, and physical proximity — can all be ruled out. The differing appeal rates are not results-driven; there are not more appeals from some provinces because of an empirically based expectation of a higher probability of success or fewer appeals from others because their appeal courts are seldom reversed. The Western provinces are appealed *more* often, and Quebec *less* often, than a results-driven logic would justify. Population might be expected to have an influence, both in the crude sense that large provinces have more people to press disputes to any given level and in the more subtle sense that large provinces are statistically more likely to have a new legal problem or issue arise in justiciable form for the first time, with its resolution obviating the need or the incentive for similar appeals. Yet, the numbers do not support this hypothesis. In appeals per hundred thousand of population, the West (especially Manitoba) has been consistently overrepresented and the central provinces (especially Ontario) consistently underrepresented. Finally, one might have expected that physical proximity would make appeals to the Supreme Court at least marginally less expensive and inconvenient for parties in Ontario and Quebec than for parties in the rest of Canada and that this factor would discourage appeals from provinces outside the centre, but the appeal rates from the central provinces are lower than those from the periphery. Neither success rates nor population patterns nor physical proximity carries adequate explanatory weight in the differential appeal rates from the various provinces.

From the point of view of a provincial court of appeal, unusually high rates of appeal have both negative and positive aspects. On the negative side, the more often one is appealed, the more likely one is to be reversed; and since the media tend to report individual reversals rather than overall or comparative reversal rates, the reputation of a provincial court of appeal can be hurt in the eyes of its own legal public by an unusually large number of appeals. The flip side of the coin, however, is that a strong provincial appeal court has the advantage of more frequently putting its point of view before the Supreme Court. Granted, Supreme Court judges read widely, but presumably the cases they read the most closely include those before them on appeal. If there is a distinct regional flavour or component to the resolution of legal issues and if there are unusually capable and articulate judges on the provincial appeal court to explain and justify their point of view, then the larger number of appeals from a specific province represents a greater opportunity to influence Supreme Court doctrine.

If the source of the Supreme Court caseload has been changing over time, so has the balance of the various types of law. The caseload can be divided into three distinct categories — criminal, private, and public law[1] — and the results for each of the Chief Justiceships are shown in Table 6.3.

Table 6.3:

Breakdown of Supreme Court Caseload in Appeals from Provincial Courts of Appeal Reported Decisions, September 1949 to June 1990

	Criminal	*Private*	*Public*	*Total*
Rinfret	32 (16.3%)	122 (62.2%)	42 (21.4%)	196
Kerwin	93 (16.4%)	332 (58.6%)	142 (25.0%)	567
Taschereau	59 (22.0%)	146 (54.5%)	63 (23.5%)	268
Cartwright	40 (19.4%)	114 (55.3%)	52 (25.2%)	206
Fauteux	53 (19.6%)	149 (55.2%)	68 (25.2%)	270
Laskin	308 (32.6%)	372 (39.3%)	266 (28.1%)	946
Dickson	283 (54.1%)	106 (20.3%)	134 (25.6%)	523
TOTAL:	868 (29.2%)	1341 (45.1%)	767 (25.8%)	2976

The trend is striking and impressive in its persistence. Under Chief Justice Rinfret and every Chief Justice for the next quarter century, the Supreme Court of Canada had a massive private law caseload that accounted for more than half of its reported decisions, a much smaller public law caseload, and an even smaller criminal law caseload. More recently, under Laskin and Dickson, the picture has changed dramatically. Now, the Supreme Court of Canada has a massive criminal law caseload, rising above one-half of its reported decisions, a much smaller public law component, and an even smaller private law component. As a number of commentators have observed (e.g., Monahan 1987), the Supreme Court once is no longer a private law court, and appeals on issues of tort and contract that once constituted the majority of its jurisprudence have become increasingly infrequent.

Part of this change is no doubt driven by the entrenchment of the Charter; for most of the last decade, the Supreme Court has faced the challenge of coming to terms with its vastly increased responsibilities. For a variety of reasons, much of this litigation has been in the area of criminal law. This effect on the Supreme Court caseload is clear, and it might imply a future return to some less Charter-dominated norm in the future. However, even if we remove all the Charter cases, on the unlikely assumption that none of them raised questions other than the Charter issue that would warrant Supreme Court attention, criminal law jurisprudence still dominates the Supreme Court docket to an extent that was never true before.

At least as important has been the increase in the Supreme Court's discretionary jurisdiction under the amendments to the Supreme Court Act passed in 1975. According to Bushnell (1982), appeals by right dominated the Supreme Court caseload before 1975 but typically made up much less than one-fifth of it afterward. They have more recently rebounded to about two-fifths. The principal impact of the Supreme Court's increased discretion appears to have been a drastically diminished private law docket, barely a dozen or so cases a year.

The implications are highly significant for the present state and future development of Canadian law; for some, the negative conclusion is that the Court's new responsibilities "have robbed it of the time necessary to perform adequately its role as 'General Court of Appeal' for the private law systems of the provinces" (Gibson 1989), In many areas of private law, the provincial courts of appeal have become the highest court in the land, the body beyond which there is no effective right of appeal. Some provincial appeal court judges have described the change as having to learn to play baseball without a backstop. Conversely, when private law cases are accepted for hearing by the Supreme Court, they arise against an increasingly impoverished precedential background. Because they are becoming infrequent, the temptation is to try to make the judgments complete and wide-ranging, consuming more of the Court's time and attention and generating sometimes prolix and tangled decisions that lower court judges resent and deplore. To be sure, if the strangling of the private law docket is the practical product of the exercise of discretionary jurisdiction, then altered practices relating to that discretion could swing the pendulum back; straight-line projections are tempting, but they may be premature.

Success Rates: Trends and Correlates

Of the 2,976 reported appeals from provincial appeal courts to the Supreme Court, 1,281 (or 43.0%) were successful. (Appeals "allowed in part" are included as successful as are those "allowed" on the grounds that both represent "interventions" — to use Burton Atkin's [1990] phrase — that substantively alter the lower court disposition of the case.) These rates have fluctuated over time, but the expansion of leave jurisdiction in 1975 does not seem to have marked a major watershed for the frequency of successful appeals; figures from the United States are quite different, which suggests that its Supreme Court usually hear appeals only when there is some serious prospect of reversal.

But 43.0 per cent is just a number. What significance should we give to it? On limited statistical evidence, it would seem that the success rate on appeals to the provincial courts of appeal themselves is somewhat lower, at about 30 to 35 per cent, and the success rate for appeals to the U.S. state supreme courts is comparable (Kagan 1978, 994; Atkins and Glick 1976, 100). Appeals from state supreme courts to the U.S. Supreme Court in recent decades succeed 66.1 per cent of the time (Atkins 1990). However, the two situations are not strictly comparable; the similarity of names overstates the similarity of functions. Judges of the U.S. federal and state courts are not (while those of the Canadian Supreme and provincial appeal courts are) selected by the same political elites from the same legal communities, and elevations from the highest provincial courts dominate the Canadian Supreme Court but are almost unheard of in the U.S. The U.S. court system therefore contains a structural predisposition toward conflict and confrontation that is absent from the Canadian system. The success rate of appeals to the British Court of Appeal is much closer to the Canadian figure, hovering in the low 40s (Atkins 1990).

Table 6.4:

Success Rate of Appeals by Chief Justice
Appeals from Provincial CAs to Supreme Court of Canada
Reported Decisions, September 1949 to June 1990

Chief Justice	Appeals	Allowed	Success %	"Corrected" Success %*
Rinfret	196	93	47.4%	48.2%
Kerwin	567	224	39.5%	40.1%
Taschereau	268	120	44.8%	44.4%
Cartwright	206	78	37.9%	38.4%
Fauteux	270	121	44.8%	43.0%
Laskin	946	436	46.1%	46.6%
Dickson	523	209	40.0%	45.4%
TOTAL	2976	1281	43.0%	43.0%

Note: * = "corrected" by assuming a criminal/private/public mix of cases that exactly parallels the 41-year average.

At first glance, the reversal rate seems high, the more so as provincial appeal decisions are themselves panel reconsiderations of trial court decisions (with the exception of statistically infrequent reference cases). However, such concern misconstrues the function of a general court of appeal in a hierarchical system; as one moves "up" the pyramid, the purpose of appeals is progressively *less* the correction of error and progressively *more* the making — or, less controversially, the clarification — of law. Reversal at the hands of the Supreme Court is often less a question of error ("the lower court should have known") than an authoritative choice between several differing but defensible judicial resolutions enunciated by different provincial appeal courts or the indirect clarification of an earlier Supreme Court doctrine followed by the lower court. By the same token, the purpose of choosing to hear and decide an appeal is not the anticipation of error but the determination that the issue raised is of sufficient importance for the Supreme Court to deal with by endorsing, altering, or reversing the relevant appeal court authorities; this purpose is demonstrated by the fact that increasing discretionary jurisdiction has not led to a higher success rate, and contrasts with the practice of the Supreme Court of the United States, which seldom grants certiorari (leave to appeal) unless it is seriously considering reversing the lower court decision (Palmer 1982, Wasby 1988).

Over the forty-one-year period, the success rate for appeals from provincial courts of appeal has oscillated around the 43 per cent average. "Oscillate" is the appropriate term; there is no consistent trend either upwards or downwards, and even the apparent high/low alternation is broken by the relatively high figure for Laskin's Chief Justiceship. It disrupts a pattern of high reversal rates when the chief justice is from Quebec, low reversal rates when he is not.

Table 6.5:

**Success Rate by Type of Law and Chief Justice
Appeals from Provincial CAs to Supreme Court of Canada
Reported Decisions, September 1949 to June 1990**

Chief Justice	Criminal Appeals	Private Law Appeals	Public Law Appeals
Rinfret	46.9%	45.1%	54.8%
Kerwin	43.0%	38.6%	39.4%
Taschereau	37.3%	45.2%	50.8%
Cartwright	42.5%	36.8%	36.5%
Fauteux	30.2%	49.7%	45.6%
Laskin	36.7%	50.3%	51.1%
Dickson	32.9%	54.7%	43.3%
TOTAL:	36.4%	45.5%	46.3%

These figures need to be qualified, however, in light of the changing proportions of the components of Supreme Court caseload indicated in Table 6.3. If there are consistently different reversal rates for criminal, private, and public law, then the reversal rate for any period results as much from the differing mix of appeals as from a general propensity to reverse. As Table 6.5 shows, there are persisting differences in the success rates for the varying types of appeal. For the period as a whole, and for every Chief Justiceship except those of Kerwin and Cartwright, success rates on criminal appeals have been ten or more percentage points lower than the success rates for other appeals. This difference survives — indeed, has been enhanced by — the recent changes in Supreme Court caseload: as the proportion of criminal law appeals rises, the success rate continues to fall; while the dwindling percentage of private law appeals are reversed more frequently than ever.

The fourth column of Table 6.4 therefore shows a "corrected" success rate for appeals from provincial courts of appeal. This figure applies that court's success rates for each type of appeal (criminal/private/public) to a mix of cases that parallels the long-term proportions (roughly 30/45/25). The difference is substantial only for the Dickson Court, which was characterized less by an unusual reluctance to reverse the lower courts (as the 40% reversal rate suggested) than by a surge of the seldom-reversed criminal cases. Given a more "normal" mix of appeals, the Dickson Court would have reversed more often than the long-term average and almost as often as the Laskin Court.

Table 6.6:

Success Rates on Appeal, by Province
Appeals from Provincial CAs to Supreme Court of Canada
Reported Decisions, September 1949 to June 1990

Province	Appeals From	Appeals Allowed	Success Rate
P.E.I.	11	4	36.4%
Newfoundland	29	11	37.9%
Ontario	868	330	38.0%
Alberta	301	124	41.2%
B.C.	438	184	42.0%
Quebec	796	350	44.0%
Saskatchewan	163	78	47.9%
Manitoba	188	96	51.1%
Nova Scotia	90	49	54.4%
New Brunswick	92	55	59.8%
TOTAL	2,976	1,281	43.0%

Table 6.6 compares the success rates for appeals from the various provinces.[2] The range is striking, with three provinces suffering

reversal less than 40 per cent of the time and one province doing so just under 60 per cent of the time. In general, a cluster of five provinces (P.E.I., Newfoundland, Ontario, British Columbia, and Alberta) are reversed about two-fifths of the time, a cluster of three (Manitoba, Nova Scotia, and New Brunswick) are reversed more than half of the time, and the two others (Quebec and Saskatchewan) fall in between.

There are two obvious limitations to the table. First, there are difficulties in suggesting a comparison between P.E.I.'s 36.4 per cent reversal rate on 11 appeals and Ontario's 38.0 per cent on 868 appeals; the smaller the numbers involved, the less confidence we can put in them and the more subject they are to dramatic alteration given a "run" of successes or failures. Second, the figures present overall averages for an eventful four decades, and the general observations should therefore be unfolded for developments over time. Specifically, the reversal rate for the Atlantic provinces has been high (except under Kerwin) and that for Ontario has been low throughout the entire period. The large number and low reversal rate for Ontario confirms the image of its appeal court as a "lead" provincial court, or at least as one that tends to be more "in step" with the Supreme Court. The reversal rate for the Prairie appeal courts generally declined until Laskin, and it has fallen again subsequently (especially for Alberta). The relatively low reversal rate for British Columbia is the culmination of a pattern that has built steadily — that is, the B.C. court is now a "lead" court for the English-speaking provinces, second only to Ontario. In contrast, the high reversal rate for Quebec is a relatively recent development; until the Chief Justiceship of Laskin, statistics suggested that there was little to choose between Ontario and Quebec, but under Dickson a decision of the Quebec court is twice as likely to be reversed as a decision of the Ontario court.

These figures cannot, of course, be treated as if they established some "league tables" of merit or reputation. Especially now that the Court controls much of its own docket, an appeal is generally heard because the case raises legal issues of national importance. Similarly, reversal does not indicate the discovery of knuckle-rapping errors but rather the exercise of the Supreme Court's law-making capacity. That said, the figures are still of interest, if only to give some substance to what all lawyers know — that in specific areas of law, specific appeal courts and judges carry greater weight and are more likely to anticipate the future direction of the law.

It is possible to suggest objective correlates of the provincial appellate decision with some limited predictive capacity. A first relevant factor is the presence or absence of a dissent on a matter of law on the provincial court of appeal. Such a dissent indicates a degree of judicial doubt about the optimal resolution of the legal issues, and such doubt logically increases the possibility that the Supreme Court will disagree with the appeal court majority. Dissent on the provincial appeal court also makes subsequent appeal more likely. There was a dissent on almost one-third of the appeals to the Supreme Court, and no provincial court has dissent rates this high. This fact presumably affects expectations regarding the probability of success; moreover, such an appeal often bypasses the discretionary leave mechanisms the Court has had since 1975.

These expectations are fully justified; a dissent on the provincial appeal court raises the success rate of subsequent appeals from four out of ten (40.2%) to five out of ten (49.5%). Considering the number of perfunctory one-paragraph dismissals scattered through the recent volumes of the *Supreme Court Reports* (most can be summarized "notwithstanding the dissent, we uphold the decision of the lower court for the reasons given there"), the success rate for cases involving substantial appeal court dissents must be even higher. A split within the provincial appeal court panel is therefore a reasonable predictor of success in the Supreme Court.

A second relevant factor is whether or not the court of appeal itself allowed or dismissed the appeal that brought the case before it. At first glance, this seems a strange point to raise. Particularly when the provincial court of appeal reached a unanimous decision, it seems completely beside the point whether that decision upheld or reversed the initial trial judge. However, it has been suggested (e.g., Atkins 1990) that there is a "rut in the road" that strongly promotes continuity and solidarity within the judiciary. At its mildest, the ideal outcome is a trial judgment affirmed at subsequent levels of appeal because this pattern implies that there is a single objectively correct answer accessible to all trained professionals and therefore minimizes the appearance of a diversity of opinion among judges, which subjects any specific decision to the "luck of the draw." On this argument, if the court of appeal has ruffled the surface of the water by reversing the trial judge, the Supreme Court is that much more prepared to re-reverse the court of appeal.

Table 6.7:

Success Rates by Category
Appeals from Prov CAs to SCC, 1949–1990

	No dissent	Dissent	Not known	TOTAL
Allowed	44.4% (910)	58.3% (420)	51.8% (141)	49.1% (1471)
Dismissed	35.5% (800)	41.4% (420)	36.0% (222)	37.3% (1442)
Other	33.3% (27)	33.3% (18)	— (0)	33.3% (45)
Not known	100% (1)	— (0)	29.4% (17)	30.0% (18)
TOTAL	40.2% (1738)	49.5% (858)	41.6% (380)	43.0% (2976)

This expectation is also supported by the results. When the provincial appeal court affirms the trial court's decision, it is reversed only three times out of eight (37.3%); when it reverses the trial judge, it itself is reversed almost four times out of eight (49.1%). The difference is substantial across a wide range of cases, and it is in the predicted direction. Indeed, the predictive value of knowing whether the appealed decision of the provincial court of appeal affirmed or reversed the trial decision is slightly better than knowing whether or not the court's decision was unanimous, even though the reverse might seem more likely.

The two factors can be combined to generate even stronger predictive capacity. Appeals to the Supreme Court of Canada from a unanimous appeal court decision upholding the trial court make up about one-third of the caseload, and they are reversed barely one-third of the time; appeals from a divided appeal court or from a reversal of a trial decision (but not both) make up about one-half of the caseload and are successful more than 40 per cent of the time; and appeals from a divided appeal court reversing the trial decision make up about one-sixth of the caseload and succeed almost 60 per cent of the time. Curiously, although dissent in the provincial appeal court is statistically connected with higher rates of reversal in the Supreme Court, it is not connected with higher dissent rates in the higher court; in 31.7 per cent of appeals from split provincial panels and 32.1 per cent of appeals from unanimous provincial panels the Supreme Court decision includes one or more dissents.

Judges and Votes on the Supreme Court

To consider things from a different angle: the decisions of the Supreme Court on appeals from the provincial courts of appeal can be considered as a string of votes by individual Supreme Court justices for or against the decision of the provincial court. This viewpoint is slightly distorting because it is a critical feature of appellate decision-making that it issues from a collaborative and interactive process involving all members of the panel, not from the recording of a discrete series of decisions arrived at privately and independently. With this reservation, however, the numbers can still be useful.

The individual judges of the Supreme Court can be divided on a number of objective criteria, the most obvious being province of origin, prior judicial experience, and the prime minister who appointed them. Any one of these factors might, on some models of judicial decision-making and the predictability of general patterns of behaviour, create enduring differences in the exercise of the supervisory role of the Supreme Court. These expectations are realized only to a limited degree, as shown in Table 6.8.

The differences are modest and do not identify any discrete minority on the Court that votes significantly differently on appeals from the provincial courts of appeal. It is particularly striking that none of the factors identified relate to voting differences on appeals from the various regions of the country. All groups of judges, whatever part of the country they came from, whatever their prior judicial experience, and whoever appointed them, vote less often to reverse the Ontario Court of Appeal and more often to reverse appeals from the Atlantic courts than any other set of appeal courts. Judges without prior judicial experience are modestly more ready to reverse than judges elevated from a provincial appeal court, and Liberal appointees, more ready to reverse than Conservative appointees, but these effects are too limited to suggest a strong causal relationship.

The figures are interesting for the absence of what might be called a "homer" effect. Judges of the Canadian Supreme Court are appointed on the basis of regional quotas — formalized for Quebec, informal but almost equally rigorous for the other parts of the country — and most judges have served on their respective provincial court of appeal before their elevation to the Supreme Court. One might therefore expect certain consistencies in the way they vote on appeals from their own region, either being somewhat more sympathetic to their former colleagues or "leaning over backwards" to avoid being more sympathetic. This is not the case; the figures in italics in Table 6.8 identify the opportunity for the homer effect and demonstrate its absence. To be sure, there are regional differences in the readiness of Supreme Court judges to vote to reverse their provincial counterparts — judges from Quebec do so the least often judges from Ontario, the most often — but these differences affect their voting across appeals from all regions, including their own.

Table 6.8:

**Relative Frequency of Supreme Court Votes to Reverse
By Source of Appeal and Characteristics of Judges
Reported Decisions, September 1949 to June 1990**

Judges:	TOTAL	WestCAs	OntCA	QueCA	AtlCAs
Atlantic	42.4%	45.2%	35.1%	44.2%	*50.9%*
Quebec	40.6%	41.1%	34.4%	*42.4%*	49.9%
Ontario	45.5%	47.4%	*41.6%*	44.7%	53.2%
West	43.6%	*45.5%*	37.6%	43.7%	55.1%
Experience					
yesCA	42.6%	46.0%	38.3%	40.8%	49.7%
noCA	43.7%	43.5%	37.7%	47.3%	55.1%
Apptd by					
Liberal	44.1%	45.2%	39.9%	44.3%	53.1%
Cons.	41.0%	44.2%	34.5%	40.8%	50.7%

Where a regional effect does reveal itself, however, is in the delivery of decisions. Were the designation of the judge delivering the decision of the Court totally random, one would expect that an appeal from a particular region would be delivered by a judge from that region 27.6 per cent of the time. (That is, Western members of the Supreme Court would deliver the decision on two-ninths of the appeals from the Western courts of appeal, which make up 36.6 per cent of the total caseload; and so on for the other regions.) In fact, this effect occurred 56.2 per cent of the time — twice as often as it would have occurred at random. For example, 72.7 per cent of the decisions delivered by the Quebec judges on the Supreme Court were on appeals from the Quebec Court of Appeal/Cour d'Appel, and these constituted 78.8 per cent of all the Supreme Court decisions on appeals from that court, 82.0 per cent of all authored judgments. If we develop an "index of regionalization of decisions" by dividing the proportion of regional decisions by the proportion of all decisions rendered by a set of judges, then the figures are as follows: West, 1.71; Ontario, 1.65; Quebec, 2.72; Atlantic, 3.11. There has been a voluminous literature in the United States on the strategy and tactics of opinion assignment in the Supreme Court; any comparable analysis in Canada would begin with, and possibly be overwhelmed by, the basic rule that most decisions on appeals to the Supreme Court should be delivered by a judge from that region.

Table 6.9:

**Participation of Supreme Court Judges, by Region
As Percentage of Total Panel Appearances
Reported Decisions, September 1949 to June 1990**

Judges from	Delivered Decision	Separate Concurrence	Dissent
Atlantic	15.7%	10.9%	7.5%
Quebec	14.9%	7.0%	7.0%
Ontario	17.6%	8.4%	12.0%
West	15.8%	7.9%	8.0%
TOTAL	16.1%	8.1%	9.0%

But there are also long-term differences in the participation rates of judges from the different regions, differences that persist over such a timespan that they may well reflect structural factors. These are illustrated in Table 6.9. Expressed in terms of total panel appearances,[3] judges from Quebec are less likely than the judges from any other region to deliver the decision of the Court, to issue or join in a separate concurring opinion, or to issue or join in a dissent, even though a Quebec judge has had the more active and high role as chief justice for one-third of the period. Judges from Ontario are the most likely to deliver the decision or to dissent; judges from the Atlantic are the most likely to concur in a separate opinion. These small differences add up over time; since 1949, Ontario judges have delivered 164 more decisions than Quebec judges (1,026 to 862) in an almost identical number of panel appearances.

The combination of the lower participation rates of Quebec judges and the practice of regional priorities in the assignment of opinion writing has created the Supreme Court's own version of the "two solitudes." On appeals from Quebec, the Quebec members of the Supreme Court play such a dominant role that one would think they constituted two-thirds or more of the Court's membership rather than one-third; on appeals from the appeal courts of other provinces, they play such a muted role that one would think they had only a single judge rather than three. This is a simple observation rather than a colourful exaggeration. On the appeals from the Western and Ontario courts of appeal, which make up well over half the Supreme Court's total caseload, the judges from the Atlantic provinces combined to deliver *more* decisions of the Court than all the Quebec judges put together. The same observation can be generalized: compared with the three judges from Quebec, the two judges from the West delivered more than twice as many decisions of the Court on appeals from Ontario and the Atlantic, and the three judges from Ontario delivered more than three times as many decisions on appeals from the West and the Atlantic. Although this observation may be less significant than dramatic differences in voting behaviour would be, the over-visibility of Quebec judges on Quebec appeals and their virtual invisibility in other appeals suggests a bifurcation in the supervisory role of the Supreme Court and in the development of Canadian law.

At first glance, there appears to be an obvious explanation: Quebec is the only province that is formally guaranteed representation on the Supreme Court because it is the only civil-law province in a common-law country. Until recently, much of the work of the court involved private law appeals, and it would be inappropriate for a common-law judge to deliver a civil-law judgment. If this were the explanation, we would expect regionalization in the assignment of judgments to be a declining factor as the private law share of the caseload declines and the civil law share declines even more. The figures compiled by David Wheat (1980) chart this steady reduction — from ten or so a year in the late 1960s to fewer than eight per year since the beginning of Laskin's Chief Justiceship; and the numbers have continued to fall. A contributing factor may well have been language facility; for much of the life of the Court, it is probably true that some anglophone judges would be at a serious disadvantage coping with an appeal involving extensive French language documentation and possibly oral argument in French as well. This factor too should be in decline, given the appointment of such French-speaking non-Quebec judges as LaForest and LeDain and the greater efforts of anglophone judges to attain facility in French.

Table 6.10:

Proportions of Quebec Appeals Delivered by Quebec Judges By Type of Law and Chief Justice Appeals from Quebec CA to SCC, Sept 1949 to June 1990

Chief Justice	Private Law Appeals	Public Law Appeals	Criminal Appeals	TOTAL
Rinfret	76.9%	71.4%	70.0%	75.0%
Kerwin	84.5%	85.7%	56.3%	82.1%
Taschereau	90.9%	90.0%	81.8%	89.1%
Cartwright	90.3%	95.2%	66.7%	90.9%
Fauteux	93.3%	91.7%	100.0%	93.5%
Laskin	84.5%	81.4%	47.9%	76.8%
Dickson	81.8%	89.2%	75.8%	82.6%
TOTAL	85.5%	85.8%	63.5%	82.0%

Note: all figures exclude *per coram*, or anonymous unanimous, judgments.

But these commonsense explanations fail on two grounds. First, the regional assignment of opinion writings has not been concentrated in the private law area; over the last forty years, the Quebec members have delivered 85.5 per cent of the private law appeals from the Quebec Court of Appeal, 85.8 per cent of the public law appeals, and 63.5 per cent of the criminal law appeals, all of these figures being well above what one would expect from a random opinion assignment process. Second, the regionalization of opinion assignments is not a declining pattern in Supreme Court decisions but an enduring one. There are fluctuations from one Chief Justiceship to the next, but these are more variations of the pattern than a consistent movement toward a new one.

If there is a pattern, it is a peak in the regionalization of opinion assignment under Taschereau, Cartwright, and Fauteux, followed by a significant drop under Laskin. This link seems plausible because

Laskin always scornfully rejected any notion that Supreme Court judges performed any sort of representative role for the provinces or regions from which they were appointed, and one would expect to find a reflection of this in the practices of his Court on the delivery of judgments. However, although the decline in regionalization is consistent across all types of law, it is not large. Under Laskin, Quebec judges continued to deliver more than three-quarters of the decisions on appeals from their own province, more than 80 per cent of the non-criminal appeals. And the decline did not continue under Dickson: for both the public and criminal appeals that now dominate the Supreme Court docket, the Quebec/Quebec proportions are well above the forty-year averages; and only for the declining numbers of private law appeals (ironically, the only one for which a solid legal argument can be made) is it below the long-term average.

One could suggest a political argument to add to legal specialization and language facility reasons for a regionalization of opinion assignments, especially for Quebec appeals. According to this line of reasoning, it is so provocative for the Supreme Court to be providing the final legal statement on an appeal from Quebec that prudence dictates the selection of a Quebec judge to deliver the message. Presumably, the message will be more palatable to Quebeckers if it comes from one of their own. But if this were the case, then one would expect the argument to apply more often when the Supreme Court decision reverses the ruling of the Quebec Court of Appeal than when it affirms it — if the Supreme Court is upholding the Quebec decision, it would not seem to matter as much who leads the applause. But the figures do not suggest that this consideration weighs heavily in the opinion assignment equation; Quebec judges delivered 83.6 per cent of the decisions when the Supreme Court dismissed the appeal from the Quebec Court of Appeal, but only 79.1 per cent when it allowed the appeal. The differences are not large, but they are enough to discount the political argument. All that is left is an observable pattern toward the regionalization of opinion assignment without any apparent explanation.

Dissent and Concurrence on the Supreme Court

Not all Supreme Court decisions are unanimous, although most of them are. Some judges disagree on the outcome, others on the reasons for the outcome, and they issue dissenting and separate concurring opinions respectively.

Table 6.11:

**Frequency of Dissenting Opinions, by Chief Justice
Appeals from Provincial CAs to Supreme Court of Canada
Reported Decisions, September 1949 to June 1990**

Chief Justice	Dissent	Total	Dissent%
Rinfret	81	196	41.3%
Kerwin	148	567	26.1%
Taschereau	84	268	31.3%
Cartwright	57	206	27.7%
Fauteux	97	270	35.9%
Laskin	233	946	24.6%
Dickson	104	523	19.9%
TOTAL	804	2976	27.0%

Dissenting opinions have occurred in 27.0 per cent of the reported Supreme Court decisions since 1949. Dissents are more likely for criminal cases (30.1%) than for private law (25.2%) or public law (26.7%) appeals, and more likely for Supreme Court reversals of provincial appeal decisions (30.8%) than for decisions upholding the lower court (24.1%). However, they are no more likely for appeals from divided (31.7%) than from unanimous (32.1%) provincial appeal panels.

The most noticeable feature about dissents is the progressive reduction of their frequency over time: dissents are now far fewer than they were forty years ago, the result of a continuous evolution rather than an abrupt turnaround. It is somewhat ironic that Bora Laskin, himself known as the Canadian Supreme Court's "Great Dissenter," should have led the Court to the lowest frequency of dissents since World War II; under Dickson, dissenting continued to decline. The contrast between the Rinfret Court, with dissents in over 40 per cent of all decisions, and the Dickson Court, with dissents in fewer than 20 per cent, makes the point. Progressively since World War II, and even more obviously since the increase in discretionary control over caseload in 1975, the Supreme Court has been speaking to the provincial courts of appeal with a more united voice. The trend is all the more pronounced because it has been accompanied by a sharp rise in the proportion of criminal appeals, the type that have traditionally drawn a higher rate of dissent. Madame Justice L'Heureux-Dubé, (1990) is right to reject criticisms of the plurality of Supreme Court judgments as historically uninformed and to identify the Supreme Court under and after Cartwright with a more unified decision-making style.

Table 6.12:

Average Number of Opinions, by Type and Chief Justice Appeals from Provincial CAs to Supreme Court of Canada Reported Decisions, September 1949 to June 1990

Chief Justice	Criminal	Private	Public	TOTAL:
Rinfret	2.81	2.70	3.93	2.98
Kerwin	2.30	1.81	2.04	1.95
Taschereau	1.64	1.52	1.65	1.58
Cartwright	2.03	1.31	1.31	1.45
Fauteux	2.09	1.36	1.60	1.57
Laskin	1.48	1.39	1.38	1.42
Dickson	1.54	1.39	1.54	1.51
TOTAL:	1.71	1.62	1.71	1.67

The same general observation can be made about separate concurring opinions, which have been following a parallel but less precipitous decline. Table 6.12 tracks the steady decrease in total number of opinions — decision of the court, plus dissents, plus separate concurring opinions — since 1949. Again, the trend is consistent: the Rinfret Court wrote an average of almost three opinions for every case it considered; the Dickson Court wrote only half as many.

It has been a general finding of American research that a strong correlate of the plurality of decisions is the simple and objective factor of caseload: put crudely, if one wants judges to write fewer decisions, then one need simply arrange things so that they have more cases to decide, which will absorb the time and energy that they would otherwise be able to devote to writing dissenting or separate concurring judgments. But this conclusion does nothing to explain the Supreme Court of Canada performance; the decline in the plurality of its decisions accompanied a *reduction* in average annual caseload from 130+ in the early 1970s to 80+ in the 1980s.

It has also been suggested that plurality of opinions is a function of the size of the panel. On purely logical grounds, the more judges serving on a panel that hears a series of appeals, the fewer decisions the average judge is obliged to prepare and, therefore, the more judicial hours are available to research and write separate opinions. As well, the more people there are sitting around a table, the more likely it is that one or more will not agree with the decision or the reasons for the decision or that dissenters will be encouraged by finding allies. In addition, Atkins and Green (1976) have proposed that there are psychological barriers to expressing dissent on smaller panels, which depresses dissent frequencies on appeal courts that are obliged by policy or caseload to limit panel size. But the decline in the plurality of opinions for the Laskin and Dickson courts was accompanied by an increase in the size of the average panel. None of the five Chief Justiceships preceding Laskin had an average panel of more than 6, and three had an average panel size below 5.5; but the average panel size for Laskin was 6.84, for Dickson 6.61. To put it in different terms: we can exclude the judge who delivered the opinion of the Court and then ask how often the other members of the panel felt obliged to deliver their own explanation of the reasons for the decision. Under Rinfret, this figure was 41.9 per cent; for the Kerwin Court, 21.5 per cent; for Taschereau, 13.5 per cent. For Laskin, it was only 7.2 per cent and for Dickson, it was slightly higher at 9.1 per cent.

Both of the usual correlates of the plurality of opinions — size of caseload and average panel size — mispredict the recent perform-ance of the Supreme Court of Canada. Yet, the parallel comment about the provincial courts of appeal — an increasing tendency toward a single opinion — has clearly been correlated with rising caseloads and the increasing rarity of panel sizes greater than three. That being the case, one must assume that the long-term decline in the plurality of Supreme Court opinions is the product of other factors and possibly of intentional policy.

The obverse of fewer separate opinions, of course, is more unan-imous decisions. Since 1949, 1,786 (or 60%) of the reported deci-sions on appeals from the provincial courts of appeal have been unanimous, but this proportion has risen steadily from less than one-quarter for the Rinfret Court and less than half for the Kerwin Court to more than two-thirds for the Laskin and Dickson Chief

Justiceships. The emergence of a "new" style of judgment in the form of the *per coram* (or anonymous unanimous) decision highlights the change. It was used in only nine reported decisions (one-half of 1 per cent of the total) before Laskin's term as Chief Justice, for fifteen (1.6%) under Laskin (none of them before December, 1979), and for 51 (9.8%) under Dickson, most of them before 1988. This large increase may be an aberration rather than a directly evolutionary stage, since the Dickson Court faced the first developments in Charter doctrine and strove for unanimity rather than public division on these basic questions. This goal may also be a partial explanation of a further development, namely, that under Laskin and Dickson, unlike the earlier Courts, a plurality of opinions no longer correlated with a reversal of a provincial court of appeal. Before Laskin, unanimous decisions were, disproportionately, dismissed appeals, but under him and Dickson the success rate on unanimous decisions has been very close to that for all decisions. This is even more the case in *per coram* decisions under Dickson; only 2 of the first 24 reported *per coram* decisions, but 19 of the most recent 51, reversed the lower court decision.

In general, then, plural opinions, particularly dissents, have become progressively less common in Supreme Court decisions on appeals from the provincial superior courts, and, concomitantly, unanimous opinions have become more and more the rule, most markedly with regard to the reversals of lower court decisions. This trend suggests that the Supreme Court has become more unified and cohesive in its supervisory role over the provincial courts of appeal and more coherent and consistent in the signals it sends for those courts to follow in their supervision of the trial courts "below" them.

Conclusion

The responsibilities of the Supreme Court as Canada's "General Court of Appeal" include a supervisory role, exercised through its decisions on appeals from the ten provincial courts of appeal. This connection is increasingly tenuous as the Supreme Court's annual caseload falls and the collective caseload of the courts of appeal rises (to 6000+ per year in 1990). Each appeal considered by the Supreme Court carries behind it an increasingly large "tail" of similar cases and related issues that the Court cannot consider separately. Logically, each Supreme Court decision is a message that it is trying to send down the hierarchy to the ultimate consumers, the trial courts and the parties that appear before them, and the appeal process is the

Appointing Judges

Obviously an important aspect of the court system is how judges come to be sitting on the bench. The simple answer in Canada is that they were appointed by the government of the day — the provincial government in the case of the "purely provincial" courts, and the federal government in the case of the provincial superior courts, the federal courts, and the Supreme Court of Canada. But not all countries approach the staffing of judicial positions in this way, and because there is a close logical connection between how judges are selected and how we expect them to behave, it is worth exploring some of the alternatives.

Alternative Modes of Judicial Selection: France

In continental European countries, taking France as a specific example, judges are considered part of the government bureaucracy. "The administration of justice in France is assured by a corps of professional civil servants which is centralised and hierarchical" (Radamaker 1988, 136). If you want to be a judge, you take a law degree, which in Europe is always a first degree, then you compete for admission to the National School of the Magistracy, usually taking intensive preparatory courses to improve your chances. Upon completion of the program twenty-seven months later, you apply to compete again for appointment as judge. Judicial appointments, like other civil service appointments, are made on the basis of competitive examination. If there are two hundred vacancies, then the most qualified two hundred applicants will be appointed, and the two-hundred-and-first is out of luck.

Virtually all "new" judges start at the bottom of the system, dealing with lesser cases in smaller centres. Their performance is subject to regular review, not just in the form of appeals by parties dissatisfied with the outcome of specific cases but also by their superiors in the judicial hierarchy. Every six months or so a formal evaluation of their performance is added to their file. When there is a vacancy in a larger centre or on the next higher court, judges are promoted to fill them on the basis of these evaluations; the better your evaluations, the sooner you move on to bigger things.

One result of this procedure is that judges as a group are not particularly well paid. The magistracy is an "entry level" job, and the junior judges who staff the lower echelons are recent graduates, not lawyers with decades of experience who must be persuaded to leave high-paying partnerships. In consequence, there tend to be much higher ratios of judges to the total population (and of judges to lawyers) than in the Anglo-American systems. This fact, in turn, contributes to a system that is more accessible and more efficient in terms of case-flow.

The major advantages of the continental system are that judges specialize in the branch of the court in which they serve and that they specialize as judges rather than as lawyers. *Access* and *specialization* are the guiding values of the French system; the price is an exceptional degree of complexity (Abraham 1986, 268). All judges on the senior benches are experienced (that is, they have served for years on the lower benches to earn their promotions), and all of them have demonstrated their judicial competence (because they would not have been promoted without positive evaluations by their professional superiors). There are no amateurs on the continental bench, and the higher the bench, the more established and entrenched the professionals are.

The major disadvantage of the system, from our point of view, lies in the implications for judicial independence. It is not the individual judges who are independent — the ubiquity of supervision and evaluation has them continually looking over their shoulders — but the judicial hierarchy as a whole. And in Anglo-American eyes, even that independence seems potentially compromised by the ability of the political administration to affect the promotion process on an ongoing basis. The Superior Council of the Magistracy, which oversees judicial promotions, includes the minister of justice, the judicial members are appointed by the government, and the evaluations of prosecutors as well as senior judges are considered. Indeed, recent reforms to the French system have tried to place the decision on promotions more firmly within the judicial hierarchy (Lafon 1991), the very fact of reform implicitly conceding that the concerns are to some extent justified.

Most Canadians would not approve of the idea of the "judge as civil servant," answerable to faceless superiors and rewarded or punished by rapid or delayed advancement. At the same time, the French system is popular worldwide; more countries have judicial systems modelled on the French than on any of the alternatives. As Abraham (1986, 266) points out, "if imitation may be regarded as indication of approval, the popularity and acceptance of the French judicial system among the older as well as the newer states of the world represent such approval in the highest degree." Be that as it may, Canadian judges are not bureaucratic officials, nor are their processes or priorities closely meshed with those of the government of the day.

Alternative Modes of Judicial Selection: United States

Many state judges are directly elected, but generalization must not be accepted too casually. The American states display a bewildering diversity of selection methods for the 18,252 state and local courts that dispose of more than 99 per cent of civil and criminal cases in the U.S. (Holland 1988, 11). Twelve states use partisan elections, and another twelve use non-partisan elections; in four states judges are elected by the legislature, in eight they are appointed by the governor, and in the remaining fourteen they are appointed by a neutral merit plan. Some of the states in the last three categories also have "retention elections" that decide whether a judge should continue to serve. And, of course, all federal judges are appointed, their appointments sometimes requiring ratification by the U.S. Senate. As a basis for comparison, we can say that some state judges in some states are elected and that in other states the voters have the more limited democratic power to remove judges.

The advantages of election are straightforward. The first is that the people get the kind of judges that they want; if an incumbent says or does things that the majority finds outrageous, then they need only wait until the next round of elections to find a replacement. The most fundamental democratic power is the power to "throw the rascals out." At a less apocalyptic level, the self-importance that judicial office tends to promote is discouraged by the knowledge that the people in the courtroom will be among those who decide how long the tenure of the particular judge will be. The second advantage is the direct legitimacy established by popular selection, the popular basis of the authority of elected judges, which makes them something other than a bastion of professional privilege. A third advantage, slightly more indirect, is the extent to which the public may be better informed because candidates have to explain the office in the process of persuading voters to elect or re-elect them.

The disadvantages, however, are equally obvious. The first has to do with judicial independence; in general terms, it is a good thing that judges should be aware of public feelings and public values, either by making concessions to them or by explaining explicitly why they should not, but there are situations in which we would want judges to be less flexible. For example, suppose that a judge who is facing re-election is confronted with a case involving a horrendous crime that has inflamed community feelings; suppose the evidence is rather flimsy and that its weakness hinges on technical questions that cannot easily be explained to a lay audience. Is it possible that public sentiment may influence the judgment? One could multiply such hypothetical situations without difficulty; the point is that there are situations in which the democratic impulse and justice head in two different directions. A second disadvantage relates to qualifications; factors that drive voting choices often hinge on matters other than the candidates' professional credentials. A marginal lawyer with a good campaign and the right party connection can thump a first-rate lawyer without the same advantages. This consideration is compounded by a third problem, namely, that the turnout in judicial elections is often incredibly low, even by the standards of the U.S., where voter turnout is generally lower than in Canada. In a recent *reductio ad absurdum* of this problem, a teenager managed to orchestrate a write-in campaign that made him a county judge. His case is extreme, but the basic point remains: when turnout is low, small groups or special interests can have an enormous influence on the outcome. More generally, elections cost money, and campaigns need organizations; if judges are elected, then they will in the process pick up obligations and commitments that the general public may not be fully aware of.

Canadians would be inclined to dismiss the idea of electing judges, the more so in this age when elected representatives are held in such low regard, but there is no serious long-term trend away from judicial elections in the U.S. Those states that elect judges seem quite happy with the way the system is working, which is possibly the product of American hostility towards and suspicion of authority without accountability. In other words, there is no perfect judicial system; different judicial systems suit different societies for different purposes.

Judicial Selection in Canada: Executive Appointment

Canadian judges are neither career bureaucrats nor elected officials. Instead, in Canada as in the United Kingdom, judges are appointed from the ranks of practising lawyers by the government of the day, holding office on good behaviour until they retire.

In the past, that was all there was to it. Indeed, for much of our history, provincial judges — or "magistrates" as they were usually called — did not even have to be lawyers. They simply served at the pleasure of the provincial government, a situation that seems to beg for abuse. For provincial and federal appointees alike, patronage was the order of the day; your chances of becoming a judge were dramatically enhanced by the electoral success of the party you supported and cast into sudden and complete eclipse when they were defeated. It is now a commonplace to observe that Sir John A. Macdonald kept the power to appoint provincial superior judges for the federal government partly in the interests of establishing a coherent national law but also partly in order to keep that very important element of patronage in his own hands (Simpson, 1988). It should be stressed that the patronage was open, assumed as a matter of course by both government and opposition, and accepted without visible revulsion by the politically concerned public. It is only recently that patronage has come to be the target of public outrage, and it would be wrong to read modern attitudes back into earlier decades.

Since the late 1960s, however, there have been clear signs of "an increasing tendency among provincial governments to move to a more impartial selection process" (Heard 1991, 135). It is now normal to require at least five and, more typically, ten years of practice as a lawyer before appointment and in most provinces to have a non-partisan council comprised of judges, lawyers, and lay-persons screen potential appointees. Although generalizations are difficult — the composition, powers, and practices of these judicial councils are highly diverse (McCormick 1986) — in several provinces lawyers now apply to become judges (although the application may have been solicited, usually by the chief judge of the province), and their qualifications must pass muster before they can be considered for appointment. A personal interview is usually part of the process, although the council reports its recommendations confidentially and only to the provincial attorney general. In some provinces, the council serves only a "veto" role, receiving the nominations of specific individuals from the attorney general and either approving or rejecting them.

Both procedures have the same effect — lawyers cannot become judges unless an impartial council of professionals has agreed that their qualifications merit their appointment. Of course, other things being equal, Conservative governments will still prefer to appoint lawyers who supported that party, and Liberal governments, lawyers who supported them. It would be naive to expect anything else. But it does provide the public with some assurance that other things are indeed equal and that, either way, only good lawyers are making it to the bench. Partisanship may supplement ability, but if the process is working, it does not replace it. Patronage is not eliminated, merely contained.

The appointment process for judges on the provincial superior courts (both trial and appeal) has also been in the process of evolution. The Trudeau government instituted new practices in the 1970s, involving a wider consultation net in the initial consideration of candidates and the informal practice of submitting names of potential appointees to the National Committee on the Judiciary of the Canadian Bar Association. These changes led to excellent appointments, many of people without political connections (Ratushny 1976); but the limitations of the process were revealed in the rash of partisan appointments that marked the last days of the Trudeau era. After an even more partisan record of appointments in its first years in office (Russell and Ziegel 1991), the Mulroney government moved to create judicial nomination committees for each province (including a provincial superior judge, representatives of the provincial law society and the Canadian Bar association, and appointees of the provincial and federal attorneys general). The results have been somewhat disappointing, partly because the committees are excluded from considering sitting judges, a serious limitation given the high proportion of judicial appointments that take the form of elevation (Russell and Ziegel 1991).

For the Supreme Court of Canada, the apex of the judicial pyramid, we ironically find the most open and "freewheeling" of the appointment processes. Basically, the appointment of a justice to the Supreme Court, or the designation of which individual on that Court will become Chief Justice, is the unilateral choice of the prime minister, unfettered by any save the formal requirement that the person will be a practising lawyer and certain expectations (formally entrenched only for Quebec) about the provincial and regional balance of appointments. The referee of federalism is the creature of one of the levels of government that appears before it; the final interpreter of the Charter is staffed by people chosen without review or ratification by one of the governments whose activities it reviews.

Not that this flexibility has been seriously abused. As Dyck (1993, 532) notes, "Patronage has not been much of a problem on the Supreme Court since the appointment of Finance Minister Douglas Abbot in 1954." Nonetheless, the Supreme Court appointments have recurrently been part of the constitutional reform process; from the Victoria Charter through Meech Lake to Charlottetown, there has been a regular demand for provincial participation in the selection to create a more truly federalized highest court. Judges like Laskin and Wilson have been constant reminders to the provinces of how much is at stake, of how a string of carefully crafted appointments could alter the decisional tendencies of the Supreme Court to the advantage of some actors (most likely the level of government doing the appointing) and the disadvantage of others (most likely themselves).

Why Judicial Selection Matters: The Problem of Discretion

Does appointment matter? Of course it does. At the structural level, the hurdles that are set up for individuals to clear before they become judges are themselves a statement of the type of people the judges will be and the style of performance they will aim at — bureaucratic-minded professionals in France, opinion-responsive politicians with an eye open to the next step up the electoral ladder in the U.S., professional lawyers with political connections in Canada. Both the formal surroundings and the informal expectations of the judicial process reflect and reinforce these presuppositions. What is taken for granted in one regime can be subtly or glaringly out of place in another.

Appointment also makes a difference in terms of the capacity to impose more pervasive ideological or behavioural criteria. The more focused and direct the discretion of selection, the more immediate this consideration is — a single prime minister has more control than the collegial French Superior Council of the Magistracy, which in turn can act in a more organized and consistent way than a widely defined electorate — but these are simply variations on a basic theme: the selector of judges can choose judges on the basis of the values they will tend to support in their decision-making. A prime minister who is so minded has a considerable capacity to fill the Supreme Court, and the upper levels of the provincial courts, with individuals whose values and ideological style he or she finds appropriate and so to have an impact on the interpretation of the law that will linger long after the next election.

This observation is not intended to have a negative implication or to insult either the prime ministers who do the appointing or the judges who are appointed. It is a matter of common sense, blindingly obvious once it is pointed out. This is especially the case for judges who are being considered for elevation, a surprisingly large category (Russell and Ziegel 1991). The record of judges' reasons for their decisions indicates the way they will tend to exercise their discretion, and the high priority that judges give to consistency makes them a good indicator of how they will perform in the future (Lawlor 1968).

"Stacking" a court is not a question of sordid deals or compromised standards, only of choosing from among the ranks of qualified individuals those whose values match those of the appointer. To exercise the potential power the appointer need only be aware of objective and readily available information. In any jurisdiction, lawyers and other judges can identify the hawks and the doves, can distinguish Charter enthusiasts from legislative differentialists, can label centralists and provincialists. In the United States, the presidential exercise of value-selective judicial appointment has become a fine art that is exercised as a matter of routine (see, e.g., Davis 1986; Gottschall 1983; Gottschall 1986; Tomasi and Velona 1987). Once the information is available, it would be irresponsible for the appointer not to use it; an accidental skewing of the bench is not preferable to one that is intentional. In this context, it is particularly frustrating that the federal judicial nomination commissions cannot comment on precisely the situation that gives the prime minister and the minister of justice the greatest capacity for conscious value selection — that is, in the elevation of people who are already judges.

If the Canadian system gives appointing authorities the most focused and unaccountable exercise of discretion, it logically follows that it demands the most scrutiny. There are two separate concerns that arise as a result — patronage and representativeness — and these will be considered in turn.

The Appointment Power and the Patronage Issue

The history of judicial appointment in Canada is the history of political patronage. The documentation is abundant; the biographies of premiers and prime ministers show the doling out of positions, the tables meshing the partisan connections of appointees with the political stripe of the appointing government are impossible to ignore. Most judges appointed by both federal and provincial Liberal governments are Liberal, judges appointed by Conservative governments are Conservative, and the general trend is merely qualified by the minor disturbances constituted by cross-party and nonpolitical appointments. As Dyck (1993, 532) notes, patronage raises three main problems: "Unsuitable individuals are appointed because of their partisan connections; well qualified candidates are overlooked because of their lack of service to the party in power; and partisan judges may favour their former political colleagues."

The recent reforms to the appointment process are a belated response to growing public distaste for blatant patronage. However, they have blunted rather than broken the edge of patronage appointments. The final decision still rests in the hands of members of the political executive — typically the prime minister/premier and the minister of justice/attorney general — individuals who are accustomed as a matter of routine to balancing official obligations with party considerations. Canada has never evolved a functional equivalent to Britain's Lord Chancellor, the formal head of the court system and chief decision-maker in appointments, whose reputation for professionalism and impartiality has historically neutralized concerns about partisan considerations (although Pannick [1987] warns that we should take these assertions with a grain of salt and that the system only works because the English bench exhibits a class uniformity that would overwhelm the exercise of discretion in any event). At most, we can say that it is now far more difficult for a Liberal or Conservative government to appoint to the bench a poor Liberal or Conservative lawyer, not that governments cannot crowd the benches with individuals from their own ranks.

To some, this fact means the revolution is unfinished (Russell and Zieber 1991; Heard 1991). But patronage — to the extent that the appointing authority chooses from among the ranks of objectively qualified and competent lawyers and judges those whose values and priorities are the same as its own — is not a necessary evil but an essential and functional part of the way the system operates. This conclusion derives from a string of premises that I will expand upon below.

First, the decisional processes of legal professionals are, must be, and should be influenced by their values and convictions. These are not biases, or prejudices, or prejudgments but settled convictions about which values should carry greater weight when the issue hangs in doubt. There is at the core of the judicial function an ineradicable element of discretion, using "discretion" in the way suggested by Barak (1987, 7): "Discretion is the power given to a person with authority to choose between two or more alternatives, when each of the alternatives is lawful." That is to say, judges are not and cannot be computers, and for a portion of the judicial caseload that is neither overwhelming or trivial, there will always be an element of choice. The more rigorously consistent and true to his or her values the judge is, the more surely we can use the patterned exercise of that discretion to place the judge in the appropriate category — "hawk" or "dove" or "Charter enthusiast" or whatever. This fundamental ambivalence and discretion at the core of law is the reason why appeal panels frequently deliver dissents and divided judgments — although some questions of law can be reduced to purely mechanical processes that generate only one correct outcome, many important and fundamental ones cannot be.

Second, the choice of specific individuals to serve as judges can never be totally objective, purely professional, so formalized that citizens will never have legitimate concerns about who is selected. Although the legal profession should be involved in certifying basic legal and judicial competence, purely professional standards are not enough to make the final choice of which individuals deserve elevation to the bench for two reasons. The first argument is logical: it is impossible to designate a standard for judicial potential or excellence that does not include some of the values I have indicated. We cannot decide whether Duff or Rand or Martland or Laskin or Wilson or Dickson deserves to be considered the best judge in the history of the Supreme Court without reading in some notion of federal questions or the balance between law and order and prisoners' rights or between "black letter" mechanical law and judicial creativity. The second is practical: if we take the decision away from the politicians and give it to the lawyers, we simply substitute for the politics of the House of Commons the in-house politics of the Canadian Bar Association or some other surrogate; and this body is by definition one that is bound to be less visible, less accountable, and less representative than the overtly political one we would be abandoning.

Third, if all judges can objectively be assigned to some specific location on continuum of fundamental values and if any selection process is going to wind up creating courts that collectively embody some combination of those preferences, then the most legitimate selection process is one grounded in the democratic political process. Assuming a screening process that ensures competence, elected governments with a democratic mandate are better suited than random processes or professional elites to make the final choices. This is especially true if the heightened sensitivities of modern public opinion militantly guard against the exercise of blatant patronage — for example, the appointment for partisan reasons of a less than adequate judge.

Fourth, partisan control of appointments constitutes a method of evolving arms-length responsiveness. Political parties are organized around the different values and priorities, and the replacement of one party in office with another often reflects the shifts in the values of the general public. Such changes should not be directly imposed upon sitting judges, either by wholesale removals or direct instructions on how to handle certain cases. However, it is quite appropriate to "add to the mix" by appointing individuals who are closer to the new political centre of gravity. This process makes the relationship between political executive and judiciary like steering a supertanker; turning on a dime is out of the question, but over time it is possible to change direction. In the United States, such observations are a commonplace; as George and Epstein (1992, 326) say, "The relationship between the Court and other branches of government, throughout history, has revolved around the ebb and flow of partisan politics." This ebb and flow are just as important in Canada; the swing of power from Conservative to Liberal (or New Democratic Party, or Reform, or whatever) indicates a shift in public values, and every time the new government is re-elected that shift is confirmed. It would be unrealistic to pretend that the courts have nothing to do with "political" issues, and it is both realistic and functional to accept such an automatic but indirect mechanism of adjustment. Perhaps oblique, it is still a form of judicial answerability to democratic will that prime ministers should leave their fingerprints on the substance and style of the upper judiciary. The longer their tenure, the more fingerprints there will be.

Fifth, this argument applies even to the appointment of those individuals who have served in a federal or provincial legislature or cabinet. If anything, the case for them is even stronger. There is an element of judicial decision-making, especially at the appellate levels, that has less to do with the mechanical application of basic principles than with the balancing of values and priorities. Consequently, we are better served by a bench containing some individuals who have experienced the same choices from the legislative side of the fence. Appellate judges are now more than ever before policy-makers and policy-reviewers because the combination of their official duties and the demands of the Charter of Rights leaves them no choice. This being the case, we need some judges who are accustomed to the compromises and the balancing of judgments that are a part of policy decision-making, rather than inexperienced "policy virgins" who pretend (or even believe) they are making technical and professional conclusions based on "black-letter" law.

For all these reasons we are, I believe, best served by an appointment process that blends professional evaluation of competence with politically directed final selection. Supporting a political party is not a crime, nor (current public opinion notwithstanding) is serving in Parliament or a provincial legislature. If patronage gives us bad judges, then the problem is not the party link but the poor quality; we are not well served either by assuming that the only bad judges are those with prior political connections or by pretending that there is such a thing as a perfectly neutral system that would impartially generate the "best" choices. A political hand on the wheel of the judicial supertanker is the way to ensure, over the long run, a consistency between the political values of the democratic majority and the values and priorities of the independent judges who seek to serve them as impartially as possible.

The Appointment Power and Representativeness

The second major issue about Canadian judicial appointment practices centres on the type of people who get appointed. Canadian judges have historically come from within a select group — upper middle class males of French or British backgrounds with political connections. Simply reading the list of names of Supreme Court justices makes the point eloquently, and the same general observation extends to all levels of the judiciary, although less so to the lower ones.

Since the World War II, the mix has begun to change. Recent Supreme Court justices have had such names as Laskin and Sopinka and Iacobucci. The same is true of provincial appeal court judges, among them Bayda, Lieberman, Sherstobitoff, and Friedman. The multicultural realities of Canadian society have finally begun to reveal themselves in positions of high status and privilege. Even more recently, women have begun to appear on the benches of the nation. Three women have served on the Supreme Court of Canada;

most provincial appeal courts have at least one woman judge, and at least four provinces have more than one; and in 1992 the appointment of Madame Justice Rosalie Abella of the Ontario Court of Appeal marked the one hundredth federal appointment of a woman judge (Abella 1992). The basic elements of the old generalization — white, middle-aged, upper middle class, French or English — are still over-represented, especially on the higher courts, but the monopoly is clearly finished.

The new mix is perfectly appropriate. There is no reason to think that the academic capacity, the practical achievements, and the demonstrated judgment that merit judicial appointment are the special preserve of middle-aged upper middle class white males of French and English descent. The appearance of "other Europeans," women, and visible minorities on the bench is a practical statement of the open boundaries of status and privilege in our society and, at the same time, an example and inspiration to other members of these previously excluded groups. The recruitment to visible positions of power of a more representative cross-section is an important and functional form of democratization. However, there is another side to the question. A representative judiciary has one set of implications if we stress the "sameness" of the previously excluded groups — their intelligence, their judgment, their education, their legal knowledge and experience. It has a different thrust if we stress how they are "different," if we suggest that no male judge can fully understand the significance of sexual assault, no white judge really grasp the injury of discrimination, no nonaboriginal truly experience that anguish of the loss of culture. Such questions are all the more important given that some groups, such as the aboriginal peoples, are the subject of court action far more often than others and that male defendants far outnumber females in the criminal courts.

This second face of the representativeness issue raises very serious questions. For example, as Supreme Court Justice Bertha Wilson (1990) asked, "Will Women Judges Really Make a Difference?" In one sense, it is insulting to ask if women are so different from men that women judges will have a different decision-making behaviour. In another, however, it trivializes the "judicial representativeness" agenda *not* to ask — if women judges will not make a difference at least for certain types of legal issues or certain kinds of defendants, then what indeed is the point? As Menkel-Meadow (1986, 913) says: "If women demand equality to men on the basis that they are the same as men, more women in the profession should be no more

significant than more blue-eyed lawyers." Wilson (1990, 522) qualifies her remarks, but she closes with the hope that "women lawyers
and women judges through their differing perspectives on life can
bring a new humanity to bear on the decision-making process."

A study based on five years of criminal appeals to the Alberta
Court of Appeal (McCormick and Job 1993) suggested that gender-
difference expectations can be formalized in a pair of hypotheses.
First, given that women are generally more liberal than men on a
range of matters that typically includes law and order issues (Gruhl,
Spohn and Welch 1981,311) and given that feminist literature suggests that women are more compassionate and conciliatory and less
punitive than men (Gilligan 1982), it should be the case either that
mixed-gender panels generate a lower proportion of Crown wins, or
that they result in a steeper reduction in successful defendant sentence appeals, or both.

Second, the major (and quite possibly the only) exception to the
preceding generalization is that mixed-gender panels should result in
a higher proportion of Crown wins on appeals involving sexual
assault and related offences, on the assumption that women judges
are more likely to sympathize or identify with the victim and more
likely to regard the offence as serious.

Neither hypothesis was confirmed by the data. Panels with women
judges were very slightly more likely than all-male panels to support
the Crown case — allowing Crown appeals or defeating defendant
appeals — and this general pattern held for a wide variety of cases
including sexual assault offences (and excluding only drug offences).
The same study also considered whether the gender of the trial judge
appealed from and the gender composition of the appeal panel had
any identifiable effect on appellate outcomes; the only observable
tendency was for women trial judges to be reversed slightly less often
than men, regardless of whether or not women judges sat on the
appeal panel. This study parallels findings from the United States,
which reported no differences on measures of judicial equality or
acceptance, no indication of a greater openness to the policy goals
of the disadvantaged (Walker and Barrow 1985, 614), and no significant differences in women's decision-making tendencies as trial
judges (Gruhl, Spohn and Welch 1981).

The American experience with black judges is similar, which
suggests that the findings may be generalized to other groups. To
push the parallels between "women judges" and "black judges" too
far is potentially offensive, but up to a point it is useful since both

provide examples of previously excluded groups now represented within the ranks of elite decision-makers; for these reasons a number of U.S. studies (e.g., Walker and Barrow 1985; Spohn 1990) have juxtaposed studies of the two groups. The general observation is that black judges tend to behave much the same as white judges. Uhlman (1978, 884) examined the sentencing practices of black and white judges on a major urban trial court and concluded that "as a group black judges establish sanctioning patterns only marginally different from their white colleagues." In another study, Spohn (1990) found only small disparities between black and white judges, concluding that "judicial race had little predictive power."

All of these studies conclude that their findings are easily explained. The triple recruitment hurdles of law school, bar, and bench are powerful tools for making sure that those who succeed will adhere to the established standards of the profession, and the first appointees from a previously excluded group will likely be those who have proven themselves in terms of precisely these standards. Once on the bench, they have every incentive to maintain those standards, to be the judicial equivalent of "*plus royaliste que le roi,*" and not to confirm cynics' doubts by becoming "oddballs" or "loose cannons." Even if, as feminist scholars suggest, the values of the existing system are essentially "male" values presupposing a male world, the successful members of the "first generation" from previously excluded groups will probably come from the ranks of those who have internalized those standards.

This probability leads in turn to another critical point: to make the courts more representative of women, of Canadians other than French and English, of visible minorities, and so on perhaps simply disguises, and may well reinforce, the extent to which they continue to be unrepresentative on a class basis. If the upper middle professional and managerial classes have only so many sons capable of and interested in becoming lawyers, they can double those numbers by opening the doors to their daughters as well. Since we have not doubled either the capacities of law schools or the employment opportunities of lawyers in recent decades (indeed, indications are that the expansion of the professions that characterized the 1960s and 1970s has levelled off), women candidates may have displaced members of the lower classes, and this displacement will show up in the pool from which future judges are recruited. As Abel (1988, 83) concludes on the basis of a large-scale international comparative study, "Because the entry of women has doubled the number of potential entrants from upper-class backgrounds, it appears to have narrowed the class composition of the legal profession." And if women judges do not perform substantially differently from men judges, then in the long run the narrower basis of the legal profession may have the more profound consequences. A more representative judiciary may be the substitute for, rather than a means of, democratizing the judiciary; to the extent that class, more than gender or ethnic background, implies values that are differentially treated by the legal status quo, this is by far the most likely outcome.

Again, we need to ask what we mean by a "representative" judiciary: Who are we representing, in what way, and for what purposes? Virtual representation is at best a starting point and often appears to concede more than the substantive reality justifies. The feminist response to the accession of Prime Minister Kim Campbell makes the general point: to place women among the ranks of the decision-makers is a necessary but by no means a sufficient requirement for the genuine representation of women and women's interests.

Conclusion

Judicial appointment is something like an Escher painting: at first glance, it seems straightforward, but the closer you look, the trickier things get. In fairness to our judges, we must point out that there is no reason to believe that we have been badly served, or that the overall quality of the Canadian bench does not compare well with that of other countries, or that that quality has not been improving. At the same time, it would be naive not to acknowledge the concerns that have surfaced about the impact of patronage and about the extent to which the present judicial appointment process generates a bench that is sensitive to the concerns of women, of the aboriginal peoples, and of cultural minorities. The problems are more easily stated than resolved; and the message of this chapter is to warn against a posture that sees the selection of "good" judges as a function of purely neutral and professional processes or that brands the mere fact of political connections as incontrovertible proof that there are rotten apples in the barrel.

The tone of this discussion may seem somewhat at odds with the notion that one of the functions of the courts is to protect us from government. On the other hand, if there is no judicial accountability, no control even at arm's length, then the question becomes: Who is going to protect us from the judges? This, in a nutshell, is the promise and the problem of judicial independence.

Judicial Independence

The notion of judicial independence is at the core of the Anglo-American idea of justice; it is "central to the conventional prototype of courts" (Shapiro 1981, 65). It is, however, more complex than it appears at first glance and requires a considerable amount of unfolding. It operates within a more specific context, with more built-in constraints, than orthodox descriptions suggest. My purpose is to explain the Anglo-American conception of judicial independence, to discuss its recent exposition in Supreme Court decisions growing out of the Charter, and then to fill in the contextual background that those decisions imply or, more correctly, that they take for granted.

The Orthodox View

The basic logic of judicial independence starts from the fact that courts exist for the resolution of conflicts in accord with established legal values. However, the resolution cannot be convincing to the loser unless the third party is genuinely a *third* party, without ties to either of the disputants. Minimally, this requirement calls for strict measures to prevent the bribery or the threatening of judges. That this aspect of judicial independence is so obvious does not reduce its enormous importance. It also means that the judge must not have any connection, any personal or business ties, with either party. If the judge is a relative, or a personal friend, or a business associate of one or both disputants, we expect that judge to step down — to recuse herself, to use the technical language. In practice the matter is left to the discretion of the individual trial judge, and appeal courts are reluctant to reverse a decision or to send it back for retrial because one of the parties argues that the judge should have exercised the option of recusal.

But for all its logical and practical importance, independence from private parties is only a small part of the problem; independence from government is far more critical for two reasons. First, government is the single largest litigator — as the Crown in criminal cases, as the enforcer in regulatory cases, as the defendant in a variety of lawsuits for injuries or damages, and, more indirectly, in any lawsuit involving one of the hundreds of federal and provincial Crown corporations that are such a distinctive component of the Canadian way of doing things. Take away the court cases involving government, and there would be no backlog of cases, no caseload crisis — probably no need for many of the courtrooms and judges we now have in place. Moreover, government tends to be a very successful litigator, which means that questions about influence and advantage are highly relevant. Second — more indirectly — democratic government is by its nature endlessly subjected, and endlessly responsive, to pressures transmitted through a wide range of channels. Without some insulating prohibition, some effective *cordon sanitaire*, it is only to be expected that this pressure would simply be passed on to the courts whenever the stakes were high enough to make it worthwhile. Such a consideration could potentially cloud any decision, disturb any loser, and thereby undermine the legitimacy of the process.

The logical core of judicial independence is therefore *the independence of judges from government itself* — the government that appoints judges, maintains their facilities and services, and appears so often before them. The practical applications of the principle have gradually developed within the Anglo-American tradition. One important element is a general prohibition that politicians should not directly contact judges about cases that are in process. This issue surfaced in Canadian federal politics during the 1976 "Judges Affair," which involved three different members of the Trudeau government — one had met with a judge during a trial to express concern about the possible international implications of a trial; a second had telephoned a judge to ask when a decision would be handed down; and a third called a judge about a contempt citation against a colleague who had reacted angrily in public to a court decision (Russell 1987, 80). There have occasionally been similar examples at the provincial level as well.

The furious reaction of the public and media to these events demonstrates that the notion of boundaries is firm. As a result, the federal government issued more formal and specific guidelines for the instruction of ministers and government officials, and some provinces, most notably Ontario, have done so as well. The understandings that surround these rules have been evolving and becoming stronger over time. The close personal friendship and frequent exchanges of advice between a politician and a Supreme Court justice that characterized the relations between, for example, Prime Minister Mackenzie King and Chief Justice Lyman Duff would no longer be acceptable (Snell and Vaughan 1985).

The most practical aspect of judicial independence is, of course, job security — security of tenure and pay, regardless of the pleasure or displeasure of any government official. Judges serve neither probationary periods nor fixed and limited terms; instead, once they are appointed, they serve until retirement age — indeed, until the constitution was amended in 1961, federally appointed judges served for life. Nor do judges negotiate their salaries with government; rather, levels of remuneration are established by legislation and apply to all the judges on the court. Judges do not enjoy perfect security — the constitution provides that federally appointed judges can be removed by joint resolution of both Houses of Parliament, something that since 1969 would happen only after an investigation by the Canadian Judicial Council — but since no federally appointed judge has ever been dismissed, we certainly should not think of this possibility as something that looms over every judge's deliberations.

A minor but significant corollary of the above is that all judges on the same court — except the chief justice, who receives an additional stipend — are paid at the same rate. This makes being a judge an unusual profession; the judge with one day's experience and the judge with twenty years' experience are paid exactly the same amount. The logic is that a system of merit bonuses adjusting the salaries of individual judges involves a discretionary process that opens up the possibility of influence, of judges worrying about offending their evaluators as the date of the annual assessment approaches. This principle is important enough that when Justice Beauregard of the Quebec Court of Appeal discovered that recent changes to a pension plan involved larger deductions for recent than for senior members of the court, he took the matter all the way to the Supreme Court on the grounds that this distinction compromised judicial independence. The Supreme Court was not persuaded that it did (although both the Federal Court Trial Division and the Federal Court of Appeal had accepted Beauregard's arguments), so this practice slightly qualifies the general principle, which still protects judges from "arbitrary" or "discriminatory" alterations to their rate of pay.

It used to be routine to argue that the career patterns of judges constitute another insulation from potential influence or from judges having any incentive to seek the favour of officials. More specifically, we thought of judges as being appointed to a specific court and serving on that court until retirement, with "elevations" (that is, promotions to higher courts) being so rare as to be irrelevant for practical purposes. This view was probably always an oversimplification; my research suggests that about half of all the judges ever appointed to the provincial courts of appeal were elevated from the provincial superior trial court. Certainly in recent years almost every appointment to the Supreme Court of Canada has been an elevation from a provincial or federal appeal court, Justices Pigeon and Sopinka being the only exceptions (Russell 1987, 138-39); and Russell and Zeigel (1991) report a sharp increase in the frequency with which provincial judges are elevated to the provincial superior trial courts. The positive aspects of this practice are obvious — it ensures high levels of experience and competence on the higher courts, and it rewards meritorious performance on the lower benches. The other side, which we should be aware of, is that it gives trial judges some incentive for not angering the government that decides who to elevate and provides the appointing politicians with firm evidence (in the form of reasoned decisions) of the views of specific judges on a wide range of issues.

Judicial Independence in the Age of the Charter

Historically these comments bear directly on the federally appointed judges of the provincial superior trial and appeal courts and by extension — although the constitutional underpinning is a little less clear — to the judges of the Supreme Court and the Federal Court. For much of our history, the status of judges of the provincial inferior courts has been less exalted, a story not for the squeamish. Since the late 1960s, statutes and political practice have progressively improved the status and the professionalism of lower court judges in one province after another. Now all lower court judges must be lawyers with five to ten years of experience in the practice of law; in many provinces, neutral judicial councils (or, as in Quebec, committees specially established for the purpose) comprised of judges, lawyers, and laypersons screen the candidates for potential appointment; and in most provinces such judicial councils are part of the process of discipline or possible removal in order to prevent casual political interference (see McCormick 1986).

The same evolution was dramatically advanced by the entrenchment of the Canadian Charter of Rights and Freedoms in 1982. Section 11(d) of the Charter provides that "Any person charged with an offence" has the right "to be presumed innocent until proven guilty according to law in a fair and public hearing by an independent and impartial tribunal." This compact phraseology invokes a number of important principles of our judicial system, including judicial independence.

The Charter's high public profile constitutes a standing opportunity for the higher courts to inform the Canadian public of the principles involved and the practical implications of those principles. The impact of entrenchment is twofold: first, it constitutes a basis against which the practices of any specific jurisdiction can be measured, a standard that the political authorities who administer any court system can be called upon to recognize. Second, it provides a constitutional foothold for specific judges or courts who feel that some action of their political masters jeopardizes the principle. Both sorts of occasions have already occurred, the first in *R. v. Valente* (1985) and the second in *MacKeigan v. Hickman*.

In the Valente case, the defendant's lawyer argued that the trial could not take place in an Ontario provincial court because that court was not the "independent and impartial tribunal" required by the constitutional guarantee. The alleged delinquencies included the fact that judges were appointed by the attorney general and that the attorney general had the discretionary power to designate higher paid "senior judges," to authorize leaves of absence and paid extra-judicial work, and to decide whether or not a specific judge would continue to serve on the bench in a supernumerary capacity after reaching retirement age. Although the argument persuaded the provincial judge before whom it was originally made, it did not convince the higher courts, and the Supreme Court of Canada used the occasion to describe the "essential conditions" of judicial independence.

The first was "security of tenure," which required that a judge be removable "only for cause related to the capacity to perform judicial functions." The second was financial security, which required a salary or pension fixed by statute or by regulation rather than by individual negotiation. The third was "institutional independence" in all matters bearing directly on the court's "judicial function." Although the Supreme Court was critical of some details of the Ontario scheme for administering its provincial courts, such as the process for designating supernumerary judges, it had no difficulty in affirming that provincial judges in the province — and by extension provincial judges in other provinces, whose organization and administration generally conforms to the same principles — constituted the sort of independent and impartial tribunal required by the Charter (see Hogg 1992).

Five years later, in *R. v. Lippé,* the Supreme Court also rejected the argument that the requirement of independence and impartiality was violated by Quebec's practice of using part-time judges on its municipal court. This decision is intriguing because the judges on the Supreme Court differed on — and did not conclusively resolve — the question of whether or not the phrase "independent and impartial" implies two logically separate requirements (raising the spectre of judges who might be independent of government but not impartial) or a single set of overlapping requirements.

The more recent case of *MacKeigan v. Hickman* is more problematic (see Russell 1990). It emerged from the aftermath of the Donald Marshall case, which involved a Nova Scotia Micmac Indian who was convicted and sentenced in 1971 for a murder that, on the basis of evidence that emerged later, he did not commit. In 1983, the Nova Scotia government submitted a reference case (a process whereby a government can refer general or specific questions to the province's highest court without having an original trial in lower court) to its own court of appeal to try to sort out what had gone wrong in the justice system to generate such an error. The appeal court's answer to the question was generally harsh and unsympathetic to Mr. Marshall — blaming the outcome on Marshall's own actions and saying that any miscarriage of justice was more apparent than real. This response was thought to have influenced the amount of money the provincial government was willing to pay Mr. Marshall by way of compensation, which provoked further controversy. Then the government of Nova Scotia set up a royal commission, headed by Chief Justice Hickman of the Trial Division of the Newfoundland Supreme Court to look into the entire matter more thoroughly. In the course of the committee's proceedings, Justice Hickman sought to summon the members of the appeal court (including Mr. Justice MacKeigan) to answer some questions about the court's procedures in general and about the panel formation and the admission of material for the Marshall reference in particular.

When the appeal court judges refused to appear, the case went all the way to the Supreme Court of Canada, which upheld in strong terms their absolute right to refuse. The critical feature of the Hickman enquiry was that it was established by the political executive of the province; it was a violation of judicial independence that the judges should be called to account in such a direct way by their political masters. It was always implicit in the notion of judicial independence that measures to protect judges from casual interference by politicians might also involve shielding judges individually or collectively from being called to account for lapses — even possibly wilful lapses — from the standards of performance expected from them; behind the principled statements of *MacKeigan v. Hickman* lurks this real possibility.

Towards a Realistic View

There is, however, something a bit odd about the arguments for judicial independence — not so strange that we should reject them but strange enough that we should wonder if we are getting the complete story. In this section, I will try to suggest what parts of the puzzle are missing.

To illustrate the strangeness of the confident certainties of Canadian judicial independence doctrine, I will make two logically separate points. The first is that the justice system in most of the Western democratic industrialized world operates perfectly well without this doctrine. It is not true that the only alternative to the maximal independence of the individual judge is the self-interested calculation of the ambitious politician or the whim of the bureaucrat. Judicial independence in the continental European systems is not a function of the individual judge but of the judicial system as a whole — a system with more specialization, more separate hierarchies, and a proportionally larger number of professionally trained judges than our own. (As Blankenburg and Schultz [1987] note: "Germany traditionally has had the highest ratio of judges to population of all countries with a developed formal legal system.") Since the system as a whole is independent, the insulation of specific decisions from political pressures is perfectly consistent with the regular and routine supervision of lower court judges by their higher court superiors, which is linked to a merit system of promotion that rewards (or deliberately fails to reward) individual judges for their performance. The only way that judges can get to the higher courts is by progressing through the ranks. No continental European judge is the monarch of the courtroom in the same way that a Canadian (or American or British) judge expects to be, yet this does not necessarily condemn Europeans to a substandard system of justice.

My second observation is that the logical core of the notion of judicial independence — that is, the idea that a total lack of any formal accountability to any superior ensures the highest standard of performance — is rejected out of hand for every other office in modern society. (The only obvious exceptions are the concepts of tenure and academic freedom for academics). In politics, we have long since abandoned absolute monarchy, with power vested in a ruler who is answerable only to God, in favour of democracy, which assumes that our politicians must be answerable in periodic elections and will retain their office only if they persuade enough of us that they deserve to. Indeed, a significant body of opinion in Canada has responded to recent events by endorsing more immediate mechanisms whereby citizens can call decision-makers to account, such as the referendum and recall. The normal human response to an arrogant bureaucrat or an incompetent sales clerk or a rude official is "I'm going to report this to your superior"; and we do so because we expect that some negative consequences will follow. Only for judges do we reject this everyday logic and assume that the process will work better if there is no superior to whom things can routinely be reported, no negative consequences that can quickly follow. Surely *impartial* judges are what we want; independence of itself merely guarantees that the judges have the opportunity to be as partial or as impartial as they choose, which is a different question altogether. Green (1988) has made the argument that impartiality is the principle value and that independence in the traditional sense is a derivative and therefore contingent value; and the Supreme Court briefly flirted with the same logical problem in *R. v. Lippé*.

Structural Constraints on Judicial Independence

My point is not that judicial independence is a conscious fraud; I do not think that it is. Nor am I suggesting that there is nothing valuable about the concept or the attempt to make it work; on the contrary, I agree completely with Rosenberg that "interposing courts and set procedures between government officials and citizens has been a hard fought-for and great stride forward in human decency" (Rosenberg, 1991). My concern is that the standard defences seem to answer only parts of the question and leave out the broader context that makes the process reasonable. To put it bluntly, the principle of judicial independence is defensible only because of several critical background factors that severely limit the scope of that independence and thereby the purposes to which it could be directed. There are at least three of these limiting factors, and they imply real professional, procedural, and political constraints on how judges will use their independence.

By *professional* constraints I refer to the fact that judges are appointed from the ranks of lawyers and that lawyers constitute a closed, self-regulating profession, which requires a strict educational process as a prerequisite for admission. More than any other professionals, lawyers learn not a set of facts or ideas but rather a particular way of looking at the world, and their professional reputation derives from how well they live up to the expectations this training engenders. Judges are drawn from the ranks of successful lawyers, and every jurisdiction in Canada draws input from judges and other lawyers as part of a screening process that regulates the kind of people who become judges. Thus, the professionals are trying to regulate in advance what individuals will do with the undeniable power that judges wield. This part of the process, the implicit and explicit requirement of technical expertise and professional evaluation, deserves to be taken seriously.

As Shapiro (Shapiro 1981, 94 ff.) has convincingly argued, the emergence of judicial independence in the unique circumstances of seventeenth-century England involved a reconceptualizing of the role of the judiciary that took judges out from under royal authority and made them independent from royal policy. However, this change could only be defensible if the judges came quickly under another umbrella. Historically and logically the English legal profession, with its organizational independence and technical expertise grounded in a comprehensive and applicable objective law, possessed the necessary qualifications. English courts (and by direct linear descent, American and Canadian courts) could be seen as independent because their judges were "members of a private and autonomous professional guild rather than officers of a hierarchical governmental bureaucracy" (Shapiro 1981, 69).

In practice, therefore, judicial independence means that the judges must be as independent as possible of the government of the day — and as dependent as possible upon the autonomous legal profession that alone can master the mysteries of the law. As Shapiro puts it, "In an important sense, what we mean by judicial independence in England is that judges were more closely linked to lawyers than to the government." It is ultimately misleading if we should forget the second half of this logically linked pair. Complete independence would be acceptable to the parties, and functional as a decision-making mechanism, only if our judges were demi-gods, above bias or whim or caprice and totally devoted to justice. Since they cannot be, it is a workable "second best" if they are competent and conscientious lawyers.

As we have seen, it is not a global norm that judges should be drawn from the ranks of practising lawyers. Most of the world does not staff its judiciary that way and does not describe the requirements of judicial office in a way that limits it to relatively senior members of the practising bar. I have in the past suggested (McCormick 1986) that we should begin thinking of judges as a separate profession rather than as a small component of the broader legal profession, but the practice of the continental European systems, as well as the vigorous and cogent arguments of Shapiro, have long since convinced me to recant. Instead, I believe it is a critical part of the operation of judicial independence that judges should be drawn from and should regard themselves as remaining within the legal profession. Typically, judges remain members of their provincial law society, but they are inactive members, they are not eligible to serve as benchers (members of the governing body of the law society), and they attend only those meetings specifically designated as "bench and bar."

This fact has ongoing implications for the way that judges perform their duties and use their powers. Carter has said that we can better understand what judges do in artistic or aesthetic terms, that we should think of a judicial decision as a kind of performance presented for an audience composed primarily of other lawyers, including lawyers who are judges (1985). The notion of performance does not deny individual differences or the opportunity for creativity, but it places them within the context of professional expectations and implies standards that transcend purely subjective reactions. The whole process of becoming a lawyer accentuates the importance of living within the values and standards that define the profession, and judges are not appointed from the ranks of the mavericks whose behaviour suggests that they treat such expectations casually.

The second set of constraints on judges are *procedural*, and there are three different branches to this consideration. First, judges can deal only with issues brought to them by parties with a justiciable dispute. They can answer only the question they are asked and not some other question, no matter how pressing and important they might think that other question is. Our system has built-in protections against "crusading" judges with a cause to push (See Galanter, Palen, and Thomas 1979). The impact of the Canadian Charter of Rights and Freedoms may give us future cause to qualify the terms in which this limitation is expressed, but it does not do away with it entirely.

Second, judges are obliged to give us not just answers to our disputes but also reasons for those answers — reasons built on the statutes and on the decisions of other judges. Because an enormous volume of routine cases flow through the court system, it is probably correct to state that in the large majority of them, statute and precedent direct a single possible outcome. Even where this is not the case, it is still a significant limitation that, no matter how innovative they are, individual judges can only provide decisions based on the precedents that are available. By the same token, as Schauer has pointed out, because judges are aware that their decisions may have precedential value for the future, they are constrained in the way they characterize actors or situations when they reach a decision. "Today is not only yesterday's tomorrow; it is also tomorrow's yesterday" (Schauer 1987, 573).

Third, the courts have no enforcement or follow-up mechanisms under their control; their decisions are always entirely dependent upon the actions of other parties or other actors within the system. For the cases that make up most of the judicial caseload, compliance is routine (if the appeal court finds the person not guilty, the jail will release him) — so much so that we tend to take it for granted, but we should not. The courts have no institutionalized process for following up on their decisions to see if their orders have been obeyed, no officials who will go out and make sure they have been obeyed. Only the co-operation of other actors, political and bureaucratic, provides this enforcement. (This consideration is so important that I will develop it at greater length in Chapter 11.) This absence of an enforcement power is a major reason why long American tradition, dating all the way back to the *Federalist Papers,* has defended the role of the courts by describing them as the "least dangerous branch" of government; the phrase itself constitutes the title of one of the classic American books on the subject (Bickel 1962).

The third set of constraints is *political* — specifically, the appointment process. The basic argument is nicely summarized by Rosenberg (1991, 13), who points out that "the appointment process, of course, limits judicial independence. Judges do not select themselves. Rather, they are chosen by politicians [who] tend to nominate judges who they think will represent their judicial philosophies. Clearly, changing court personnel can bring court decisions into line with prevailing political opinion." That is, as I have argued in Chapter 7, it is not criticism but common sense to suggest that judges must ultimately ground their decision-making on their own values and priorities. Objective information about these patterns — revealed, for example, through the decisions of a trial judge over several years — is available to the appointing authority as part of the basis for its selection decision.

This political constraint does not mean compromising the standards of competence, or seeking signed pledges, or making furtive phone calls on important cases. Instead, it operates on a level that is at one and the same time more subtle and more transparent. For example, Bora Laskin and Brian Dickson are widely regarded as two of the most outstanding judges to serve on the Supreme Court of Canada. Each marked out vigorous positions on a wide range of legal issues — such as Laskin supporting a generous, and Dickson a more circumscribed, role for the national government on division-of-power questions. Clearly, a Supreme Court with nine judges like Laskin would take Canada in a somewhat different direction — would decide some important subset of cases differently — from a Supreme Court composed of nine judges like Dickson. In a similar vein, some scholars have suggested that the "Mulroney Court" reflects a different philosophy, a different slant on the reading and application of the Charter, from the "Trudeau Court" that it replaced (Beatty 1991), and we can expect such arguments to increase as we bring the courts under increasing scrutiny.

It is in this sense that the political constraint on judicial independence is significant; it provides an ongoing mechanism whereby the judiciary in general will be "in sync" with the government. When a new government takes office, presumably imbued with a new sense of the slant the courts should take on the issues that come before them, it can use the power of appointment to ensure that vacancies and new positions are filled by judges who are basically sympathetic with the general tone of its values. Nor should we overlook how rapidly judicial turnover takes place. Although there were only 1,017 federally appointed judges in this country in 1989 (McCormick and Green 1991, 21), Russell and Ziegel (1991, 11) point out that the Mulroney government made 228 judicial appointments in its first four years in office.

In the United States, this whole line of argument is transparent. Parties come to power with lists of actual and potential judges carefully ranked on a variety of criteria, and analysts track the appointments to unravel the priorities of the new administration. As I wrote this chapter, the U.S. media were awash with speculation about the implications for abortion rights and criminal process and states rights because a U.S. Supreme Court justice has indicated an intention to retire. However, this is merely an extreme manifestation of a logic that lies at the core of political appointment. The whole point of being in power is to deploy the legislative, executive, and appointment opportunities that present themselves in a way that shapes the policies and the institutions of government. Citizens have every right to be annoyed if presidents or prime ministers abuse the appointment power to compromise the standards of the higher courts or to undermine their quality, but they have no right whatever to object if they choose from the ranks of qualified candidates those who represent a certain set of values, a particular grouping of priorities. In a democratic society, who has a better claim to making these choices?

The Recent Evolution of Judicial Independence

Even the courts, the most traditional of social institutions, are evolving, far more pervasively and far more quickly than most people realize. The "first wave" of court reform was the professionalization of the purely provincial courts in the late 1960s and early 1970s; the "second wave" was the unification of the provincial superior trial courts in the late 1970s and early 1980s; the more recent formation of the "Court of Ontario" and the "Court of Quebec" (see Lachapelle et al. 1993, ch. 12) may point the way to even more significant structural changes in the near future.

However, some of these changes have also had an impact on the theory and practice of judicial independence. Consider, for example, what we might call the judicial councils movement — the Canadian Judicial Council, comprised of the chief justices of all the federal and provincial superior courts, was established in 1971; the first provincial judicial council was established shortly after in Ontario as a result of the McRuer Commission report, and the idea had rippled to every other province in Canada except P.E.I. by the late 1980s. Although some of the judicial councils are not involved in the appointment process, they all have a role in dealing with complaints against the performance of provincially appointed judges. The various provinces have devised different structures and procedures for the purpose, but it is generally true that no provincially appointed judge can be removed from office without a formal investigation and an appropriate recommendation from the judicial council, and some councils are also involved in disciplinary procedures of a less serious nature.

The Supreme Court decision in *MacKeigan v. Hickman* explicitly approved of judicial councils. Although the Court ruled that it is a violation of judicial independence for a judge to be called to account by a government-created royal commission or committee of enquiry (even one whose membership is comprised exclusively of judges), the same does not apply to judicial councils with their long-established and ongoing involvement in the process of evaluating complaints. This situation may be reassuring to people who worry about the implicit licence lurking in the more generous and sweeping interpretations of judicial independence, but the solution is not without its own difficulties.

The "Berger Affair" of 1981-82 is a case in point. Tom Berger, then a justice of the British Columbia Supreme Court, gave an interview to the Toronto *Globe and Mail* in which he denounced the 1981 constitutional agreement for neglecting the native peoples and for abandoning the principle of a Quebec veto. When a fellow judge complained to the Canadian Judicial Council about Berger's public remarks, the council conducted an investigation and privately reprimanded Berger, suggesting that similar actions by any judge in the future might well justify removal from office. The exchange became public when Justice Berger released the information to the press and resigned. (There has been serious argument about whether the Judicial Council has the power to issue a reprimand, formal or informal, public or private; it is not explicitly indicated in the empowering legislation, and although Chief Justice Laskin argued that it was implicitly contained within the larger power of recommending removal, other experts have disagreed [Russell 1987, 89].) It is easy to agree that Justice Berger behaved somewhat unwisely but harder to ignore the political overtones of the complaint against him. The message of the Berger Affair for future judges is ambivalent, and becomes even more so when Supreme Court Justice John Sopinka argues publicly that judges should speak out on controversial issues, and "put aside the fear of somehow entering the fray." (*Globe and Mail*, 13 November 1993).

Intriguingly, Peter Russell concedes that Berger was "indiscreet," but he criticizes the use of the Judicial Council investigation route as "unnecessarily heavy-handed" because there are informal ways of dealing with such a situation, ways that revolve around the office and the powers of chief justices and, to extend the principle to provincially appointed judges, chief judges (Russell 1987, 88). Now, it is true that since Confederation every province has had a chief justice — invariably the chief of the specialized appeal court where there is one. However, more recently, and as part of the court reform process to which I have already referred, every bench in Canada has acquired its own chief judge or justice and often (where the number of judges on the bench and/or the size of the geographical area requires) associate or assistant chief judges as well. Especially on courts that do not sit regularly in panels that include the entire court (and few Canadian courts do), the role of these individuals makes them more than "first among equals." They have considerable responsibilities in recruiting judges, in assigning duties, and in supervising the activities of the dozens of judges that serve "under" them.

Most of these responsibilities are administrative and routine, and where they are not, chief judges and justices are unlikely to exercise their power in an arbitrary way. However, even the limited hierarchical organization built into each bench has implications for judicial independence. Suppose a provincially appointed judge receives a phone call from the chief judge, indicating that a number of minor complaints have been received about the way the provincial judge is handling a certain type of case. The chief judge has looked over the transcripts of some of the recent trials and seen nothing really out of order, but he or she hopes that the provincial judge will be particularly alert to this sort of problem in the future. By the way, the chief judge mentions that there is a great deal of trouble finding a volunteer for a rather gruelling northern circuit and that it may just be necessary to order someone to do it in the near future. Has the provincial judge been threatened? Has his or her judicial independence — his or her freedom in the exercise of the judicial function in the courtroom — been undermined? The example, as it happens, is not hypothetical, nor was the judge who mentioned it to me sure how to characterize the episode. The point is that hierarchical organization carries some supervisory responsibilities for the individuals at the top, accompanied by some opportunities to exert influence or pressure; no matter how benign, how principled, how professional the use that is made of those opportunities, the implications are that the traditional solo-judge-centred version of judicial independence is altered in some important way.

Juxtaposing the ideas about judicial council and chief judges suggests to me that we may be on the verge of evolving a different approach to judicial independence, one that focuses more on the functional independence of the organized judiciary as a whole rather than on the individual judge in the courtroom. Such a change in focus is completely consistent with a closer supervision of judges and with administrative procedures that reduce their discretionary control over the length of time allowed for hearing arguments or for delivering judgments. But it puts us on a slippery slope that might have no comfortable stopping point. As Justice David Marshall recently warned (*Globe and Mail,* 9 June 1993), "The country's chief judges have amassed such power over promotions, reprimands and the allocation of cases that they are in a position to exert ideological control of the courts they oversee."

The increasing rationalization of the court system and the need to adopt more efficient administrative techniques present problems to judicial independence of either variety that cannot be ignored. "It is not improved administrative procedures that create unease within the ranks of the judiciary; rather, it is the perceived threat of executive intrusion, as disguised in the garb of the court administrator" (Millar and Baar 1981, 51). It would be most unfortunate if we were forced to choose between independent judges who were not efficient and efficient judges who were not independent, and more unfortunate still if we slid into the choice without realizing that we had reached such a critical crossroads.

Explaining Judicial Decisions

This chapter's title may suggest that it is dauntingly abstract, but that appearance is misleading. The principles of judicial decision-making and the standard method that judges use to explain their decisions are both logical and practical. Moreover, there are practical reasons for pursuing the topic. First, it helps to penetrate and to render more understandable the process of judicial decision-making — what it is that judges do when they "make a decision" and how they go about it. Second, it helps to make sense out of the two-way relationship between the resolution of individual cases and the development of general rules or doctrines that guide that resolution, a relationship that lies at the heart of the common-law system of the Anglo-American democracies and that defines and limits judicial power.

Citations, Authorities, and Modes of Persuasion

Examining citation practices makes judicial decision-making more comprehensible. The term "decision" has more ambiguity than is obvious. For those directly involved in a case, of course, the decision is the outcome: that is, all that usually matters is which side won and which side lost. But to judges and lawyers, that is only part of the process, and not necessarily the more important part; the decision also includes the logical reasons that explain the outcome, that re-trace the intellectual process of decision-making so that other legal professionals can understand the "what" and the "why" and the "how." To the larger legal community to which the judge feels professionally accountable the reasons are far more important than the outcome. And when a case is reported in law reports, what is printed is not the single outcome of the arguments of the lawyers or a summary of evidence or selections from documents but the text of the written reasons provided by the judge. Even the normal terminology of the Canadian court system makes the point explicitly: American judges write "opinions," but Canadian judges deliver "reasons for judgment."

These "reasons" have two further implications. The first grows from the fact that the major weapon in the persuasive and explanatory arsenal of judges is quotations from the decisions of other judges. A judicial decision is usually generously studded with citations: "As Judge X said in Y vs. Z," or, "It is clearly established since *Regina v. A* that ..." There is nothing mysterious about this process; it is simply the judicial variation of the way that most professionals explain their decisions to each other. "Presumably a citation means something to the person citing, and presumably he anticipates that it will have some meaning to a reader" (Merryman 1977). As a political scientist, I anchor my arguments with references to books and articles in established academic journals in my field. My fellow political scientists expect these references and would be surprised if I did not supply them. By skimming my bibliography, they have a good idea of the subject matter, the style of analysis, and the tone of my argument. In my own writings, I do not very often quote from judicial decisions, and judges do not very often refer to academic journals, but this difference in detail does not affect the basic similarity of what we are doing — we quote from the expected sorts of authority to demonstrate that we know what we are talking about and to add the persuasive authority of the people we are quoting to our attempt to present plausible arguments. However convinced you are by the suggestions I am making, you will not be any less likely (and may well be somewhat more likely) to accept the idea when you discover that Henry Merryman made a similar argument in the *Southern California Law Review* in 1977.

As Shapiro points out (1981), this practice can be seen as having a straightforward beginning. Initially, the "king's justice" was dispensed directly by the king, which explains why the term "court" refers both to the room where the king sits on his throne and the room where judges hears cases. But when his domain was large or he was away for years fighting major wars, the king could not be everywhere to dispense justice himself, so he delegated his powers to trusted officials. The possibilities for the misuse of power were enormous, and so were the officials' risk of annoying the king, so they found it useful to report their decisions in writing and even more useful to downplay the degree of choice and discretion that they exercised. "I decided this case as Your Majesty decided such-and-such a case ten years ago" was an extremely effective way of avoiding royal displeasure; almost as good was, "I decided this case as my fellow official in the south decided a similar case last year." Although this description characterizes the motives of the early precursors of judges as more selfish than modern practitioners might like, the logic of the process still works the same way, minimizing the chances of the decision-maker acting on whim by grounding decisions in the recorded results of similar past disputes.

The second implication is that judges cite other decisions not because of their outcomes but because of the reasons that were given for the outcomes. The important thing about *Regina v. Oakes* (for everyone except Mr. Oakes) is not that Mr. Oakes was acquitted by the Supreme Court of Canada of the charge of possession of narcotics for the purposes of trafficking but rather that the judges of that Court explained that outcome by developing a clear and complete doctrine for applying Section 1 of the Canadian Charter of Rights and Freedoms; to cite *Regina v. Oakes* as an authority is not necessarily to argue that a particular defendant should be acquitted but rather to reiterate that Section 1 of the Charter has a specific application. Similarly, the decision in *Morgentaler v. Regina No.1,* Dr. Henry Morgentaler's first visit to the Supreme Court of Canada in 1975, said nothing at all about the abortion law. However, it did clarify the meaning of the "defence of necessity" in criminal law, which means that it has frequently been cited in legal cases that have nothing to do with the termination of unwanted pregnancies. *Pelech v. Pelech* was the final resolution of a specific divorce, but it was also the first of the "family law trilogy" that laid down new doctrine for the judicial treatment of the rights of the two parties upon the dissolution of marriage. And as a fourth example (from a list that could extend to hundreds), the more recent case of *Regina v. Lavallée* broke new ground by establishing "battered woman's syndrome" as a defence (not merely as extenuating circumstances) against a charge of murder (Boyle 1991).

Because lawyers and judges are so familiar with these decisions, they can often simply give the citation and assume that the reader understands the point, but in principle any such citation can be expanded to include (or be replaced by) the argument that it established or clarified or reinforced. The citation is simply the professional code for the argument, which, in turn, means that the standard court decision, full of citations, can be unfolded into a more conventional argument about which is the best of several possible outcomes to resolve a specific dispute. Indeed, the way legal professionals use and think about the cases that they cite is part of the process of abstraction, the shift away from reality, that is at the core of the legal process. For lay persons, mention of a specific case evokes a real-life episode between protagonists who may or may not command their sympathy and that they may or may not see as having any parallels to their own lives. But "lawyers are trained not even to think of the reality of the case and, therefore, to pay attention to only the printed version of what occurred. As a result, over time, it has been forgotten that the printed opinion is only a representation of reality" (Katsch 1989, 36). Also, over time, professional legal attention may come to focus not on the entire written reason, which can run to many pages, but on the single page or even the single paragraph that makes a specific point. For the legal profession, *Roncarelli v. Duplessis* is not a story about a businessman courageously helping the members of an unpopular minority religion against legal harassment and persecution; instead, it establishes the principle that government officials are bound by identifiable rules and principles in the performance of their duties. (The similar case in English law is *Entinck v. Carrington.*)

It is a very important principle of our judicial process that judges are obliged (or at least expected — see Taggart 1983) to give these reasons for their decisions. They do not simply say "X wins and Y loses"; they go on to say, "And here is why this must be so." These reasons are our protection against arbitrary decisions and wilful judges, our assurance that a decision is not the casual preference of a person who happens to be wearing a black gown but a decision that grows out of the law in which it is grounded. Britain's distinguished jurist Lord Denning identified the giving of reasons as "the whole difference between a judicial decision and an arbitrary one" (Denning 1949, 91). The mode of explanation favoured in common-law countries relies heavily on references to the decisions of other judges. The civil-law world of continental Europe leans instead toward explanations buttressed by references to the legal codes themselves and to academic expositions of legal principles — academics, rather than working judges, are the favoured authorities. Although there are some intriguing systematic implications of this difference in style, for present purposes they are variations on one basic theme: judges make their decisions convincing to a legal audience and acceptable to the parties by delivering persuasive reasons for them.

Functionally, the heavy reliance on citation represents a double displacement of the responsibility for the decision. It represents a displacement in time — not, "I the judge am making this the law now," but, "I the judge find this law already existing as I pronounce it to you." And it also represents a displacement as to person — not, "This decision represents my choice, my personal preference" but, "This decision flows from the authority of the law as it has been pronounced by other judges at other times." To push the matter to the extreme of deliberate overstatement: the judges try to present themselves as puppets whose strings are the law and to persuade us that we should no more blame them for "their" decisions than we blame the dummy for the ventriloquist's projected remarks. It is never quite so simple, but if we are persuaded that this exaggeration captures this essential core of the way judges make their decisions, we are more likely to accept decisions even when they go against us, which is a very important part of what a successful judicial system is about.

The reason it is never as simple as the exaggeration implies is that the match between the principles of the cited decisions and the specific details of the immediate case is often less than perfect, and sometimes more than one principle or doctrine bears upon the individual case. Trial judges would find this an unlikely description of their work. Most cases are routine to the point of boredom, revolving around questions of fact and often quite straightforward facts at that; and any characterization of judicial behaviour that denies the low-level monotony of most judicial decision-making is highly unrealistic. As Taggart (1983, 3) points out, "In most cases at first instance and in many that reach the intermediate appellate court, the controlling rule of law is not in controversy; rather, what is disputed is the facts or the application of the rule to the facts."

However, my point is more modest. Enough cases are non-routine that mechanical models of decision-making can never totally cover the ground, and it is the non-routine cases that better reflect the essential character of judicial decision-making, the potential for innovation that lurks within every case. Whenever the case is not routine, the judge must put together, out of the legal ideas and arguments in existing decisions, that combination of elements that generates the most just resolution of the dispute that has to be resolved. This effort is a creative process, an original combining of pre-existing elements to create something that is both faithful to already established norms and a unique synthesis. What judges find in the citations to authority is often not "the answer" but rather the raw materials to draw on to fashion and explain the optimal answer.

This is the reason I am dissatisfied with standard discussions of the doctrine of "binding" precedent: that is, the argument that judges resolving a specific dispute are "bound" to "follow" the decision of any "higher" court ("higher" in this context meaning a court to which their own decision could theoretically be appealed). Since a judicial decision is more a question of reasons than of outcome, to be "bound" only means to be aware of those reasons and of the authority that should attach to them. Moreover, any single "binding" precedent may resolve only some of the legal issues into which a dispute can theoretically be divided, and thus it may contribute to a final resolution without necessarily narrowing the range of legitimate options to one.

Nor is it always a straightforward matter to decide what it means to "follow" a higher court decision. To take a relatively recent American example: suppose a judge on an intermediate appeal court knows that the Supreme Court has just quashed a verdict and returned a criminal case for retrial because the case involved a black defendant and the panel from which the jury was drawn did not include any blacks.[1] From now on, if a lawyer brings an appeal before the court involving a black defendant and an all-white jury panel, the judge would be acting subversively if he or she ignored the Supreme Court precedent and dismissed the appeal. But what if the defendant is Hispanic? The Supreme Court said nothing about other ethnic groups. So, does the judge decide that these are analogous grounds (analogy being a central part of the legal process), or does she consider that the history of the treatment of blacks in America makes them a unique category? What if the defendant is a member of the aboriginal peoples — arguably their situation is closer to the situation of blacks, but are they close enough? How about a young offender? A Satanist? A homosexual? An alcoholic? Someone who is over seven feet tall? A hypochondriac? Nearsighted?

In this hypothetical string of appeals, all lawyers will ask the court to follow the Supreme Court precedent by allowing their appeal and granting a new trial. Somewhere along the list the judge will decide that the analogy is a wearing a little thin and dismiss the appeal. But the judge would be very annoyed if someone accused her of failing to follow a higher court simply because she drew the line somewhere. And, to push the point a notch further, it seems only reasonable to suppose that how far the judge was willing to extend the principle beyond the literal starting point would be a function of how completely she had been persuaded about the merits of the basic idea itself. Explanation and persuasion are the core of the judicial citation process, and they can get lost behind technically correct but subtly misleading phrases like "binding authorities."

Precedent provides considerable illumination for a central logical point, but it gives little guidance for whether or how much it should be applied as one moves away from that meaning. It is insulting to lower court judges to suggest that their job consists simply of finding higher court precedent and "following" it, of flipping pages until they find the right paragraph. Their responsibilities are frequently much more complex, which is why looking for precedent is less like receiving orders from headquarters than like looking for help on how to unravel a difficult logical challenge.

Single Cases and General Rules: The Two-Way Street

Understanding the logic of judicial citation helps us to make sense out of the two-way relationship between the resolution of individual cases and the development of general rules or doctrines that guide that resolution. The relationship is two-way because there are two apparently contradictory statements that are equally and always true about the way that judges make decisions. On the one hand, judges explain and justify their decisions by grounding them in a previously existing body of law contained in the decisions of other judges; but, on the other hand, the decision of any judge can become a new contribution to the body of objectively existing law that will be cited by other judges to explain and to justify their own decisions. It is the simultaneous truth of these two general statements that constitutes the dynamic of the common-law tradition and gives judges an individually modest but collectively critical role in defining the meaning, and therefore the *practical impact*, of laws.

To return to an example mentioned earlier: Dr. Henry Morgentaler's first visit to the Supreme Court of Canada involved a Crown appeal of an acquittal at trial[2] in which a central element of the case had been based on the defence of necessity, "a long recognized although rarely used legal defence that excuses otherwise criminal conduct if it is performed to avoid a more serious evil or crime" (Morton 1992, 50). Dr. Morgentaler's lawyer argued that the doctor's patients were in difficult circumstances where normal procedures were not available to help them and that Morgentaler did only what was necessary to help them. This argument was a major element of the lawyer's closing comments to the jury, and the judge's summary instructions to the jury accepted it as a possible defence, telling jurors that if they believed the actions were necessary then they should acquit, which they did. But the Quebec Court of Appeal said that this was not a correct interpretation of the defence of necessity and that the judge erred in telling the jury they should consider it as a possible defence; since it was the only grounds on which the jury could have found the defendant not guilty, it follows that the appropriate remedy was not a new trial but the substitution of a verdict of guilty. On further appeal, the Supreme Court agreed with the Quebec Court of Appeal (Morton, 1992).

Leaving to one side what happened to Dr. Morgentaler, I want to look at what happened to the defence of necessity. If there had been a "Case X" somewhere in the background in which a respected trial judge or a reputable appeal panel considered a similar case and gave carefully reasoned arguments why the defence should not apply, then we have no trouble characterizing the judicial handling of the case. The trial judge goofed, and the Quebec Court of Appeal and the Supreme Court corrected matters simply by applying existing law. But there was no "Case X," so things are not that simple.[3] The trial judge was faced by an unusual situation and indicated to the jury (and thereby, indirectly, to the appeal court) why he was persuaded that extending the defence of necessity to the case at hand was a reasonable possibility and not something to be dismissed out of hand. The Appeal Court was not persuaded that the defence of necessity was relevant or that the jury should have been given this option, and in explaining why they were not persuaded, the court made it clearer for future trial judges when the defence of necessity could be invoked and when it could not. Future trial judges would cite that decision to explain why they rejected (or, much more rarely, permitted) such a defence. However, this is another way of saying that the Appeal Court changed the law — an incremental change rather than a bold creation *ex nihilo* to be sure, but a change nonetheless.

My example here involves an appeal court that changed the law in the process of reversing a trial judge, but suppose that the appeal court had instead upheld the trial judge and endorsed his reasons. We would still have a case of judicial innovation, still have an incremental change to the law, still have a new precedent that could be cited to justify future decisions. This possibility lurks within every judicial decision because every case represents the application by a specific judge of a specific set of precedents to a unique set of social circumstances. The judge will use the citations to deny any degree of novelty or originality — but the result may nonetheless be a new way of resolving some of the issues raised in similar cases and be cited itself subsequently. This endless incremental process of fine-tuning judicial doctrine in the light of specific situations, accomplished in a gradual and decentralized way by hundreds of individual judges, is one of the powerful arguments for the utility of the common-law method of judicial decision-making.

For two related reasons we tend to assume that the provincial courts of appeal and the Supreme Court of Canada play the dominant role in the creation of new legal doctrine. First, cases that raise problems calling for novel solutions are more likely to be appealed by the loser at trial to higher and higher levels of the judicial hierarchy. And second, appeal court decisions are more likely to be reprinted in the *Law Reports* and thereby brought to the attention of lawyers (who can cite them in their arguments in court) and judges (who can cite them in their reasons for judgment).

But we should not be too hasty in centralizing the common-law process of judicial innovation. By definition all new problems (or lawyers' suggestions of new ways to resolve old problems) must be considered and provisionally resolved by trial judges before they wend their way to appeal judges, who are just as likely to refine or to endorse the trial judge's suggestions as they are to substitute their own. Moreover, although any single trial decision has a statistically lower prospect of being reported than any single appellate decision, the sheer volume of trial decisions means that more of them are reported. Nor is it the case that all doctrinally important decisions by trial judges are cases that have not yet been appealed; indeed, a trial decision applying an innovative adaptation of doctrine that was not appealed arguably carries some presumption that the new explanation was persuasive to both sides. Citations of trial judges make up a substantial component of the judicial authority used by judges at all levels to explain their decisions.

Current Canadian Citation Practices

What does citation look like in practice? In 1987, the ten provincial courts of appeal delivered just over 6,000 decisions, of which 1,402 were reported in one or more of the standard reporting services. In those decisions, provincial appeal court judges made 6,213 references to judicial authorities; a preliminary breakdown of these authorities is indicated in Table 9.1.

Table 9.1:

Citations to Judicial Authority, by Type of Authority Reported Provincial Court of Appeal Decisions 1987

Province	Supreme Court Canada	Own Court of Appeal	U.K.	Other Court of Appeal	Cdn Trial	Other	Total
B.C.	21.8%	25.3%	19.8%	13.6%	15.2%	4.4%	237
Alberta	26.5%	24.3%	14.4%	20.5%	11.4%	2.9%	174
Sask.	28.9%	23.2%	13.1%	17.9%	12.6%	4.4%	202
Manitoba	25.4%	16.9%	19.9%	16.1%	17.1%	4.5%	104
Ontario	24.2%	27.4%	11.1%	11.4%	12.8%	13.0%	177
Quebec	31.1%	37.2%	3.6%	7.9%	14.0%	6.2%	137
N.B.	29.4%	17.1%	14.1%	18.6%	17.1%	3.7%	102
N.S.	27.5%	30.9%	8.6%	18.9%	10.9%	3.3%	188
P.E.I.	19.5%	14.6%	7.3%	31.7%	26.8%	0.0%	19
Nfld.	35.4%	10.8%	11.9%	25.0%	11.9%	5.0%	62
TOTAL	26.6%	25.6%	12.9%	15.4%	13.6%	5.9%	1402

Some of the details are not surprising; others are. For example, as could be anticipated, the largest single supplier of judicial precedent was the Supreme Court of Canada, with just over one-quarter of all citations (26.6%), although the range is wide — from a high of 35.4 per cent (Newfoundland) to a low of 19.5 per cent (Prince Edward Island); British Columbia is also strikingly low at 21.8 per cent. This average is higher than the frequency with which U.S. state supreme courts cite the U.S. Supreme Court (about 19%) (Merryman 1977, 419), although neither the existence nor the direction of the difference is surprising. In Canada, but not in the U.S., criminal law is a matter of federal jurisdiction with a strong natural role for the national court of appeal; and in Canada, but not in the U.S., all areas of law (provincial as well as federal) are subject to appeal beyond the highest provincial court.

The second most commonly cited authority by provincial courts of appeal, with 25.6 per cent of all citations, is previous decisions of their own court. Indeed, for four provinces, these self-citations are more frequent than Supreme Court citations. (These four are Ontario, Quebec, Nova Scotia [the "lead court" of the Atlantic provinces, and British Columbia [the "lead court" of the Western provinces].) The range is from a low of 10.8 per cent in Newfoundland to a high of 37.2 per cent in Quebec. (Quebec's unique civil-law system correspondingly reduces the practical relevance of decisions from the other jurisdictions.)

U.S. state supreme courts also cite themselves frequently; indeed, "the cases most often cited by state supreme courts are their own prior decisions" (Friedman et al., 796). However, they do so at a much higher rate than the Canadian provincial courts of appeal: about two-thirds of all state supreme court citations are to their own decisions or to the decisions of their own intermediate appeal courts (Merryman 1977, 394). The big difference between Canadian provincial practices and those of the American state courts is therefore not that federal courts are cited so often but that the provincial courts' own decisions are cited so seldom. The smaller area of self-citation is not offset by a corresponding increase in citations of the Supreme Court. What differentiates Canadian provincial appeal judges from U.S. state supreme court judges is less a centralized fixation on the Supreme Court than a pluralistic openness to a variety of judicial authorities.

The third major source of citations to authority is the other provincial (and territorial) courts of appeal; taken collectively, these accounted for almost one citation in six (15.4%) ranging from a high of 31.7 per cent (P.E.I.) to a low of 7.9 per cent (Quebec). Again, these levels differentiate Canadian from American practice; Canadian provincial courts of appeal are twice as likely to cite other provincial appellate courts as a U.S. state supreme court is to cite other state supreme courts (Merryman 1977, 400). Naturally, not all provincial appeal courts are equally likely to be cited; as one would expect, the Ontario Court of Appeal leads the way with more than 40 per cent of all such citations. The B.C. Court of Appeal is a distant second, and Alberta, an even more distant third. A partial breakdown (combining into a single category Atlantic and Western appeal courts respectively) is shown in Table 9.2. More than in the United States, the judges of the highest provincial courts are taking part in an ongoing conversation with each other about the content of the law, and new ideas are that much more likely to ripple across the country rather than to differentiate specific jurisdictions.

Province	Atlantic	Ontario	Quebec	West	All
Table 9.2: Citations of Other Provincial Appeal Courts Reported Decisions of Provincial Courts of Appeal 1987					
B.C.	21 (13%)	85 (54%)	4 (2%)	49 (30%)	169
Alberta	14 (9%)	70 (49%)	8 (5%)	51 (35%)	143
Sask.	19 (11%)	73 (73%)	2 (1%)	74 (44%)	168
Manitoba	5 (7%)	26 (40%)	2 (3%)	31 (48%)	64
Ontario	20 (14%)	—	13 (9%)	102 (75%)	135
Quebec	8 (12%)	34 (54%)	—	21 (33%)	63
N.B.	12 (24%)	16 (32%)	2 (4%)	20 (40%)	50
N.S.	6 (6%)	51 (55%)	1 (1%)	34 (37%)	92
P.E.I.	7 (27%)	8 (31%)	0	11 (42%)	26
Nfld.	12 (18%)	27 (42%)	1 (2%)	25 (38%)	65
TOTAL	124 (13%)	390 (40%)	33 (3%)	418 (43%)	965

Caldeira (1985) suggests a number of characteristics relevant to the patterns of judicial reference across state boundaries, two of which — population size and geographical proximity — seem useful in explaining this pattern. Population size would help to explain the apparent leading role of the Ontario Court of Appeal, and geographical proximity, the clustering of citations within the Western and Atlantic courts of appeal.

The argument from size is as follows: a larger population means a larger trial caseload; therefore, there are more appeal cases and a larger number of legally significant appeals. The larger numbers in turn suggest that an appeal court in a large province is likely to have already dealt with cases of a type arising for the first time in a smaller province and to have developed the doctrine to accommodate them consistently. Further, a larger population means more lawyers and more trial judges and, therefore, a better opportunity to recruit a higher proportion of outstanding appeal judges. Finally, it may be that the Ontario-based specialized law reports pick up Ontario cases more quickly than others, giving them a head start for frequency of citation. The same factors do not operate for Quebec because of language and because that province has a different legal system for the non-criminal cases that make up most of the reported decisions.

The argument from geographical proximity suggests that physical closeness makes it more likely that judges will know each other personally or by reputation and will be more familiar with styles or with areas of expertise that particular judges have developed; it may also mean that provincial law reports are available more regularly. In addition, neighbouring provinces are more likely to have similar problems and similar attitudes towards their resolution. This factor is mildly in evidence within the Atlantic and Western provinces, accounting for roughly 25 per cent of all interprovincial citations.

What the figures do show is the lead role of Ontario, which is cited by every other province much more often than it cites in return. Also illustrated graphically is the isolation of the Quebec Court of Appeal, which hardly ever cites any Canadian provincial appeal court except that of Ontario and which is hardly ever cited by any Canadian provincial appeal court except (again) Ontario.

Canadian trial courts — almost exclusively the provincial superior trial courts — account for about one-seventh (13.6%) of total citations, highest in P.E.I. (26.8%), New Brunswick, and Manitoba (17.1%) and lowest in Nova Scotia (10.9%) and Alberta (11.4%). Ontario trial courts are cited more frequently than those of any other province, but own-province trial citations are also common, especially in Quebec, where most trial citations are of this type. These numbers are higher than might have been anticipated; it seems natural to think of a court looking for guidance and leadership "up" or "across" the judicial hierarchy rather than "down." Some studies of appellate citation practices exclude citations to trial courts on the question-begging grounds that they are not "really" precedent (Landes and Posner 1976, 251). It makes better sense to take the judges' actions at face value: if appellate courts cite trial decisions as part of the explanation of their decisions, then they constitute part of the body of judicial precedent and are not to be excluded by a priori definitions.

More than one citation in eight (12.9%) is from a British court, more than any other single authority except the Supreme Court or the specific court of appeal itself. Some of these citations are to venerable cases, dating back as early as the sixteenth century, and some (about one-tenth) are from the period before 1949 when the Judicial Committee of the Privy Council was Canada's final court of appeal. Most, however, are more recent, suggesting an ongoing rather than a largely historic interest in British ideas and the British legal style. Generally, the most frequent references to British courts are made by the appeal judges of the four Western provinces.

Again this finding clearly differentiates the Canadian style from that of the U.S. state supreme courts, where citations to English authorities have virtually vanished. The persistence of such a high level of English citations is perhaps mildly surprising since most of today's provincial appeal judges took their legal training and were admitted to the bar after the abolition of appeals to the J.C.P.C. The pattern of English citations may change as the new generation of lawyers comes to the fore or as Charter litigation moves the focus of attention to American Bill of Rights jurisprudence.

Noteworthy more for their low frequency than for anything else are citations of American authorities. Barely 3 per cent of all citations are to U.S. courts, which is all the more surprising because Charter issues arise in about 15 per cent of all cases. For them, U.S. authorities should be attractive and instructive — not necessarily to be followed closely but certainly providing a survey of relevant issues and a warning of possible pitfalls. As well, American law is similar to Canadian law in a number of specialized areas, such as petroleum law and insurance law, which creates an unfulfilled expectation that U.S. authorities would be routinely canvassed in such areas. Bushnell (1986) indicates that the Supreme Court of Canada does tend to refer to U.S. authorities fairly frequently in specific areas of law, which emphasizes the sparse appeal court citation of U.S. jurisprudence.

Equally striking is the fact that a single court — the Ontario Court of Appeal — accounts for fully one-half of all the U.S. citations made by all the provincial courts of appeal. In fact, American references make up over 10 per cent of all citations for that court. (Only two other courts — those of Saskatchewan and British Columbia — approach the 3 per cent figure; for the other seven provincial courts of appeal, U.S. citations are negligible, and U.S. authorities are almost as infrequent as, say, Australian.) Combining this fact with the apparent "lead court" role of the Ontario Court of Appeal suggests an interesting dynamic — American influences on the development of Canadian law are not directly upon the various courts of appeal, but indirectly through the mediate authority of the Ontario Court of Appeal (and, of course, the Supreme Court of Canada).

The reason why this matters at all, why these patterns are of anything more than casual and passing interest, is that they reveal the footprints of judicial influence. To cite another court is to acknowledge its authority, to accept that its ideas and its solutions to problems of evidence and definition and procedure deserve to be followed and emulated. To turn the coin over, to be cited is to exercise leadership over the courts that find merit in the arguments and analysis contained in the reasons for judgment. This is not the leadership of a general over an army, not command backed up by enforcement, but it remains important notwithstanding these softer edges. It is significant as well that the citation patterns show considerably stability over time; they do not show judges shopping around for authorities to cite to rationalize prior positions but instead demonstrate an enduring consensus within specific judicial communities of the appropriate sources for the precedential bricks from which to construct decisions. A complete picture of the patterns of influence thus established would require information about the citation patterns of the trial courts and the appeal courts of every province, and of the Supreme Court as well; such information is simply not available now. What has been presented instead is a glimpse at one segment of the larger story in the consideration of provincial appeal court citation patterns over a single year and some indication of how they differ from their American analogues, the U.S. state supreme courts.

Precedent Today and Tomorrow

What I have tried to provide is a "modern" (that is, late twentieth-century) version of precedent that is true to the intentions of the judges who employ it. If I had been writing fifty years ago (and perhaps as recently as twenty years ago), the emphasis within this discussion would have been different. I would have stressed "binding" authority (decisions from courts to whom the citing court could be appealed) more and "persuasive" authority (decisions from all other courts) less. Paradoxically, although the citation of precedent appears to be a method of decision-making that attempts to conquer time by linking today's decisions to yesterday, it is in fact itself the prisoner of time as it adjusts to changing social expectations on the way that past and present and future bear on today's decisions.

More specifically, the modern world and the technology that increasingly characterizes it are having an impact on judicial citation as on every other aspect of society, and therefore there is a time-bound character to any discussion of precedent. Some of the comments I have made are more accurate as providing a way of understanding precedent today than they would have been twenty or thirty years ago; by the same token, they describe the practices of today better than they will catch the realities of tomorrow.

For example, even while the number of judges and the number of cases that they decide has been steadily rising, computer technology is making more and more of these decisions widely and immediately available. This has a double effect on the use of judicial citations; either one would be significant on its own, but the "one-two" punch of the combination is even greater.

The first effect is a product of the volume of available precedents that can be accessed by computer data-base techniques. Modern judicial citation has its roots in a time when the number of reported decisions was modest and manageable; judges and lawyers could identify from a finite body of reported cases the smaller set of cases that made useful contributions to knowledge and then use the citations as a kind of professional shorthand to build their own decisions. But this process depends upon a sort of equilibrium point, a delicate balance in the volume of cases that need to be processed and assimilated. "A system of precedent is unnecessary when there are very few cases that are accessible; it will be unworkable when there are too many cases" (Katsch 1991, 44). If the universe of citable precedents is a manageable size, then citations are a way of meshing the immediate decision with a stable and coherent background. If that universe becomes too large, then we are in danger of the confusion that can be created by what Neil Postman describes as "precedent overload" (Postman 1992, 121). The use of judicial citations becomes a "mix and match" game limited only by the imagination of the lawyer and the power of the computer that is searching the data-base. As Grant Gilmore bluntly warned three decades ago, "When the number of printed cases becomes like the number of grains of sands on the beach, a precedent-based case-law system does not work and cannot be made to work" (Gilmore 1961). This observation replicates the irony that surrounds the first uses of any new technology; although it is initially used in ways that seem at first glance to allow old things to be done in a much better way, in fact over time it often undermines the old things themselves.

The second effect is a result of the *speed* with which new precedents become available. The impact of this factor is somewhat more subtle. As Katsch suggests: "The authority of case law is promoted by a process that does not rapidly modify reported decisions. 'Landmark' decisions not only settle a particular point of law, but add to the general authority of judicial decisions because they seem to settle a problem with some finality" (Katsch 1989, 46). Under the old technology of printed reports, it took time for other judges to respond to and adjust the modified doctrines laid down in landmark decisions; under the new technology, the feedback loop is measured in days.

Our society is sufficiently "hooked" on newness that it will be difficult for many to see this as a problem, but newness subtly and significantly alters the meaning of precedent and the way that it is used. Merryman's study of citation practices in the United States suggested a cycle whereby new precedents displaced old ones at a fairly steady rate, balancing the stability of legal doctrines with the capacity for adaptation to changing circumstances. As the speed with which new cases are reported goes up, however, this cycle becomes much shorter; the fact that newer cases are available increases the pressure to use them, and "older" citations date quickly. "Such a trend is a natural response to pressure to be less behind the times and to make use of the increased accessibility to cases. It will also lead to a perception of the judicial process as a system in which questions are not settled finally but are continually raised for reconsideration" (Katsch 1989, 46).

Many lay people probably think of the judicial citation process as quaintly antiquarian, of lengthy and often dreary judicial dissertations studded with references to cases that were already old when inventors began to muse about steam power and ships made of iron. This conception is very wide of the mark; not only are many appeal court decisions short and tightly written, but also most citations are to recent decisions. For example, more than one-third of the citations of the Manitoba Court of Appeal have been to decisions delivered within the last five years, more than half to cases that are less than ten years old (McCormick 1992). Even more to the point, the average age of the judicial citations in Canadian appeal decisions has been declining fairly steadily, from 34.3 years in 1927 to 19.8 years in 1987.

Given the technological possibilities and the public expectations of modern society, this decline is hardly a surprise, but a focus on the frequent re-examination of recent decisions is logically antithetical to the idea of precedent. As Frederick Schauer pointedly argues, precedent does not mean following the good ideas of past decisions because they are good ideas; it means following past decisions because of their historical pedigree. "Only if a rule makes relevant the results of a previous decision regardless of a decisionmaker's current belief about the correctness of that decision do we have the kind of argument from precedent routinely make in law and elsewhere" (Schauer 1987). The cult of newness precludes understanding this assumption, let alone being persuaded by it.

In this context, it is highly relevant that two of the first "big" decisions applying the Charter — *Big M Drug Mart* and *Therens* — both explicitly rejected ten-year-old Bill of Rights precedents to initiate a bold new style of interpretation. Given the widespread disappointment with the Supreme Court's handling of the Bill of Rights and the high expectations that surrounded the Charter, this is not reprehensible; but at the same time, it is surely a symptom of a new approach to precedent that sharply depreciates that particular currency. By way of contrast, the Supreme Court of Canada and the Judicial Committee of the Privy Council spent decades trying to reason their way around the roadblock created by the famous (or infamous) case of *Russell v. R,* rather than simply admitting that it was an aberration or an error.

Conclusion

This discussion of judicial citation began by suggesting that judicial citation is not a unique practice locked into its own realm of discourse, and that it is conceptually similar to the way other professionals refer to written material. I suggested that a judge's reasons for judgement are in many ways like a professor's publication in a learned journal; both are laying out a line of analysis and attempting to persuade their fellow professionals that it represents the best way to tackle a specific intellectual problem. The discussion progressed to a statistical study of citation practices, looking at which courts cite which other courts how often and how new or old those citations tend to be, on the grounds that this suggests the patterns of influence that link Canadian judges to various sources of ideas. This is sharply at variance with the normal analysis of judicial decision-making, which tends to focus more narrowly on intellectual content, on the specific ideas in the individual cases cited, and the adequacy of the logical reasoning that links them. Finally, the discussion placed itself within the context of limits on judicial authority, on the idea that the power and discretion of judges are significantly circumscribed by requiring them to give reasons for the outcome.

This last point is the most important even though it is at first glance perhaps the most curious of the three. Nevertheless, the logic is simple. We are all subject from time to time to the decisions of others, but (in Posner's terms) the giving of reasons is what distinguishes authority from tyranny. The decision may still stand, but the capacity to request reasons — for the student to ask the professor why a term paper received a particular grade, for the employee to ask the supervisor why someone else got the promotion, for the applicant to ask the bureaucrat why benefits were denied — remains important for two reasons. The first is that the reasons, especially if they are in writing, can themselves be subject to review and possible reversal by yet higher authorities. The second is that they constitute a foundation for success on future occasions if the identified omissions (a better grounding in the relevant literature, or the taking of appropriate training programs, or the provision of missing documents) are corrected.

But this in turn suggests that judicial decisions are not to be understood simply in themselves but as part of a much larger system. Individual decisions build on and refer to that larger system in the provision of written reasons, just as they contribute to it by becoming part of the background of future decisions. This general system operates to reward certain types of actors and certain types of behaviour and to deny comparable rewards to other actors and behaviours. These larger patterns themselves need to be examined.

Winning and Losing in Canada's Courts

Like other Western countries, Canada has tried to design a judicial system in which independent, professional judges operate under rigorous procedures to make decisions in accordance with established law. Still, we know that the overall operations of the legal and judicial system tend to favour some segments of society more than others — some interests therefore approach the courts willingly and with enthusiasm, while others do so only with reluctance. In other words, we know that the outcome of this independence, professionalism, rigorous impartiality, and established law is, by and large, to perpetuate privilege and "to protect the interests of dominant groups" (Wanner 1974, 437). The general label for the study of how this situation comes about is "party capability theory" (Galanter 1975, 360). This label must be applied with caution. It is misleading, even question-begging, because it takes one possible explanation and turns it into a definition of the phenomenon.

Party Capability and the Trial Courts

The shift from viewing the operations of the judicial system as a neutral process to seeing it as one where general advantage is perpetuated has several logical components, first explored systematically by Wanner (1974, 1975). Although an enormous range of human disputes is theoretically subject to judicial resolution, in fact a large part of the courts' workload is derived from a relatively narrow number of areas. Moreover, some types of individuals and groups are much more likely to use the courts to resolve disputes — they appear more frequently as a plaintiff, the party that has initiated the court action. "Not everyone exercises his right to a day in court. Some individuals and some organizations predominate as court users" (Wanner 1974, 423). Working from a two-year sample of civil trials in courts of general jurisdiction in Baltimore, Cleveland, and Milwaukee, Wanner found that only ten types of action were litigated frequently, those being (in order of frequency): collection of delinquent debts; money damages for breach of contract; liens of various kinds; divorce-related actions; personal injury and property damage torts; foreclosures (including taxes and mortgages); evictions; administrative agency appeals, usually workers compensation; petitions for bail; and various injunctions.

Business organizations were the most frequent plaintiffs, usually in debt or contract-related matters, and next were individuals involved in a wide variety of cases. However, the burden of the defence was not similarly distributed because most defendants were individuals, usually male. "Individuals, particularly men, are most often chosen as defendants by each category of plaintiffs" (Wanner 1974, 431). This observation is important because "success and failure in litigation are distributed unequally among litigants in such a way that the court generally ratifies the demands made by plaintiffs" (Wanner 1975, 297). Wanner found that plaintiffs succeeded outright 50 per cent of the time, suffered complete defeat less than 10 per cent of the time, and either settled or were deflected to another forum the rest of the time. In general, organizations are uniformly more successful than individual litigants, and government plaintiffs significantly more successful than businesses. Organizations were also more efficient litigators; their cases were cleared in less than half of the time it took for individual-initiated cases. As a result, Wanner concluded that the neutrality of civil trial courts, "if it exists, is not incompatible with results which are heavily skewed in terms of different benefits and burdens to different groups in society" (Wanner 1974, 438).

To be sure, legal representation makes a difference; as Marc Galanter bluntly concludes, "Parties who have lawyers do better" (1974, 114). But having a lawyer does not even the odds for several related reasons. First, organizations are more likely to be represented than individuals, which is part of what it means to be able to "overinvest" in a case relative to the immediate stakes. Second, the lawyers who represent organizations do so on a regular basis and help develop the long-term strategies that repeat players use. The lawyers who represent one-shotters, even when they are specialized and competent, are constantly preoccupied with mobilizing their own clientele, endlessly replacing a string of small-stake litigators unwilling to invest in long-run strategies or elaborate preparations. Third, the lawyers who represent "one-shot" clients tend to be clustered in the lower echelons of the profession, while talent and ambition typically rise to the large firms that represent organizations. The Canadian legal profession, like that of the United States, features an upper echelon of large elite law firms whose clients "are mainly wealthy institutions" (Arthurs, Weisman, and Zemans 1988, 153). The organization of the legal profession enhances, rather than offsets, the edge that goes to advantaged litigants.

Galanter also argues in more general terms that we should consider all litigant types as organized along a continuum that has two ideal ends. One, which is made up of those actors in society who have many occasions to use the courts to make or defend claims, he called "repeat players"; the other, including those who utilize the courts only rarely, he called "one-shotters." Repeat players have considerable advantages; they have low stakes in the outcome of any one case, and the resources to pursue long-run interests by, for example, "overinvesting" in a single case. They have built up knowledge of how the system works, which implies both economies of scale and low start-up costs, and they have opportunities to develop helpful informal relations with institutional incumbents. Because of their long-term interests, they can "play for the odds," working for changes to the rules as well as for immediate outcomes. The reactive nature of the court system — someone has to choose to bring the dispute to the appropriate forum in the appropriate form — rewards repeat players, and the overload endemic to all Western court systems further plays into their hands. The routine nature of litigation and the low stakes involved in any single case makes them better able to cope with the frustrations and the costs of delay since they are strategically better placed to seek the most favourable settlement terms.

The interaction of these two types of litigants creates a taxonomy of four different types of litigation. Cases involving two "one-shotters" (Type I) tend to involve either divorces (frequently pseudo-litigation in which a settlement has already been worked out between the parties) or between parties with some ongoing tie whose litigation has overtones of spite and irrationality. Type II accounts for "the great bulk of litigation" and involves a repeat player plaintiff against a one-shotter defendant, the general outcome being that "the law is used for routine processing of claims by parties for whom the making of such claims is a regular business activity" (Galanter 1974, 108). With the single exception of personal injury cases, "one-shotter" plaintiffs challenging "repeat player" defendants (Type III) are unusual and usually unsuccessful. Finally, litigation involving two repeat performers (Type IV) tends to be unusual because such actors find it more convenient to work out formal or informal bilateral arrangements rather than to resort to the courts constantly. (There are special circumstances, such as those involving governmental litigants, that stand out from this generalization.)

Subsequent research (Galanter 1975) applied this framework to a wide range of trial court settings (mostly in the U.S., although also including some Ontario provincial court data) with remarkably consistent results, both for the relative proportions of litigation that fell within each of the four types and the relative successes for each. In general, Type II litigation (repeat performers using the courts for the routine processing of claims against one-shotters) is the largest category with the highest success rates ("in something in excess of two-thirds of all litigation in American courts, the strategic configuration of the parties is RP v OS" [Galanter 1975, 356]); and over all, the data strongly support the proposition that repeat performers (generally organizations) do better as both plaintiffs and defendants than one-shotters (generally individuals).

Both Wanner and Galanter suggest that given the way the system operates, the trial courts are really a forum in which advantaged groups invoke a status quo that embodies and reinforces their advantage, while disadvantaged groups confront the impartial enforcement of their disadvantage. Their comments are not criticisms of the motives or the competence or the performance of the judges because at one level the judges' impartiality and independence are part of the system that successful litigants exploit. At another level, that professionalism helps to validate a fair and impartial legal regime that generally serves to validate the status quo. The fact that judges are generally drawn from the ranks of advantaged groups further contributes to the stability and predictability of the system. For that matter, the same is true of lawyers; "for at least the past generation ... entry into the legal profession, and especially access to its most prestigious positions, has been enjoyed disproportionately by individuals from professional families and other privileged socioeconomic groups" (Arthurs, Weisman, and Zemans 1988, 134). The alleged democratization of the professions in general, and of law in particular, is largely mythical.

Party Capability in the Courts of Appeal

If judicial decisions are a valuable resource for which parties compete, this is even more true of appellate decisions with their stronger and more wide-ranging precedential implications. The rewards of victory are not just success in the immediate case but also favourable interpretations of statutes or definitions of legal categories or favourable variations in the rules that guide the applications of those principles, which will affect the way trial courts resolve similar controversies in the future. But just as in trial courts, some types of litigants win more often than others. There is nothing mysterious about the nature of the advantages these parties enjoy, just as there is nothing mysterious about the fact that the taller basketball team usually wins, and we do not impugn the judges by pointing out these advantages any more than we impugn the referees by knowing in advance which team is favoured to win. Such predictive capacity simply follows from knowing what factors go together to make a "good" team, a winning team — similarly, by analogy, to knowing what a "good" appeal case looks like and what resources allow one to put it together.

The categories and generalizations that Wanner and Galanter sketched for the trial courts were fairly broad — that government would do better than other actors and that business would do better than individuals. However, the same principles can usefully be applied to appeal courts (Wheeler 1987; Songer 1992) and the general categories can be refined — not government in general, but specific governments (federal/provincial or municipal governments) or government acting in a specific capacity (as the Crown in a criminal case); not business in general, but "big" business as opposed to ordinary business interests. The basic logic remains the same: court decisions are sought by a variety of groups to protect or to advance their interests, and some groups are more successful than others in this quest.

Party capability theory applied to the courts of appeal leads to the expectation that governments will do better than other parties, that the senior levels of government will do better than their municipal counterparts, and that the Crown will do better still because it acts against isolated individuals in a clearly defined legal background that maximizes returns to experience and organization. "Big" business, a small subset of unusually powerful and active major interests, will be much more successful than "small" business, and individuals will be successful less often than either. Put in such terms these assertions may seem obvious, but not so uncontestably so that there is no need to verify them empirically. Orthodox legal mythology would have it that all types of litigants stand equal before the appeal courts, while some people argue that we should see the courts as the champion of the underdog. It also follows, of course, that if differences can be found in the success rates of the general classes of litigant, then more pervasive differences might render at least subtly unequal almost every confrontation between every appellant and respondent.

Table 10.1:

Success Rates, by Litigant Category
Reported Provincial Appeal Court Decisions, 1920–1990

Litigant category	Reversal rate as appellant	Reversal rate as respondent	Combined success rate	Net Advantage
Crown	74.6% n= 696	43.8% n=1729	61.4%	+ 30.7%
Big business	55.9% n= 392	34.8% n= 405	60.6%	+ 21.1%
Fed/prov governments	51.5% n= 237	38.4% n= 450	58.1%	+ 13.0%
Municipal governments	52.2% n= 345	45.9% n= 477	53.3%	+ 6.3%
Other businesses	45.2% n=1536	50.0% n=1391	47.5%	– 4.8%
Individuals	46.4% n=5579	53.6% n=4324	46.4%	– 7.2%
Unions	39.3% n= 89	48.9% n= 90	45.3%	– 9.6%
Other	29.6% n= 27	37.1% n= 35	58.4%	– 7.5%

Table 10.1 considers the performance of various categories of litigants on the basis of a sample of provincial appeal court decisions (including all reported decisions for the second and seventh year of every decade since 1920). The categories are self-explanatory except that federal and provincial governments are combined in a single

category because of the very small number of cases involving the former and that a separate "big business" category (comprising banks, insurance companies and major corporations, such as the C.P.R., C.N.R., Hydro Quebec, Hydro Ontario, and the Irving interests in the Maritimes) has been broken out from business litigants. The first column indicates the number of cases in which the appellant fell within each of the categories identified and the frequency with which their arguments in favour of altering the lower court decision were successful. The second column shows the other half of the story, indicating the number of cases in which the respondent fell within each category and the frequency with which their arguments supporting the lower court decision were overridden. The third column indicates the combined success rate for litigants in each category, expressing as a percentage of total appearances their successful appeals plus their successful defences against appeal. Because the ratio of appellant appearances to respondent appearances is quite different for the various litigant categories, this column is not simply the average of the first two.

The results strongly confirm the party capability thesis. The government category was the most successful as both appellant and respondent; appeals by governments succeeded well over 50 per cent of the time. The rank ordering within the government category (Crown, federal/provincial, municipal) was also as expected. Business as a whole was slightly less successful, with a combined success rate just over 50 per cent. However, the spread between "big business" and "other business" is surprisingly large, so much so that big business litigants rank above the federal/provincial government category and second only to the Crown. Unions and individuals bring up the rear, with combined success rates well below 50 per cent. The rational actor hypothesis, which assumes that all parties compete more or less equally at the appellate level because they receive comparable legal advice and base their litigation decisions on careful assessments of their prospects, is not supported by these significant long-term differences in the success rates of different classes of litigant.

Although the number of cases is small, the apparent weakness of trade unions is particularly striking. Many unions are large organizations with considerable resources and access to first-rate legal advice. Their operations are such that recurrent interaction with judicial and quasi-judicial bodies is unavoidable. One would expect them to reap some of the benefits of size and repeat player status, at

least in relation to ordinary business operations if not in direct conflicts with big business opponents and with major government regulatory activity. In fact, unions are relatively effective when they
appear as respondent, successfully defending the trial court decision
more than half of the time. However, they seldom manage to persuade the appeal court when they appear as appellant, and their
combined success rate is even lower than that of individual litigants.
Wheeler et al. (1983) argue that one factor contributing to differential
outcomes may well be a "normative tilt of the law," which favours
one type of interest over another, and that the weakness of trade
unions before the courts — in the Anglo-American court systems
generally — might well be a case in point. As Glasbeek (1990) has
said: "In the past, courts have sided with capital when it clashed with
labour. This well-established fact is central to the argument of those
who oppose the *Charter* as an instrument to achieve a better society."
By contrast, the large spread between big business and other business
cannot be explained in terms of any such normative tilt; instead, it
suggests a straightforward vindication of the party capability thesis
— large organizations for whom litigative activity at the appellate
level is a routine activity can both develop the expertise and deploy
the resources to maximize their performance.

Provincial Appeal Courts: International Comparisons

One of the advantages of party capability analysis is that it facilitates
comparisons between the operations of the judicial systems of different countries. But there are two complicating factors. The first is
that appeal courts tend to affirm rather than to reverse the lower
court; the second is that litigants can appear before the court as either
appellants or respondents, and the ratio of such appearances is not
the same for all groups. Governments, for example, seldom appeal,
but they are often appealed against; individuals appear as appellants
far more often than as respondents. The fourth column of Table 10.1
refines the analysis by calculating the "net advantage" (Wheeler
1987, 407) for each category, calculated by taking the success rate
when that party appears as the appellant and subtracting from it their
opponents' success rate when they appear as respondent. This index
has a triple advantage. Unlike the combined success rate, it is independent of the relative frequency with which each type of litigant
appears as appellant or respondent. It also reduces the extent to which
intra-category litigation pulls the combined success rate toward 50

per cent, thereby understating relative advantage. Finally, "It is also independent of the relative propensity of different courts to affirm" (Songer 1992, 241) and is therefore a better measure to use for comparisons between countries, different sets of courts, or different time periods. Using this fourth column, we can proceed to a comparison with other countries.

Table 10.2:

Party Capability Analysis
Net Advantage: U.S. Courts

Type of litigant	State Supreme Courts	U.S. Courts of Appeals
U.S. government	n.a.,	+45.1%
Government (state and city)	+29.9%	+11.8%
Big business	+ 6.4%	+ 5.9%
Business organizations	+ 3.1%	+ 1.6%
Individuals,	- 1.5%	-18.2%
Government (small towns)	- 1.6%	n.a.
Business proprietors,	- 5.4%	n.a.

Note: figures calculated from data in Wheeler (1987) and Songer and Sheehan (1992)

In the United States, Wheeler et al. (1987) looked at the performance of state supreme courts over an extended period, while Songer and Sheehan (1992) investigated U.S. courts of appeals decisions for the single calendar year 1986. Their findings, summarized in Table 10.2, are extremely similar. In general, government litigants show the strongest performance on appeals, this advantage being the most pronounced for the national government, less so for state and city governments, and much less so for the governments of smaller centres. Business organizations fared less well. Big business concerns (where they could be identified and their appellate performance isolated) do somewhat better than their smaller counterparts, although significantly less well than state governments. Individual litigants tend to be less successful, their status as residual net "loser"

being somewhat disguised by the disproportionately large share of
appellants and respondents they constitute.

There is a notable difference in the magnitude, not the ordering,
of these advantages. Wheeler et al. found only modest (although
significant and persistent) advantages and disadvantages; the maximum advantage or disadvantage is just over 17 per cent. In contrast,
Songer and Sheehan found massive differentials — the spread between the most and least advantaged class of litigants is 66.3 per
cent. They suggested that the most likely reason for the difference is
that state supreme courts typically have significant control over their
own docket while courts of appeals do not. As a result, in courts of
appeal, "frivolous appeals by individuals inflate the winning percent-
ages of governments and businesses," while "repeat players with
substantial resources are less likely to bring appeals to any court if
they have little realistic chance of winning" (Songer 1992, 256). The
leave process of most state supreme courts allows them to devote
their decision-making to substantial questions. The long-term success rate of appeals to state supreme courts was under 40 per cent
(Wheeler 1987, 407); the similar figure for appeals to the courts of
appeals in 1986 was only 16 per cent (Songer and Sheehan 1992,
240).

Comparing these two sets of data to the figures derived from the
provincial courts of appeal is appropriate because within the single
hierarchy of the Canadian judicial system, a provincial court of
appeal combines certain functions of the U.S. courts of appeals and
the state supreme courts — that is, it is at one and the same time an
articulator of federal law under the appellate supervision of the
supreme court and the highest court in the judicial structure of the
province. Typically, courts of appeal exercise little control over their
dockets, but the screening of the reporting services could be expected
to offset the insubstantial, even frivolous, appeals that would otherwise pad the advantage of superior litigants unrealistically. Functionally as well as procedurally, the provincial courts of appeal fall
somewhere between the two U.S. courts, as is clearly reflected in the
figures; all three are variations on a single theme. One significant
difference is the much greater degree of net advantage for big business interests in Canada.

Employing blunter litigant categories and measuring direct inter-
category competition rather than overall figures, Atkins (1991) has
examined the English Court of Appeal and discovered parallel patterns: government litigants are significantly advantaged (+25%–

+30%) relative to both business and individual litigants, and business litigants are comparably advantaged (+15%) relative to individuals. (Atkins provided no breakdown between the various levels of government or between different types of business, nor did he isolate data for trade unions.) The persistence of patterns "across the pond" as well as "across the border" further strengthens the likelihood that we are identifying structural features of courts (or at least of Anglo-American appeal courts) rather than some incidental feature unique to a specific bloc of data derived from a specific component of Canadian judicial experience.

These comparisons should, of course, be made with some caution because the scope of the projects differs. The U.S. state supreme court study sampled the reported decisions of sixteen state courts for every fifth year over a hundred-year period ending in 1970; the court of appeals study included all decisions, both published and unpublished, from three circuits in a single calendar year; the English study reviewed all cases, reported and unreported, over a three-year period; and my comments on appeal courts survey seventy years of the reported decisions of those courts. Even with these qualifications, however, the general similarity is great, which suggests that the insights of party capability theory can be generalized beyond the boundaries of a single country and therefore provide a useful basis of comparisons.

Party Capability Theory and the Supreme Court of Canada

By the same logic, the output of the Supreme Court of Canada can be assessed in similar terms. The discussion that follows (summarized and abridged from an article that appeared in the *Canadian Journal of Political Science*) is based on an analysis of the 3,993 decisions of the Supreme Court of Canada between 1 September 1949 and 30 June 1992 that were reported in either the *Supreme Court Reports* or the *Dominion Law Reports*. Reference cases (directly to the Supreme Court or to provincial appeal courts subsequently appealed) are omitted. The categories employed are the same as those used in discussing the provincial courts of appeal except that "federal" and "provincial" governments now appear as two separate categories.

Two methodological reservations must be made. The first is that a dramatic and event-filled period of more than four decades is treated as a single block for counting purposes. Over the time period, the role of the Court changed greatly, culminating in the dramatic and public leadership of Laskin and Dickson; the procedures of the Court changed, particularly with the sharp reduction in appeals by right in 1975; the caseload of the Court has changed in recent years, with a dramatic increase in criminal law appeals and a sharp drop in private law appeals; and the ideological climate that affects the prospects of litigants such as trade unions has changed significantly in their favour. The second is the abstract arbitrariness of counting each case as one, from one-paragraph dismissals refusing the appeal for the reasons given in the lower court through lengthy formal decisions making significant contributions to established legal doctrine to measured arguments from various members of a divided court explaining their own disagreements. These concerns qualify, but do not disqualify, the findings from party capability analysis.

Table 10.3 summarizes the success of the various categories of litigant in cases decided by the Supreme Court of Canada since 1949. Again, the results confirm the party capability thesis. The general category of government was the most successful as both appellant and respondent; appeals by all four government categories succeeded more than 50 per cent of the time. The rank ordering within the government category (Crown, federal, provincial, municipal) was also as expected. Business as a whole was slightly less successful, with a combined success rate just under 50 per cent. However, the spread between "big business" and "other business" is so large that big business litigants rank above provincial governments.

Unions and individuals bring up the rear, with combined success rates well below 50 per cent. The ongoing disadvantage of labour unions, in the Supreme Court as in the provincial appeal courts, again raises the spectre of a "normative tilt in the law" (Wheeler 1987) favouring the concerns and interests of management.

Moreover, the rational actor hypothesis is again not supported by the significant long-term differences in the success rates of different classes of litigant. This finding parallels the U.S. experience, where their persisting success as litigants has prompted closer investigation of the U.S. national government (Ulmer 1985; Sheehan 1992), of its administrative agencies (Canon and Giles 1972), and of state and local governments (Epstein and O'Connor 1988; Kearney and Sheehan 1992).

Table 10.3:

**Reversal Rate As Appellant and Respondent
By type of litigant; Supreme Court Decisions 1949-1992**

Type of litigant	Reversal rate as appellant	Reversal rate as respondent	Net Advantage	Combined success rate
Crown	56.8% n=227	29.9% n=739	+26.9%	67.0%
Federal government	54.2% n=229	33.7% n=406	+20.4%	61.9%
Big business	49.6% n=137	34.7% n=127	+15.0%	57.2%
Provincial government	47.5% n=139	43.8% n=208	+ 3.7%	54.3%
Municipal government	42.9% n=84	45.3% n=150	- 2.5%	50.4%
Other business	39.6% n=1075	45.5% n=953	- 5.9%	46.6%
Union	40.6% n=69	48.9% n=45	- 8.3%	44.7%
Natural person	40.4% n=2017	50.0% n=1352	- 9.6%	44.2%
[Other]	37.5% n=16	30.8% n=13	+ 6.7%	51.7%

The Supreme Court figures establish a long-term background against which the judicial system operates, but it would be disingenuous not to put them in the context of 1982. The entrenchment of the Charter has created new expectations of the relationship between social advantage on the one hand, and Supreme Court success on the

other. Table 10.4 presents the empirical evidence by showing the
success rates for each category of litigant before and after 1981.

Table 10.4:

**Combined Success Rates, by Litigant Category
Reported Supreme Court Decisions, Pre- and Post-Charter**

Litigant Type	1949–1982	1982–1993
Crown	69.4%	65.7%
Federal government	63.6%	56.1%
Big business	59.3%	54.6%
Municipal government	51.6%	44.9%
Provincial government	50.2%	56.9%
Business	46.3%	46.0%
Individuals	44.9%	41.2%
Unions	44.6%	42.3%

The apparent anomaly — that almost every category of litigant is
less successful after 1982 — is explained by the fact that criminal
cases increased from about one-sixth to almost one-half of the
caseload, displacing private law cases to such an extent that business
litigants make up only half the proportion of total litigants that they
did before 1982. This aside, there is very little change. The Crown
is still successful about two-thirds of the time, and other government
litigants suceed more than half the time, while success rates for
business (combining the two categories) are unchanged and the rates
for unions and individuals have fallen, by 2.3 per cent and 3.7 per
cent respectively. The general message remains the same, during as
before the age of the Charter: governments, especially the Crown,
are more successful than business litigants, who in turn are more
successful than unions or individuals. The gap between government
and business may have narrowed slightly, but the gap between business and other litigants has grown.

Conclusion: Toward a Better Understanding of Appeal Courts

If we think of appeal court decisions as "a resource that appellants, dissatisfied with rulings in lower forums, attempt to mobilize to their advantage" (Atkins 1991, 884), then we must recognize that this is a resource that not all litigants are comparably successful in acquiring. The reported decisions of the Supreme Court of Canada since 1949, and of the provincial courts of appeal over an even longer period, show patterns of advantage so strong and so internally consistent that we can statistically "predict" the probability of appellate success from a knowledge of the relative status of the two parties. This statistical reality links the behaviour of Canadian appeal courts to the observed performance of their counterparts in the United States and Britain, a generalization that supports the utility of party capability theory.

This analysis is an attempt to understand, not a cry for reform. The appeal courts are not to blame for these patterns, any more than the basketball referee is to blame when the taller team grabs more of the rebounds; nor should they "do something" to level the playing field any more than the referee should help the shorter team by not calling fouls against them. The constitutional formalities, strict procedures, and formal neutrality of the court system are important both in themselves and for their consequences, but we must not be blind to the extent to which the court system remains embedded in the broader socioeconomic and sociopolitical system. The privilege-reinforcing tendencies of an extended run of decisions cannot be excluded from a full understanding of the political implications and social consequences of even the most professional, independent, and impartial judicial system, even if that broader context does not (and should not) intrude explicitly within the process.

The question is how much significance should be attached to these numbers. It is not the case that governments and corporations always win and individuals always lose, only that governments win more often than corporations and corporations more often than individuals. That the Crown should succeed half again as often as individual litigants suggests an advantage that is pronounced rather than overwhelming, and the greater success rate of government and business does not obliterate, but merely puts in a broader context, the fact that individuals still win about two times in five. To switch metaphors: we are demonstrating that there is a current in the river and making some suggestion of how strong that current might be. This does not mean that it is impossible to paddle against the current, only that it is harder than going with it.

The Impact of Judicial Decisions

Much of this book has revolved around the central dramatic moment of the judicial process — the decision itself, when the judge pronounces the outcome, declares the winner (and the reasons for the victory), and spells out the consequences for the loser. This focus is appropriate because Anglo-American practice pivots on this single event to a much greater extent than its continental European counterparts. However, there is another critically important characteristic of this moment: it marks the point at which the judge "signs out" of the process. Judges have power because of the impact of their (at least partly) discretionary decisions. From the moment that the decision is made, however, this power is indirect — mediated through the choices, actions, and understandings of other actors — rather than direct — under the ongoing immediate supervision and control of the judge who made it.

The Indirectness of Judicial Power

The most curious feature of judicial power is that someone else must carry the judge's words into actions. The courts have no bureaucracy to carry out their wishes, no police force to ensure compliance, no inspectors to make regular reports on implementation, no official watchdogs to blow the whistle on noncompliance. This is why Alexander Hamilton, during the debate over the new U.S. constitution, referred to the courts as the "least dangerous" of the branches of government. This structural limitation does not refute the notion of judicial power, but it calls for a careful understanding of its nature and limits and the mechanisms through which it is transmitted.

The impact of any single decision travels down two different channels. The first — the most important if you have the misfortune to be directly involved, but in grander systemic terms the least interesting — bears directly upon the immediate parties. For them, the decision may have set in train any of a series of material outcomes — a prison term, a transfer of property, a payment of fines or damages, or whatever. Any decision will be enforced by someone other than the judge, someone who is not in the judge's office or subject to the judge's supervision or directly accountable to the judge in any way. If the order is not carried out, there may well be a further proceeding in front of the same or another judge, but that will only happen if the party who gained entitlement from the decision brings it there as a new action and not because of any automatic process of the court itself. What Hodder-Williams (1980, 109) observed of the U.S. Supreme Court is equally true of all other courts:

> Words have no force of their own. All that a judicial decision does is to require the appropriate official, sometimes a lower judicial officer, sometimes a governmental appointee, sometimes a state judge or official, sometimes merely private parties like union leaders or company directors, to do, or refrain from doing, something. Normally people obey; but there are degrees of obedience, and it would be naive to imagine that judgements ensure their own fulfilment.

Most people do comply, and judges are, when called upon to do so, often prepared to deal severely with those who do not; but the assumption of compliance means that it is difficult and timeconsuming to bring to the court's attention whatever foot-dragging or delinquencies may occur.

This remoteness from the action can be a source of frustration to judges. They can sentence a person to prison, and determining the appropriate sentence is for most judges the most difficult and demanding aspect of their responsibilities, but they cannot designate a specific correctional institution or remedial program, and they have no say at all in what the parole board may do down the road to alter the length of incarceration. If you ask what percentage of parties sentenced in their courtroom actually pay the fines or do the community work ordered or whatever, not only will judges be unable to answer, but also they will be surprised that you expected them to be able to (Greene, Gabor, and McCormick 1986). And what is true of the summary conviction offence is also true at the grander level of public law; as Rabkin (1989, 20) notes, "Courts are entirely unequipped to act as ongoing, freestanding guardians of administrative performance," which means that they must rely on the litigants to take the time and incur the costs that are necessary to bring non-compliance to their attention.

But far more important are the indirect effects of judicial decisions — the long shadow potentially cast by any court's decisions and, particularly, by those of the "higher" courts. Every decision is an implicit indication of how the same court would resolve the same type of situation if it were raised again. It therefore gives a signal to everyone involved in similar activities about precisely what the rules-as-enforced mean. The higher courts — provincial courts of appeal or the Supreme Court itself — are implicitly sending the same message past the trial courts to the general categories of litigant, and sparing litigants the cost and bother of appeals that will inevitably succeed is one reason why lower court judges accept the obligation of following higher court decisions. If the message is clear enough, and widely enough communicated, then everyone knows what the rules are, and people have good reasons to behave as they think the court would order them to. As an intriguing article by Schauer (1985) says, one consequence of our system is that it turns most potential disputes into "easy cases" that are never raised because the resolution is obvious, and so interactions that would otherwise have matured into disputes do not escalate. (By the same token, however, it will call forth disputes on logically related issues to locate the precise conceptual boundaries of the "easy" question.)

But saying that legal decisions enunciate and clarify legal principles, that lower courts follow higher courts, and that most actors comply with actual or anticipated court requirements provides us with no more than an outline of the complex process whereby judicial decisions have an impact upon society. If Hodder-Williams is right to remind us that words do not enforce themselves, it is surely equally pertinent that words do not communicate or interpret themselves either.

The general point is nicely illustrated by what happened in September 1981, when the Supreme Court handed down its decision in the Patriation Reference, ruling on the constitutionality of the Trudeau government's plan for the unilateral patriation of the Canadian constitution. The decision has been both praised for its political opportunism and criticized for its juridical content (Russell 1983), but for present purposes the most striking thing about the occasion was that it was the first time the Supreme Court permitted its decision to be televised live. Because the occasion was of such historic importance, all the networks were there, the cameras were set up and ready to go, and millions of Canadians tuned in to watch the spectacle. The nine judges filed in, resplendent in their ermine-trimmed robes, took their seats, and Chief Justice Bora Laskin began to read the history-making decision. The result — anticlimax. The sound quality was terrible, Laskin's voice thin and distant and almost drowned out by background noise and static, and nothing the networks could do with the sound feed helped the audience straining to make out the words. It later turned out that another judge had switched on his microphone by mistake, but the symbolism was perfect: the Supreme Court had misplayed its own first step into the electronic age.

The episode is also a splendid metaphor for the limitations under which judicial power operates. The courts have an impact on society to the extent that other actors (judges, bureaucrats, politicians, ordinary citizens) accept their *interpretation* of the law as providing the *meaning* of the law, but other actors can only respond to the leadership of the courts if they are aware of it and understand it. The roads down which the courts' messages travel have many pitfalls, not all of them as obvious as a glitch with microphones.

Judicial Impact Theory: The Four Populations

Serious research into the question of what happens after a judicial decision began in the United States following the famous desegregation case *Brown v. Board of Education* in 1954, when it became clear that neither school officials nor many lower court judges were meekly or routinely following through on the U.S. Supreme Court's order to desegregate public education. Moreover, controversial decisions on prayer in schools, defendants' rights, and reapportionment suggested that compliance problems extended far beyond this issue. It was not enough to assume public and official compliance with court orders. Often the transmission belt slips a little and sometimes it slips a lot, which makes it important to understand the circumstances. Such was the proliferation of research on the subject (see, e.g., Wasby 1970, Becker and Feely 1973) that by 1970 Stephen Wasby was able to put together an inventory of 135 hypotheses on judicial impact, some mutually contradictory (Wasby 1973), which was perhaps too much of a good thing. More usefully, in 1984 Johnson and Canon suggested a powerful conceptual framework for organizing research into the impact of appellate judicial decisions, which the following discussion modifies to accommodate trial courts as well.

The Johnson/Canon model is summarized diagrammatically in Figure 11.1. It identifies a judicial decision-maker and four different "populations" that link in different ways to the judicial decision; "filling in" these various populations for specific decisions, identifying the nature of their links to that decisions, and unravelling their motivations and interactions is the way we apply the model to the study of judicial impact. The comments that follow apply Johnson and Canon's ideas to judicial decisions at both trial and appellate levels.

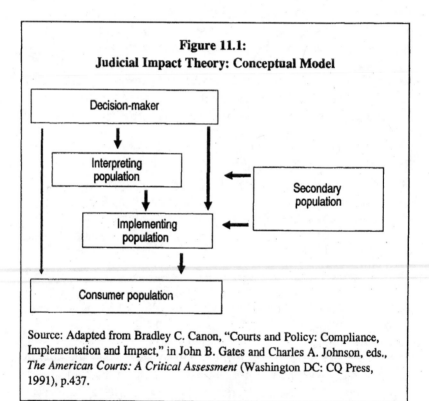

Figure 11.1:
Judicial Impact Theory: Conceptual Model

Source: Adapted from Bradley C. Canon, "Courts and Policy: Compliance, Implementation and Impact," in John B. Gates and Charles A. Johnson, eds., *The American Courts: A Critical Assessment* (Washington DC: CQ Press, 1991), p.437.

The Decision-Maker

In this model, the "decision-maker" is the court that has handed down a particular decision. For the bulk of judicial decisions, trial and appeal alike, the impact of the decision is far too modest to need anything like the conceptual apparatus of this model. Many trials are routine and short, revolving around relatively straightforward fact and law situations, and many appeals represent forlorn hopes that are briefly dismissed. (As one appeal judge said to me: "About one-third of the time, you wonder why they are wasting your time.") As well, most legal decisions repeat existing doctrine and add little to the body of the law. But a certain percentage of cases raise new questions or give judges the opportunity to respond in a new way to ongoing problems, and the accommodation and diffusion of this element of novelty is what we have to be able to explain.

The Interpreting Population

But for those other than the immediate parties, what is important is not the specific decision but the legal principles the decision embodies; that is, the specific decision must be interpreted to extract a general message. The set of actors who do the interpretation Johnson and Canon identify as the *interpreting population*. For appeal court decisions, an important part of this population is constituted by the "lower" courts, who will explain the meaning of the decision as they incorporate it into their own decisions. For example, when the Supreme Court of Canada hands down a benchmark decision on the division of marital assets (such as *Pelech v. Pelech*), then in a large number of cases, the lower court will explain its decision simply by citing that case (if the factual situations are sufficiently similar) or by locating their case by reference to its similarities to and differences from Pelech. To a lesser but still significant extent, the same is true of trial court decisions. Although only a minority of trial decisions are reported, trial judges try to stay current with the laws in areas frequently raised by the cases that appear before them; indeed, many judges say that one of the attractions of the life of the judge over the life of the practising lawyer is that there is so much more opportunity to study the law, to catch up on the reading of cases and commentaries (McCormick and Green 1990, ch. 4.). As a matter of course, judges will try to incorporate the principles and reasoning of recent trials into their own decisions (Canon and Baum 1981). Doing so both serves the judicial value of consistency and contributes to similar cases receiving similar treatment in different parts of the province or country. It thus reduces (although it never eliminates) the difference that the judge on the bench makes in a particular trial.

For all judicial decisions, trial and appeal alike, the interpreting population is mostly made up of lawyers. Lawyers spend far more time advising clients than they do representing them in court; and much of that advice bears on how to avoid or minimize direct contact with the judicial system. Therefore, it follows that the impact of judicial decisions on the lives of many citizens is mediated through the way that lawyers explain their practical implications — we behave the way that lawyers say we have to behave because of such-and-such a case, and usually this interpretation is not directly tested in a courtroom because we accept the lawyer's prediction of what would happen if it were. As Lewis (1988) tersely sums it up, "One fact is general: lawyers make law."

This truism does not imply a conspiracy of lawyers; it simply points out how the messages contained in law are communicated to the broader public and indicates the overlapping functional responsibilities of judges and lawyers. A trial judge once told me that the law that issued from his court was as final as that of the Supreme Court of Canada right up until the minute that someone appealed it; by the same token, your lawyer's statement of the law is as final as a judge's would have been, right up until the moment that you decide to go to court anyway.

But identifying the interpreting population is only the first step because the interpreting process can be far from straightforward. Indeed, some have provocatively suggested that there is an "uncertainty principle at work in the judicial process," so that any attempt to achieve certainty involving any major legal issue is not only unlikely to succeed but also will "inevitably create uncertainty as to more issues than it settles" (Bradley 1986, 2). Some problems stem from the way meanings are communicated. Usually, appeal courts deliver a single decision signed by all the members of the panel, but there still are dissents (judges disagreeing with the outcome of the case), or separate concurring opinions (judges agreeing with the outcome but disagreeing with the reasons), or both. When there is more than one opinion, the message of the court is garbled, especially if the result is what is called a "plurality decision" — that is, if there are so many differing opinions and the judges are so evenly divided among them that there is not a single package of "outcome plus reasons" that drew the agreement of even a bare majority of the court. The evolution of modern appellate practice is toward the delivery of a single decision, so this is less often a problem now than it was in the past (see, e.g., Bushnell 1992), but "less often" is not the same as "never." In such circumstances, lower courts and lawyers can be left scrambling for a clear understanding of the law, and the court may have to return to the issue in further decisions to clear up the ambiguities.

A good decision (appeal or trial) not only provides and explains an outcome, but also it clearly locates the immediate decision in relation to other elements of the law As Terrell (1984) argues in the interesting if off-the-wall "Flatlaw," a good decision is much more than just one more point on some notional multidimensional field, adding itself to the thousands of other points that represent other decisions. Instead, it draws the lines to connect the dots and turns them into a meaningful picture. To the extent that a decision falls short of this ideal, that it leaves lines undrawn, it can create confusion and even apparent contradiction, which makes it harder for other courts to know which decision to follow in what circumstances. Paul Weiler (1974) concludes that the Supreme Court of Canada has often performed poorly in this regard, especially on private law matters.

By the same token, it is usually more functional if "new" legal ideas emerge gradually rather than "out of the blue": messages are easier to decipher if they have been "telegraphed" in advance and if they build on a sequence of cases emerging from the same jurisdiction. Here is a possible future example whose impact would be enormous. One major case in Canadian constitutional law was the decision of the Judicial Committee of the Privy Council in the Labour Conventions case of 1937, which acknowledged that the national government had the power to negotiate any international treaty it might wish but denied it the legislative jurisdiction to implement those treaties. Effectively, if the subject matter of the treaty falls within provincial jurisdiction (and many do), then its implementation is a matter of provincial discretion and cannot be legally compelled or pre-empted by the national government. The Supreme Court of Canada has hinted on at least a dozen occasions over the last twenty years that it would be willing to reconsider that decision (see Hogg 1992), although no government has so far been willing to take it up on the invitation, Ontario's blustering over the free trade deal notwithstanding. Given the implications of such a reconsideration — which would probably result in the federal government being able to legislate in areas of provincial jurisdiction if that were necessary to fulfil international obligations — it is fully appropriate that the Supreme Court should be dropping these heavy hints well ahead of time. (Of course, the hints may well have the effect of calling forth the court case that would allow the court to do what it is hinting it would like to do.) Without such notice, other actors might well discount what such a far-reaching reversal would mean: "Surprise!" is not a productive game for higher courts to play.

Communication is one problem, and motivation is another. Judges and lawyers are trained professionals with a commitment to the law, but they are also individuals with their own values and interests, their own styles, their own priorities. What they do with the legal message embedded in specific decisions — whether they apply it expansively or restrictively, whether they enthusiastically follow through on its nuances or reach to distinguish its fact situation from those they confront — will depend on the extent to which they are in sympathy with the legal values it embodies. As Johnson and Canon (1984, 70) suggest, "A judge's willingness to accept a higher court decision depends upon whether it falls within his or her 'zone of indifference.' For most judges, the zone is broad enough to encompass the great majority of judicial policies." Outright insubordination is rare but not impossible. I once spoke with a provincial judge whose notion of the appropriate sentence for male sodomy in a public park sharply varied from that of the Court of Appeal, but he cheerfully insisted that the learned appeal judges were wrong on this one, and defendants could (and, in fact, did) always appeal if they did not agree with his sentence. More typically, sympathetic lawyers and judges can expand the legal principle of a pivotal case, or reluctant lawyers and judges can minimize its impact — subtle effects that can add up over time. This variability among legal temperaments is functional rather than deplorable, an important part of the way that the legal system accommodates changes in social views.

The Implementing Population

But only a minority of human interactions are ever submitted to judicial scrutiny or even to legal advice. The next category of actors in the judicial impact process is the *implementing population*, by which we mean the various sets of actors whose daily routine actions accommodate the law as it has been declared or modified by judicial decision-makers. If the courts enunciate new standards in the rules of evidence or the rights of the accused, then the actions of the police will change to take these into account, to jump the new hurdles on the way to their law-enforcement goals. If the courts declare stricter requirements for the consideration of refugee claims, then the officials of the Immigration Department will have to establish the new procedures and provide the facilities that permit them to be carried through. If the courts accept a new definition of the family unit (for example, including common-law or same-sex relationships), then thousands of large employers will have to renegotiate their benefits packages. Such changes are clearly the most important way that judicial decisions affect our daily world, and our lives may well be touched in some way by dozens of such decisions every month without our being directly aware of it.

But the twofold qualification applies to this link in the impact chain as well. First, the implementing actors can only respond to the law as they understand it, which means that the same principle can be conscientiously applied in different ways by different officials. (For example, in the *Mossop* case, the Supreme Court denied the claim of a same-sex couple who believed they had been wrongly treated when they were denied the same bereavement leave that a couple in a traditional marriage would have been entitled to, but the Court hinted strongly that this outcome was justified only because the case was not a Charter case. Should a conscientious employer read this as requiring or not requiring that same-sex couples be given the same benefits as traditional families? Surely both readings are defensible.) The standards and principles that judges derive are often buried in lengthy prose and sometimes opaque in their language. It is not considered proper to write a judge asking what he meant in paragraph 62.

Second, the way that implementing actors respond to the law will tend to be a function of how well it meshes with their professional values and whether it facilitates or complicates their duties. One study of the evidence exclusion rules in the United States found that sometimes the police reaction seems to be evasion rather than whole-hearted compliance, all the easier to accomplish because so much of the proceedings revolve around the way the police present their evidence (Oaks 1970). For example, when random stop-and-frisk practices were prohibited, researchers noted an astounding rise in the frequency with which accused parties happened to drop stolen property or weapons while a policeman was watching. I am not making a cynical jibe at the police, simply recognizing that they see themselves as having an important job to do and that their priorities are not always congruent with those of judges. As well, because we tend to hear what we want to hear, these professionals may firmly believe that they are responding to nuances or qualifications within the judicial decision that more neutral observers have failed to detect.

Generally speaking, the smaller the changes required, the less the expense of accommodating them, and the less they interfere with the implementors' perception of their duties and responsibilities, the greater will be the compliance. Conversely, the larger and more expensive the changes and the harder they make the implementors' job, the more likely there will be only lip-service or even evasion. This is the practical face of the indirect nature of judicial power; it can be seen as either advantage (if the concentration of judicial power in the hands of remote and possibly doctrinaire appeal courts is seen as a problem) or as disadvantage (if the judicial proclamation of rights and procedures is seen as the principled core of the legal process).

The Consumer Population

Johnson and Canon also identify the *consumer population* as directly relevant to judicial impact. By this term, they mean that set of actors whose legal position and claims are similar to those directly dealt with in specific decisions. If a case deals with prisoners' rights, then the consumer population includes all prisoners; if it resolves issues of landlord-tenant relations, then the consumer population includes all landlords and tenants; if it deals with the criminality of abortion, then the consumer population includes all women who do now or might in the future seek an abortion and all doctors who might be called upon to carry out the procedure.[1] This broad shadow of judicial decision-making is its most important dimension, but it is the hardest to come to grips with, the more so because judicial innovation is so incremental and unheralded that even alterations in the law are structured so that they stress the elements of continuity with established legal principles and practices.

The communication process is especially critical for this group, whose members are unlikely to be regular readers of law reports. It means little for the courts to proclaim a right or invalidate a statute if the target group remains unaware of the case and lacks an understanding of what it accomplished. The mass media fill some of the gap, but there are grave limitations. The popular print media tend toward encapsulization and summary, the headline and the slogan rather than the lengthy discursive argument; and the electronic media live in an "eternal present" that limits concern for context and long-term causation (Mander 1978). Both are unsuited to the complex technical arguments and fine distinctions that are made in judicial decisions; legal judgments are not produced for a mass audience or wide diffusion, and they do not always take the transformation well.

The Secondary Population

The final group is the *secondary population*, which is basically a residual category. This label does not necessarily imply that the group is indifferent to the judicial product. Indeed, some members of the secondary population may be intensely interested in the trends of legal doctrine, either because they hope to draw useful parallels to their own claims and interests or because they want to oppose what they see as wrong turns of events. The "right to life" lobby, which reacts strongly to decisions on abortion, is a case in point, as is the "Victims of Violence" movement, which responds to judicial elaboration of criminals' rights. The secondary population also includes elected officials who may be called upon to facilitate (or to limit) the exercise of newly proclaimed rights or opportunities. However, most members of the general public are indeed indifferent to most judicial decisions, and the segment that is active on any given issue will be small. The communication problem is most serious with regard to the secondary population because it is so diffuse and multifaceted and because levels of interest and self-information vary so greatly.

Three Brief "Case Studies" in Judicial Impact

By itself judicial impact theory does not answer all the questions. It is a conceptual map on which to organize the process of looking for the answers. What follows is three brief "case studies" from recent Canadian experience. As it happens, they are Charter cases, but the principles they illustrate apply much more broadly.

All three are explored as examples of problems in communication rather than in lower-court insubordination or non-compliance. This perspective is consistent with recent trends in the U.S. that have suggested that judicial impact studies should not be "handicapped by excessive attention to the relatively narrow and artificially dichotomous concept of compliance" (Songer and Sheehan 1990, 297). Since we are concerned with results rather than intentions — that is, with the question of whether or not final outcomes correspond to the initial intentions of the judicial decision-makers — non-comprehension and non-compliance are both potential contributing elements to any distortion that might occur.

Carter

Section 3 of the Canadian Charter of Rights and Freedoms affirms that every citizen has the right to vote in federal and provincial elections. It is a short step from this affirmation to the argument that every citizen has a right to cast a vote of equal value — that is, since our electoral system involves the creation of electoral divisions that elect a single representative, citizens have a right to electoral divisions of roughly equal size.[2] *Carter* represents the Supreme Court's only intervention into this debate and therefore formally states Canadian constitutional law on this question.

In both Canada and the United States, reform of the electoral boundaries process dates from the 1960s, although the process was driven by judicial decisions in the U.S. (*Baker v. Carr* 1962, *Reynolds v. Sims* 1964) and by legislative action at the federal and provincial level in Canada. These reforms proceeded on two fronts: first, to minimize the extent to which individual ridings could depart from an average size; and second, to set up independent and neutral (or at least multi-partisan) commissions for drawing the boundaries. However, the achievement of this "electoral boundaries revolution" (the phrase is drawn from Carty 1985) was uneven from one jurisdiction to another, some governments being more prone to manipulate the process to their own advantage. The entrenchment of the Charter in 1981 provided an opportunity to force the pace. The first such case was *Dixon v. A-G. B.C.* in 1989, in which Madame Justice McLachlin, then chief justice of the B.C. Supreme Court, declared the new B.C. electoral boundaries unconstitutional. Building on Section 3 of the Charter, she identified equality of voting power as the "single most important factor to be considered in determining electoral boundaries," which meant that population must be "the dominant consideration." With *Dixon,* the courts clearly signed on to the electoral boundaries revolution.

Months later came the second case, in the form of the *Reference re Saskatchewan Electoral Boundaries* (curiously renamed *Carter v. A.-G. Saskatchewan* when it was appealed to the Supreme Court of Canada), in which the Saskatchewan Court of Appeal responded by unanimously finding unconstitutional both the legislation establishing the Saskatchewan electoral boundaries commission and the commission's final report. The court reached this conclusion by applying the principle of "one person, one vote," a principle that it said was violated by dividing the province into two types of riding with different electoral quotients as well as by pervasive inequalities in the sizes of neighbouring ridings. However, when the Saskatchewan government appealed this decision, a divided Supreme Court of Canada reversed the Court of Appeal. The majority decision interpreted Section 3 of the Charter as providing a guarantee for "effective representation," which did not necessarily require perfect mathematical equality; it stressed that the departure from proportionate representation for urban and rural seats was small, and (rather perversely[3]) it accepted categories of seats with different electoral quotients as traditional practices posing no problems. The decision concluded that "deviations from absolute voter parity may be justified on the grounds of practical impossibility or the provision of more effective representation" and that these were the only circumstances under which the "dilution of one citizen's vote as compared with another's" should be countenanced.

The decision was widely taken as a repudiation of judicial commitment to "one person, one vote" and something of a carte blanche to provincial governments to pursue more flexible redistribution procedures, typically favouring rural voters over urban voters (see e.g., Morton and Knopf 1992; Baillie and Johnson 1992). In Alberta, in the aftermath of *Carter,* several intervenors withdrew from a reference on Alberta's redistribution legislation, which transparently underrepresented urban voters, and the provincial government vigorously defended its legislation as fulfilling the Supreme Court's requirements. When the new boundaries emerged from the process, they were not even challenged in the courts until the election was under way, although the chief electoral officer reported that the boundaries failed to satisfy even the rather generous limits suggested by the court of appeal. If *Dixon* and the *Saskatchewan Reference* rallied proponents of democratic equality, *Carter* threw them into retreat.

But there are two striking things about *Carter,* and adding them to the equation suggests that the message might be rather different. The first is that the case arose in Saskatchewan. Of all the electoral boundaries drawn for provincial elections in the history of Canada, the closest to "one person, one vote" were the 1979 boundaries in Saskatchewan, and the second closest were the 1989 boundaries challenged in *Carter*. The second is that it was delivered by Madame Justice McLachlin, the same judge who decided *Dixon v. A.-G. B.C.* The decision in *Carter* refers to *Dixon* about a dozen times but never repudiates it; quite the contrary, it quotes from *Dixon* to reinforce points and underline arguments.

If Madame Justice McLachlin did not think she changed her mind or contradicted herself, one possible response is to take her at her word. An interpretation of *Carter* that preserves the basic thrust of

Dixon would run along these lines: The Charter establishes a right to vote with real implications for the drawing of electoral boundaries, the most important being a strong expectation of numeric equality. This is not the only principle implied by the Charter, and others must be acknowledged; for example, it permits accommodation for sparsely populated regions and, possibly, special provision for groups such as the aboriginal peoples. Nor does this expectation imply that courts must become number-crunchers; minor inequalities will be tolerated, as witness *Carter,* but major and pervasive inequalities will not, as witness *Dixon.* If we look at *Carter* alone, the implications are, of course, rather different.

Only time will tell which side of the *Carter* message is the correct one — whether it mandated "effective representation" even at the cost of voter inequality or "relative parity of voting power" with departures tolerated only if they are not very large. If it turns out to be the latter, then "what the court meant" has been effectively eclipsed by "what people thought the court meant"; and the immediate reaction to *Carter* by the interpreting population (such as the Alberta Court of Appeal), the implementing population (such as the Alberta government), and the consumer population (such as the voters of Alberta who might have wished to challenge the process) has delayed the implementation of Charter rights.

Askov

Section 11(d) of the Charter gives accused persons the right to be tried "within a reasonable time," but the phrase does not interpret itself. For several years, the Supreme Court was willing to deal with the matter on an ad hoc basis, and in a string of cases beginning in 1986, it indicated whether a specific delay was or was not unreasonable, at the same time laying down the general factors that should be taken into consideration in assessing this reasonableness. Apart from the simple length of elapsed time, the Court said that it was relevant to consider whether the accused had waived any time periods, what the reasons for the delay were, and whether there had been any prejudice to the accused as a result. However, in 1989, in *Askov v. The Queen,* it took the bull by the horns and (apparently) gave an unusually cut-and-dry answer.

The case involved a Mr. Askov, who, with several colleagues, was accused of attempted extortion in connection with a series of threats against an owner of a nightclub. The preliminary hearing (the enquiry process that precedes the laying of an indictment in the case of a serious crime) was originally scheduled for the spring of 1983, but it could not be concluded until September of that year. At the conclusion of the preliminary hearing, the case was committed for trial at the first available date, which was October 1984. When that date arrived, the case could not be accommodated, and it was put off until the next available date, another year later. When the trial was finally held, Mr. Askov was convicted. He then appealed on the grounds that the delay between charge and trial was unreasonable; the Ontario Court of Appeal denied the appeal on the basis of the standards laid down in previous Supreme Court decisions — there was no indication that the case of the accused had in any way been prejudiced by the delay. On subsequent appeal to the Supreme Court of Canada, however, that decision was reversed, and a clean and definitive definition of "reasonable delay" was put forward.

Although the length of time between charge and trial seems long, figures submitted to the Supreme Court suggest that it was not atypical for the particular Ontario district in which the trial was held. The Judicial District of Peel has the dubious distinction of being one of the most heavily backlogged jurisdictions in North America, and a year's delay in scheduling a trial is not unusual. The trial judge had even referred to this fact when rescheduling the trial. Although the accused made some objection to the delay, the judge indicated that an earlier date was not possible without delaying other scheduled trials, which would simply shift the problem to another case rather than resolving it. Similarly, the Ontario Court of Appeal accepted that such an accumulation of delays was not so unusual as to suggest particular incapacity on the part of the Crown, and it focused on the critical element of whether or not the defence's case had suffered from the wait.

The Supreme Court upheld the appeal from the Ontario Court of Appeal, saying that the delay was so unreasonable that the charge against Mr. Askov should be dismissed. Mr. Justice Cory spoke of the "exquisite agony" of a person awaiting trial and the strong presumption of prejudice against the accused from the simple fact of delay. In what came to be critical element of the decision, he suggested that "a period of delay in a range of some six to eight months between committal and trial might be deemed to be the outside limit of what is reasonable." As some commentators have pointed out (Manfredi 1993, 110), one of the ironies is that a major cause of the increased length of time that it took to bring cases to trial was the stricter procedural guarantees that the Supreme Court itself had been reading into other sections of the Charter.

The impact of *Askov* was massive. In Canada, there were tens of thousands of accused who had been awaiting trial for six to eight months, and most of these immediately applied for a stay of proceedings on the grounds of unreasonable delay; "in the twelve months that followed the *Askov* decision, over 47,000 charges were stayed or withdrawn in Ontario" (Hogg 1992, 1126). Hundreds of these stays were appealed by the Crown. The appeals were dismissed by some provincial appeal courts because the Supreme Court's numbers were so specific that there was little leeway, but they were allowed by other courts (including that of Ontario), which insisted on taking them as guidelines that amplified rather than replaced the earlier criteria. So great was the outcry that Mr. Justice Cory took the unusual step of using the occasion of a speech in England the following summer to respond to some of the complaints, indicating, first, that the Supreme Court had never been informed that the impact of a six-to-eight month limit would be so great (although the figures were in the brief of the Ontario attorney-general), and, second, that the figures had been intended only as a guideline, not as an absolute limit (although the specific numbers were volunteered by Cory and did not arise from any detail of the specific litigation). Subsequently, in *R. v. Morin* (1992), Mr. Justice Sopinka committed the Supreme Court to the proposition that the numbers were a guideline rather than a fixed limit and appears as well to have reopened the door to a need to prove prejudice to the accused before a delay can be deemed excessive.

There are three different ways to look at the *Askov* episode. The first is simply that the Supreme Court goofed, misunderstanding the expert testimony (Baar, 1992), casually laying down a rigid number, and then retreating (with poor grace) from the consequences of its ruling. The second, and the one that is most directly relevant to the thesis I am pursuing, is that the Supreme Court was misunderstood; it was a victim of the uncertainties built into the process of communicating a judicial decision and was honestly surprised at consequences it neither intended or anticipated. The third is that the Supreme Court deliberately gave a sharp message to induce a response that earlier hints had failed to elicit and then retreated once the message landed; two of the undeniable results of *Askov* were the expansion of resources made available to the court system and the appointment of more judges in Peel and other congested judicial districts. Whichever is the case, decisions like *Askov* need to be included in any assessment of judicial impact and judicial power.

Morgentaler

Regina v. Morgentaler, Smoling and Scott is arguably the highest profile decision of the Supreme Court since the Patriation Reference, and this discussion builds on the excellent treatment by Morton (1992). The case arose out of charges made against three individuals who operated an abortion clinic in Toronto; it provided the opportunity for the defendants to challenge the current law on abortion, Section 251 of the Criminal Code. After a lengthy and dramatic trial, the jury found the defendants not guilty, but the Crown appealed the acquittal and successfully persuaded a unanimous five-judge panel of the Ontario Court of Appeal to order a new trial. It was Morgentaler's appeal from this decision that brought the case before the Supreme Court. In the event, they surprised most observers by reversing the highly regarded Ontario Court of Appeal and finding unconstitutional the Criminal Code sections dealing with abortion.

This is the outcome: what of the decision? In fact, the seven judges delivered not one opinion but four, none of which gained the support of a majority of the Court, and the diversity of views that emerge from those opinions make it difficult to know with any certainty what the final message really was.

Only two judges, McIntyre and Laforest, would have upheld the Ontario Court of Appeal and left the relevant sections of the Criminal Code standing. They reasoned that the history of debates surrounding the Charter clearly showed that none of the politicians involved believed that entrenchment would resolve the abortion issue one way or the other, and they thought arguments about women's rights and women's freedoms were largely irrelevant to criminal charges against three males for conspiring to break the law. Since none of their colleagues would go this far, McIntyre wrote and Laforest signed a dissent.

Two judges, Beetz and Estey, had some reservations about the actual operation of the existing abortion law and felt that the unfairness and inequality built into its application required a finding of unconstitutionality, but they indicated that with relatively minor amendments a revised version might pass constitutional muster. Most importantly, they saw nothing wrong with the existence of therapeutic abortion committees or with limiting abortions to situations that threatened the life or health of the mother.

Another pair of judges, Dickson (the Chief Justice) and Lamer, found that the abortion law imposed serious violations of procedural fairness, so much so that requirements such as approval by a therapeutic abortion committee were inherently unfair and could not be part of a constitutionally acceptable law. They also found that the references to "health" were unconstitutionally vague and that varying interpretations of its meaning had further contributed to unfairness in the application of the law in different provinces.

A single judge, Wilson, interpreted Section 7 of the Charter as including a constitutional right to an abortion (although not after some stage of fetal viability and therefore possibly limited to the first trimester of pregnancy) and saw the decision of a woman to terminate her own pregnancy as an important element of personal autonomy deserving constitutional protection.

The difficulties of determining what the Court decided are obvious. Five of the seven judges found that Section 251 of the Criminal Code was unconstitutional; this much is clear. However, four judges would have found the same provisions constitutional had they been linked to a more streamlined procedure for determining whether an abortion application should be approved, and two more would have signed on if vague terms like "health" were clarified and the number of required physician approvals were reduced. At the least, one must conclude that it is difficult to say whether Dickson/Lamer or Beetz/Estey has the best claim to supplying the court's reasons; and it is something of a leap to conclude, as did a headline the next day in the *Globe and Mail*, that the abortion law had been completely scrapped and women guaranteed free choice (29 January 1989, A1). The irony was that the scrapping of the abortion law had indeed given women more choice than even Wilson intended, but that this was done by a fragmented court that was willing to accept new legislation that might closely resemble the recently invalidated provisions. It is hard to see how these subtleties could be reduced to a newspaper headline.

The ambiguities of the divided decision meant that there was still logical room to argue not that the abortion law had been too restrictive but that it had been too permissive. The *Borowski* case, which was on the Supreme Court docket at the same time as the *Morgentaler* case, was directed at getting the court to declare that the fetus was a rights-bearing human being within the meaning of the Charter; the obvious implication was that abortion was murder and that the abortion law offended against the rights of fetuses by permitting their death. The Supreme Court finessed this possibility by declaring the question moot — since the *Morgentaler* decision, there was no *Criminal Code* section on abortion to challenge — and they declined to consider the matter in its more general terms. When the same question subsequently returned to the Court — in the later case of *Daigle v. Tremblay* — the Supreme Court ruled that the fetus was not a person for such purposes.

The Mulroney government struggled to deal with the resulting controversy, and after several false starts, they introduced amendments to the Criminal Code that conformed very closely to the Dickson/Lamer position — that is, they replaced the therapeutic abortion committees with a single doctor, they gave a clearer definition of health, and they avoided the accredited hospital bottleneck by allowing free-standing abortion clinics. After barely scraping through the House of Commons in May 1990, the legislation died on a tie vote in the Senate. What is striking, however, is that the legislation was widely attacked as offending constitutional principles and violating the rights of citizens. This suggests that the very ambiguity of the *Morgentaler* decision has altered its message and its subsequent impact, that it has been retrospectively turned into a confrontation between the deferential position of McIntyre and the strong position of Wilson with the latter prevailing.

If *Askov* highlights the interpreting population, *Morgentaler* arguably highlights the secondary population. The major impact of the decision has been on public opinion itself, on groups organizing themselves for and against what is now seen as a court-created right for women, on politicians being dragged into the fray, of the prestige of the court being mobilized by one side in a highly divisive issue. If one aspect of the impact of law can be discussed in terms of litigants persuading the courts to interpret words and phrases in certain ways, then another can be discussed in terms of publicists persuading the public to interpret court decisions in certain ways. To the extent that the ultimate meaning of an important court decision is its actual impact, not the precise ideas that may have been in the minds of the judges delivering it, then *Morgentaler* indicates how public and contentious this process may be.

Conclusion

These three anecdotes do not pretend to be a complete analysis of judicial impact in Canada, but they do illustrate some of the limitations of judicial power. Wielding power from the judicial benches is like steering a supertanker with a faulty electrical system; sometimes it jumps in response and sometimes nothing happens at all, but in general it goes roughly the direction you want it to as long as you plan well ahead and do not change your mind. The indirect nature of judicial power is mildly reassuring to democrats, and it goes some way to dispel the spectre of judicial tyranny because other actors of more solid democratic legitimacy provide the conduits through which judicial influence flows.

Towards Democratic Courts?

This book has a double focus. It asks why our courts are important and what concepts and methods of enquiry best equip us to understand them. It explores the impact of the courts on the "person in the street" and the opinions that those individuals hold about the judicial system. The detailed discussion of the various levels of court and of the various critical concepts for the study of judicial behaviour strikingly confirm the general outlines of the public opinion: although their immediate experience is limited and sporadic, most Canadians respect the individuals who staff the judicial system but are sceptical of a process that they believe favours the rich and the powerful and disadvantages the poor, women, and ethnic minorities. But this confirmation simply brings us full circle: since public opinion has been validated rather than refuted, to what extent and for what purposes should the average citizen care about the courts and their actual or potential impact? One context in which an answer can be sketched is the concept of "legal mobilization."

The Concept of Legal Mobilization

Black suggests that the mobilization of the law can be understood as "the process by which a legal system acquires its cases" and which therefore supplies "the link between the law and the people served or controlled by the law" (1973, 125). In the area of private law as well as public law, specific cases represent legal actors (individuals, corporations, government agencies) using the law and the court system to accomplish their purposes. The evolving patterns of legal mobilization can be seen in any longitudinal study of the caseload of specific courts. That is, from one time to another we get different answers to the questions of who is using the courts to take legal action against whom and about what (McIntosh 1981, 1983, 1985,

1991), and the general pattern of judicial outcomes may often pro-
voke legislative activity either to consolidate or to reverse it (Stookey
1990).

Courts are essentially reactive institutions, taking disputes as they
are brought to them rather than actively seeking them out. This fact
has a double implication for the power of the individual litigants
considered as a broad group. The first implication is that "within the
limits of jurisdictional rules that structure participation, individual
litigants actually set the agenda of the judicial branch of government"
(Zemans 1983, 691). The courts as an institution do not have their
own agenda; they are necessarily limited to responding to the priorities of other actors.

The second implication is that "the litigants' arguments frequently
frame the alternatives from which the judge must choose," a consideration that can often be important (Lawrence 1991, 467). That much
of this legal activity takes place in the lower courts is not a problem.
It is important to avoid "the common error of overemphasis upon
upper courts" and realize that "in most cases it is courts of first
instance that are the terminus of the legal process" (Zemans 1983,
692); that "given our commitment to stare decisis and the rule of law,
even seemingly routine trial court litigation shapes the development
and implementation of our public policies" (Lawrence 1991, 466).
Indeed, one of the things that people fight about in the lower courts
is the precise meaning, the relevant extent, and the specific application of the rulings from higher courts. "Any new authoritative rule,
whether statute, judge-made common law, or administrative regulation, merely provides opportunities" for litigation (Zemans 1983,
694), and the "real" meaning of the law-in-practice as distinct from
the law-in-theory will be in large part the product of who takes up
the opportunities successfully. "The fact is that the share of the output
of the political system that individuals receive is in part determined
by the extent to which they mobilize the law on their own behalf"
(Zemans 1983, 693).

To the legal mobilization theorists, these "opportunities" mean
that the courts are a democratic institution in the pure sense of
facilitating popular participation through individual action, rather
than through more indirect representative processes. "The legal system...provides a uniquely democratic mechanism for individual citizens to invoke public authority on their own and for their benefit.
The bulk of this activity takes place among private citizens who, in

the process of involving legal norms, employ the power of the state and so become state actors themselves" (Zemans 1983, 692).

These considerations remain relevant even if the law favours the status quo (and therefore those individuals who are advantaged by the status quo) and even if not all people have equal access to the resources that facilitate the mobilization of the law. "The equality required for direct democracy in the courts is undermined by the disparities in access to one of the tools of mobilization: attorneys" (Lawrence 1991, 441); that is, privileged groups are not only able to afford to pay for more of the legal services that lawyers supply, but they are also able to afford the better lawyers who command higher prices for their services. However, such concerns notwithstanding, it remains both true and important that the law is "a resource available to the citizenry" (Zemans 1983, 694), a way in which "individuals can mobilize the law, invoke the power of the state on their own behalf, affect the course of legal change, and escape some of the problems inherent in representative government" (Lawrence 1991, 441). The educative dimension of democracy is also served by the fact that legal mobilization involves making reasoned arguments, hearing the adversary's response, and obtaining the judge's reasons for judgment — not perfect participation, to be sure, but arguably superior to the participatory opportunities presented by, say, a political rally. One can find more than an echo of the legal mobilization argument in the Trudeau government's defence of the *Charter* as a device that would "transfer power to the people" by giving them the "right to appeal to the courts" (Government of Canada, 1982).

In a similar vein Weiler suggests that legal mobilization is a major factor in the rather surprising degree of influence that the European Court of Justice has come to enjoy within the emerging European Community. "Individuals (and the community of practicing lawyers that represent them) were not tardy in noticing" the potential of the Court and the Community law that it articulated, and, as a result, "Effectively, individuals in real cases and controversies (usually against state public authorities) became the principal 'guardians' of the legal integrity of Community law within Europe, very much in the same way that individuals in, for example, the United States have been the principal actors in ensuring the vindication of the U.S. Bill of Rights and other federal law" (Weiler 1994, 513). The influence of the European Court of Justice, it has been argued, rests less on its rather modest formal powers than on the emergence of "a whole community of interests" shared by individuals, lawyers and judges of the national courts, who have developed a real financial and professional stake in the successful administration of Community law (Burley and Mattli 1993), and the emergence of a powerful Community court is simply one facet of a broader development that has seen the European judiciary emerge as a major "conduit" for "transmitting policy-relevant issues" (Shapiro and Stone 1994, 415).

This vision of the courts as an opportunity for democracy is qualified by the fact that judges are not accountable electorally. Yet it is not completely undermined because the second-hand and round-about influences are extremely important. "In many instances legal mobilization is generated not by the writing of new laws, but by changing social perceptions of the nature of a problem and the appropriateness of the intervention of state authority." By the same token, "evolving social definitions of the circumstances in which the law is appropriately invoked" creates new interests, new demands on the legal system (Zemans 1983, 697). The treatment of drunk drivers, the way the courts deal with the division of matrimonial assets, and the growing concern with child abuse are all cases in point: the judges have moved, sometimes in advance of the law and sometimes in tandem with it, to accommodate new public definitions of the appropriate and the justiciable. This may be a responsiveness without accountability, and it may happen more slowly and selectively than some would like, but it is still responsiveness.

The involvement of interest groups can be seen as either an advantage or a disadvantage. Lawrence suggests that "interest group mobilization of law is often simply an extension of their participation in pluralist politics in the political branches" (Lawrence 1991, 425). This is a specific application of the general argument that interest groups represent ways that individuals can promote their cause more effectively by organizing into a group and pooling their resources, by doing in a more coherent and focused way the same things they could conceivably do with less effect as individuals. Certainly interest groups are active in the courts, either by providing information and other resources to their members, or by sponsoring legal cases that raise the issues they are concerned about, or as intervenors presenting legal argument and relevant material to courts considering cases that indirectly affect the interests the group is organized to promote.

But "the flaw in the pluralist heaven is that the heavenly chorus sings with a strong upper-class accent. Probably about 90 percent of the people cannot get into the pressure system" (Schattschneider

1975, 34). If some theorists see interest groups as the solution to the democratic communication of wants and interests, others see them as part of the problem, part of the way that some issues are organized into politics and others are organized out. Those who defend legal mobilization as the direct involvement of individuals tend to downplay this aspect of the phenomenon, focusing on the enormous range of opportunities available to individuals whether or not they are part of larger groups, whether or not some organized interest shares their immediate concern.

There is a further problem that cannot be overlooked. As Lawrence says, "the caseload crisis may ultimately deprive the litigation process of its unique ability to promote the education of those who participate in it" (1991, 473). Growing caseloads imply the routinization of disputes and the compressing of available court time. Judges with a large backlog and with the concomitant pressure from their chief judge to improve the case-flow by handling cases quickly are less likely to have the time and the patience to allow an unusual litigant to present unusual arguments or to make the reasoned point-by-point response that shows the arguments have been given a careful hearing. Just as "justice delayed is justice denied," so the participatory element of legal mobilization is undermined if the courts take months or years to begin to address the questions. The fit between the fast pace of the modern world and the methodical processes of the judiciary is already a serious problem; the burgeoning caseloads of the 1980s (which may or may not continue into the 1990s) exacerbate the situation.

Legal Mobilization: Examples

To make legal mobilization less abstract, consider some recent examples of how individuals have sought to use the courts. Small business owners continue to challenge the legality of the federal Goods and Services Tax, a new case having gone before the Trial Division of the Federal Court just as this chapter is being written. On another front, recent news stories have reported that one individual has brought a multi-billion dollar lawsuit against the Bloc Québécois, presumably based on the anticipated economic effects of the separation of Quebec that the Bloc advocates. Admittedly, the prospects for both cases are not good, but it is easy to sense the feelings of frustration and political helplessness that have given rise to the suits and to recognize that the litigant gets a significant degree of satisfaction simply by being able to make focused arguments, to listen to a point-by-point response, and to have a judge explain the outcome. Similarly, a few years ago, there were court challenges to several of Prime Minister Mulroney's Senate appointments, and in the 1980s Operation Dismantle asked a court to overturn the cabinet decision allowing cruise missile testing in Canada.

Therefore, even when the dispute ends in a courtroom defeat, the "loser" may well have found within the judge's decision specific comments and concessions that are subjectively very important, that respond to major elements of the original dispute. It is this, and not just after-the-fact rationalization, that explains an otherwise curious phenomenon: the extent to which many unsuccessful litigants report with pride and even triumph that the judge agreed with them on a number of points although these points did not have enough legal weight to tip the outcome.

But having the courts respond to a lawsuit is not simply cathartic, limited to the purely emotional satisfaction of being heard and answered. Recently, a group of Western farmers took the chartered banks to task for the way that interest payments on farm loans over a period of years had been calculated on a shifting basis and persuaded the lower courts that the banks had indeed overcharged them by tens of millions of dollars (Calgary *Herald,* 29 November 1993). Although the case is on its way to the Supreme Court of Canada and probably will not receive final resolution for a few years, at least in its early stages it represents a clear win for the "little guy," and a win that has important ongoing implications for the way that the banks do their business.

Most of the examples above are non-Charter cases. Although the Charter provides the purest and most spectacular examples of legal mobilization and although the Charter has been a critical catalyst in the transformation of the judicial role in Canada, the effects of this transformation ripple much wider. The potential for legal mobilization is pervasive rather than Charter-specific, and it takes a wide variety of forms. The entrenchment of the Charter is making Canadians think about the courts in different ways, and it is undoubtedly causing judges to think about their own roles in different ways. In the 1990s, we are undoubtedly witnessing the beginning of a revolution in popular consciousness that will take years to work itself out.

It is also significant that none of the examples involved an attempt to have the courts declare a piece of legislation unconstitutional. This confirms the American experience, which is that "litigation is overwhelmingly used to obtain enforcement of statutes, not their nullification" (Lawrence 1991 466). For example, according to several recent newsmagazine programs, some landlords take advantage of renters by enforcing, in the face of legislative changes, their traditional policies regarding security deposits and the payment of the "last month's" rent. Since there is no effective enforcement arm to bring such landlords into line, the courts provide a practical and effective recourse for individual renters. Again to make the general point: the law creates a pattern of rights and obligations and thereby a set of opportunities for different sets of actors to pursue their interests through the courts. The successful use of those opportunities is what "legal mobilization" is all about.

Legal Mobilization: Context and Cautions

There are two obvious and important reservations about the legal mobilization argument. The first is suggested by Mandel, who objects strenuously to the "legalization of politics," both for the "fundamental dishonesty" of the form and the "authoritarian nature" of the process (1989). Bluntly, the democracy of the courts is not much of a democracy. The problem is that the courts constitute an elitist institution, which defines itself by a self-conscious and proud denial of any form of democratic accountability. Indeed, the courts constitute precisely the same claim to privileged power grounded in transcendent authority that modern democratic regimes replaced, sometimes with violence and never without considerable effort. The psychology is wrong for a practical operationalization of the democratic ethos. Even the terminology of the courts is wrong for a democrat: one does not "demand" but rather "submits" an argument for the consideration of the court, which then "finds" for one side or the other. The oracular mode of judicial dispensation is a far cry from the self-empowerment of real democratic practice.

The second reservation about legal mobilization derives from the argument that by and large the courts are an instrument not so much for delivery of justice as for preserving a status quo already divided into winners and losers and that those winners tend to have their status reinforced, not undermined, by the application of the law.

This reservation is valid. Nevertheless, the court system undeniably presents opportunities for the mobilization of legal authority — even if that mobilization proves more difficult for some groups than others. A flawed tool can still do a lot of work, and a multi-purpose machine can make some reasonable accommodation to a variety of uses. This does not deny that an awareness of the flaws must accompany the effective use of the tool.

Conclusion

In an important sense, the foregoing objections to legal mobilization are beside the point. The argument is not that the courts are perfectly democratic, which they clearly are not, nor that they are neutral tools equally serviceable in a wide variety of causes, which again they are not. Rather, the argument is that we must acknowledge that the courts exercise power, that judicial choices carry significant practical consequences, and that an increasing number of Canadians are becoming aware of these facts. Lawrence notes that "as the courts have become increasingly, explicitly, involved in decisions about 'who gets what, when and how,' and as legal realism and behavioralism have showed us that judicial decisions are not simply neutral readings of the law, we have been forced to acknowledge that courts are political, policy-making institutions" (1991, 466). This awareness is what causes the mobilization of law — not as a perfect solution but as a pragmatic adjustment to a new reality, and one to which the legal training and professional experience of judges in recent years has progressively prepared them (Kramer 1972, 268).

Not everyone will be happy with this emerging reality. Many judges who believe in the neutrality and objectivity of their function will be dismayed at the thought of being recruited for a variety of political purposes. Politicians will be annoyed by both the thought of being "end-run" by groups who use legal cases to make their arguments and by the practical consequences of their successes, however infrequent. Democrats will be concerned about the new primacy given to a privileged and self-governing profession based on frankly elitist principles. And left-wing and progressive groups will be outraged by the covert conservatism, the entrenchment of the status quo, the invisible advantages of privileged adversaries that the judicial process carries beneath its gleaming surface. All of them, perhaps, make the same mistake of assuming that this new world of judicial power, this new reality of law and its processes as instruments to be mobilized, represents a choice that we could somehow refuse or exchange for some shinier alternative. A realistic perspective — one that is neither naive about the neutral professionalism of legal practitioners nor cynical about their conscientiousness — may provide the only mood in which the new world of judicialized politics and mobilized law can be accommodated.

Carl von Clausewitz is remembered today for his famous dictum that war is nothing more than the continuation of politics by other means. His ideas transformed the way that politicians and generals, citizens and soldiers, thought about war and prepared for war, with consequences that we can read in every page of the history books (Keegan 1993). In the 1990s, for a growing number of Canadian individuals and groups, it is increasingly the case that the law and the courts are nothing more than a continuation of politics by other means, and this discovery will inevitably work a comparable trans-formation of the way that politicians and citizens and judges and litigants thinking about how courts operate and the way that the courts respond to these expectations. A corollary of Clausewitz's statement was the idea that war is too important a matter to leave to the generals; similarly, today the law has become too important a matter to leave to the lawyers and the judges, and only an informed public can navigate effectively within this new reality.

Notes

Chapter 3

1. In P.E.I., Supreme Court (Appeal Division).
2. Variously named; in Nova Scotia only, this court is divided into two levels with a Supreme Court and a County Court.
3. In Quebec since 1988, "the Court of Quebec," which merged into single judicial body the former Provincial Court, Court of the Sessions of the Peace, and Youth Court; in Ontario since 1989, "the Ontario Court of Justice (Provincial Division)."
4. In Quebec only, there are municipal courts in Montreal, Quebec City, and Laval.
5. In several provinces — in Manitoba, New Brunswick, and Prince Edward Island, and in Ontario since 1989 — this function is assigned to the provincial superior trial court.

Chapter 5

1. The Quebec Court of Queen's Bench/Banc du Roi (renamed the Court of Appeal/Cour d'Appel in 1976) retained until that date a vestigial but not insignificant trial jurisdiction that leads Russell to list only Ontario as having a specialized appeal court in 1867; and from the 1920s, the New Brunswick provincial superior court had a Chancery Division of trial judges that doubled as an appeal panel, on which basis the Chief Justice of New Brunswick has argued for an earlier pedigree for his court.
2. For example, some appeals are "by leave of the court" rather than by right," but in several provinces the decision on whether to grant leave is heard by a panel. If leave is granted, a decision will be made simultaneously on the merits. Also a single decision of the court may resolve a batch of related appeals, leaving it unclear whether this is one case or several.

Chapter 6

1. Public law is defined for present purposes as non-criminal litigation to which government officials, departments, or boards are parties in their governmental capacity. In some usages, "public" is used in a way that includes "criminal," but the more restricted meaning is intended here.
2. Includes appeals from superior trial courts *en banc* before the formation of specialized Courts of Appeal.
3. Those panels on which a judge did not participate for any reason — a significant factor only for the Laskin Court — are excluded.

Chapter 9

1. I use an American example because the closest Canadian analogue does not work very well for these purposes: in 1972, in *Rose v. The Queen* [(1972) 19 *Criminal Reports* (New Series) 66], a male accused unsuccessfully invoked the Canadian Bill of Rights to challenge the fact that the jury before which he was being tried included no women.
2. Many Canadians are surprised to discover that an appeal court could substitute a finding of guilty for an acquittal at trial, an option that appeal courts do not have in the United States. The Criminal Code has subsequently been amended to eliminate this possibility (and to restrict the appeal court in such a situation to ordering a new trial), largely because of this case.
3. Of course, if there was a "Case X," then this paragraph would be about it, not about *Morgentaler v. Regina*, so the logical problem I am describing would still remain.

Chapter 11

1. There can be situations in which the entire population is the "consumer population" — for example, when the Alberta Court of Appeal upheld the constitutionality of the Goods and Services Tax (GST) against the challenge of the Alberta government — and more generally the boundary between "consumer" and "secondary" populations can be problematic.
2. If it takes 10,000 votes to elect a representative in one riding but 30,000 or more in another, then it follows that a vote in the smaller riding is worth considerably more than one in the large riding.
3. This finding is doubly perverse: first, only the three prairie provinces have ever created these rural/urban categories in legislation,

and they have done so for only four redistributions including the one in question, which makes the notion less traditional than the Court implied; and second, pre-Charter practices are not the best guide to the meaning of the Charter, especially on the "dark side" of politics where electoral boundaries issues have long been resolved.

Sources Cited

Abel, Richard L. "Comparative Sociology of the Legal Professions." In *Lawyers in Society: Volume III, Comparative Theories*, edited by Richard L. Abel and Philip S.C. Lewis. Berkeley, Los Angeles, and London: University of California Press, 1988.

Abel, Richard L., and Philip S.C. Lewis. "Putting Law Back into the Sociology of Lawyers." In *Lawyers in Society: Volume III, Comparative Theories*, edited by Richard L. Abel and Philip S.C. Lewis. Berkeley, Los Angeles, and London: University of California Press, 1988.

Abella, Madame Justice Rosalie Silberman. "Speech from Her Swearing-In Ceremony at the Court of Appeal for Ontario." *Ottawa Law Review* 24 (1992).

Abraham, Henry J. *The Judicial Process: An Introductory Analysis of the Courts of the United States, England and France.* New York and Oxford: Oxford University Press, 1986.

Appleby, Ronald, and A. Lorne Greenspoon. "The Tax Court of Canada and the Tax Appeal Process." *Advocates' Quarterly* 5 (1984–85).

Arthurs, Harry W., Richard Weisman, and Frederick H. Zemans. "Canadian Lawyers: A Peculiar Professionalism." In *Lawyers in Society: Volume I: The Common Law World*, edited by Richard L. Abel and Philip S.C. Lewis. Berkeley, Los Angeles, and London: University of California Press, 1988.

Atkins, Burton M. "Interventions and Power in Judicial Hierarchies: Appellate Courts in England and the United States." *Law and Society Review* 24 (1990).

————. "Party Capability Theory as an Explanation for Intervention Behavior in the English Court of Appeal." *American Journal of Political Science* 35 (1991).

Atkins, Burton M., and Henry R. Glick. "Environments and Structural Variables as Determinants of Issues in State Courts of Last Resort." *American Journal of Political Science* 20 (1976).

Atkins, Burton M., and Justin J. Green. "Consensus on the United States Courts of Appeals: Illusion or Reality?" *American Journal of Political Science* 20 (1976).

Aubert, Vilhelm. *In Search of Law*. Totowa, N.Y.: Barnes and Noble, 1983.

Axworthy, Christopher S. "A Small Claims Court for Nova Scotia—Role of the Law and the Judge." *Dalhousie Law Journal* (1978).

Baar, Carl. "Social Facts, Court Delay and the Charter." In *Law, Politics and the Judicial Process in Canada*, edited by F.L. Morton. 2nd ed. Calgary: University of Calgary Press, 1992.

———. "The Zuber Report: The Decline and Fall of Court Reform in Ontario." *Windsor Yearbook of Access to Justice* 8 (1988).

Baar, Carl, and Ellen Baar. "Diagnostic Adjudication in Appellate Courts: The Supreme Court of Canada and the Charter." *Osgoode Hall Law Journal* 27 (1986).

Baar, Carl, et al. "The Ontario Court of Appeal and Expeditious Justice." *Osgoode Hall Law Journal* 30 (1992).

Bailie, Warren R., and David Johnson. "Drawing the Electoral Line." *Policy Options* 13 (1992).

Baker, J.H. *An Introduction to English Legal History*. 2nd ed. London: Butterworths, 1979.

Bale, Gordon. *Chief Justice William Johnstone Ritchie: Responsible Government and Judicial Review*. Ottawa: Carleton University Press, 1991.

Barak, Aharon. *Judicial Discretion*. New Haven and London: Yale University Press, 1987.

Baudoin, J.L. "Chronique de Droit Civil Québécois: Session 1985–1986." *Supreme Court Law Review* 9 (1987).

———. "Chronique de Droit Civil Québécois: Session 1986–1987." *Supreme Court Law Review* 10 (1988).

Beatty, David. "A Conservative's Court: The Politicization of Law." *University of Toronto Law Journal* 41 (1991).

Becker, T.L., and M. Feely, eds. *The Impact of Supreme Court Decisions*. New York: Oxford University Press, 1973.

Bickel, Alexander. *The Least Dangerous Branch: The Supreme Court at the Bar of Politics*. Indianapolis: Bobbs-Merrill, 1962.

Blackshield, Anthony R. "Five Types of Judicial Decision." *Osgoode Hall Law Journal* 12 (1974).

Blankenburg, Erhard, and Ulrike Schultz. "German Advocates: A Highly Regulated Profession." In *Lawyers in Society: Volume II, The Civil Law World,* edited by Richard L. Abel and Philip S.C. Lewis. Berkeley, Los Angeles, and London: University of California Press, 1988.

Blom-Cooper, Louis, and Gavin Drewry. *The Final Appeal: A Study of the House of Lords in Its Judicial Capacity.* Oxford: Oxford University Press, 1972.

Bourgeois, Donald J. *Public Law in Canada.* Scarborough: Nelson, 1990.

Boyle, Christine. "A Feminist Approach to Criminal Defences." In *Canadian Perspectives in Legal Theory,* edited by Richard F. Devlin. Toronto: Emond Montgomery, 1991.

Brace, Paul, and Melinda Gann Hall. "Neo-Institutionalism and Dissent in State Supreme Courts." *Journal of Politics* 52 (1990).

Bradley, Craig M. "The Uncertainty Principle in the Supreme Court." *Duke Law Journal* 1986.

Brannigan, Augustine. *Crimes, Courts and Corrections: An Introduction to Crime and Social Control in Canada.* Toronto: Holt, Rinehart and Winston, 1984.

Brantingham, P.J., and P.L. Brantingham. *Patterns in Crime.* New York: Macmillan, 1984.

Brodie, Ian Ross. "Interest Groups and the Charter of Rights and Freedoms: Interveners at the Supreme Court of Canada." M.A. thesis, Department of Political Science, University of Calgary, April 1992.

Burley, A.-M. and W. Mattli. "Europe before the Court: A Political Theory of Legal Integration." *International Organization* 47 (1993).

Bushnell, S.I. "Leave to Appeal Applications to the Supreme Court: A Matter of Public Importance." *Supreme Court Law Review* 3 (1982). Updated annual comments have appeared in each volume since 1986.

———. "The Use of American Cases." *University of New Brunswick Law Journal* 35 (1986).

Bushnell, Ian. *The Captive Court: A Study of the Supreme Court of Canada.* Montreal and Kingston: McGill-Queen's University Press, 1992.

Cairns, Alan C. "The Judicial Committee and Its Critics." *Canadian Journal of Political Science* 4 (1971).

Caldeira, Gregory. "The Transmission of Legal Precedent: A Study of State Supreme Courts." *American Political Science Review* 79 (1985).

Canada. *Canada Year Book 1992*. Ottawa: Government of Canada, 1991.

Canada. *The Charter of Rights and Freedoms: A Guide for Canadians*. Ottawa: Government of Canada, 1982.

Canon, Bradley C. "Courts and Policy: Compliance, Implementation and Impact." In *The American Courts: A Critical Assessment*, edited by John B. Gates and Charles A. Johnson. Washington, D.C.: CQ Press, 1991.

Canon, Bradley C., and Lawrence Baum. "Patterns of Adoption in Tort Law Innovations: An Application of Diffusion Theory." *American Political Science Review* 75 (1981).

Canon, Bradley C., and Michael Giles. "Recurring Litigants: Federal Agencies before the Supreme Court." *Western Political Quarterly* 25 (1972).

Canon, Bradley C., and Dean Jaros. "External Variables, Institutional Structure and Dissent on State Supreme Courts." *Polity* 4 (1970).

Carter, Lief H. *Contemporary Constitutional Lawmaking: The Supreme Court and the Art of Politics*. New York, Oxford, and Toronto: Pergamon Press 1985.

Carter, P.B. "Do Courts Decide According to the Evidence?" *University of British Columbia Law Review* 22 (1988).

Carty, K.C. "The Electoral Boundary Revolution in Canada." *American Review of Canadian Studies* 15 (1985).

Curtis, Dennis E., and Judith Resnick. "Images of Justice." *Yale Law Journal* 96 (1987).

Damaska, Mirjan R. *The Faces of Justice and State Authority: A Comparative Approach to the Legal Process*. New Haven and London: Yale University Press, 1986.

D'Amato, Anthony. "Can/Should Computers Replace Judges?" *Georgia Law Review* 11 (1977).

Davis, Peggy C. "'There is a Book Out ...': An Analysis of Judicial Absorption of Legislative Facts." *Harvard Law Review* 100 (1987).

Davis, Sue. "The Impact of President Carter's Judicial Selection Reforms: A Voting Analysis of the United States Courts of Appeals." *American Politics Quarterly* 14 (1986).

Denning, Alfred, Lord. *Freedom under Law*. London: Stevens, 1949.

Dyck, Rand. *Canadian Politics: Critical Approaches.* Scarborough: Nelson Canada, 1993.

Dubois, Philip L. "The Illusion of Judicial Consensus Revisited: Partisan Conflict on an Intermediate State Court of Appeals." *American Journal of Political Science* 32 (1988).

Eberts, Mary. "New Facts for Old: Observations on the Judicial Process." In *Canadian Perspectives in Legal Theory,* edited by Richard F. Devlin. Toronto: Emond Montgomery, 1991.

Edwards, Harry T. "The Role of a Judge in Modern Society: Some Reflections on Current Practice in Federal Appellate Adjudication." *Cleveland State Law Review* 32 (1983).

Epstein, Lee, and Karen O'Connor. "States and the U.S. Supreme Court: An Examination of Litigation Outcomes." *Social Sciences Quarterly* 69 (1988).

Fair, Daryl R. "State Intermediate Appellate Courts: An Introduction." *Western Political Quarterly* 24 (1971).

Fallers, Lloyd. *Law without Precedent.* Chicago: University of Chicago Press, 1969.

Feeley, Malcolm M., and Deborah L. Little. "The Vanishing Female: The Decline of Women in the Criminal Process, 1687–1912." *Law and Society Review* 25 (1991).

Felstiner, William L.F., et al. "The Emergence and Transformation of Disputes: Naming, Blaming, Claiming ..." *Law and Society Review* 15 (1980–81).

Frank, Jerome. *Courts on Trial: Myth and Reality in American Justice.* Princeton: Princeton University Press, 1949.

Friedman, Lawrence M. "Lawyers in Cross-Cultural Perspective." In *Lawyers in Society: Volume III, Comparative Theories,* edited by Richard L. Abel and Philip S.C. Lewis. Berkeley, Los Angeles, and London: University of California Press, 1988.

Friedman, Lawrence M., et al. "State Supreme Courts: A Century of Style and Citation." *Stanford Law Review* 33 (1981).

Galanter, Marc. "Explaining Litigation." *Law and Society* 9 (1975).

———. "The Legal Malaise; or, Justice Observed" *Law and Society Review* 19 (1985).

———. "Reading the Landscape of Disputes: What We Know and Don't Know and Think We Know about Our Allegedly Contentious and Litigious Society." *UCLA Law Review* 31 (1983).

———. "Why the 'Haves' Come Out Ahead: Speculations on the Limits of Legal Change." *Law and Society* 8 (1974).

Galanter, Marc, et al. "The Crusading Judge: Judicial Activism in Trial Courts." *Southern California Law Review* 52 (1979).

Galloway, Donald. "Critical Mistakes." In *Canadian Perspectives in Legal Theory,* edited by Richard F. Devlin. Toronto: Emond Montgomery, 1991.

George, Tracey E., and Lee Epstein. "On the Nature of Supreme Court Decision Making." *American Political Science Review* 86 (1992).

Gibson, Dale. "Case Comment." *Canadian Bar Review* 69 (1990).

———. "The Crumbling Pyramid: Constitutional Appeal Rights in Canada." *University of New Brunswick Law Journal* 38 (1989).

Gilligan, Carol. *In a Different Voice.* Cambridge, MA: Harvard University Press, 1982.

Gilmore, Grant. "Legal Realism: Its Cause and Cure." *Yale Law Journal* 70 (1961).

Glasbeek, H.J. "Contempt for Workers." *Osgoode Hall Law Journal* 28 (1990).

Goldman, Sheldon, and Thomas R. Jahnige. *The Federal Courts as a Political System.* New York: Harper and Row, 1976.

Goldman, Sheldon, and Austin Sarat, eds. *American Court Systems.* San Francisco: W. H. Freeman and Co., 1978.

Gottschall, Jon. "Carter's Judicial Appointments: The Influence of Affirmative Action and Merit Selection on the U.S. Courts of Appeals." *Judicature* 67 (1983).

———. "Reagan's Appointments of the U.S. Courts of Appeals: The Continuation of a Judicial Revolution." *Judicature* 70 (1986).

Greene, Ian. "The Doctrine of Judicial Independence Developed by the Supreme Court of Canada." *Osgoode Hall Law Journal* 26 (1988).

———. "The Zuber Report and Court Management." *Windsor Yearbook of Access to Justice* 8 (1988).

Greene, Ian, and Paul Shaffer. "Leave to Appeal and Leave to Commence Judicial Review in Canada's Refugee-Determination System: Is the Process Fair?" *International Journal of Refugee Law* 4 (1992).

Greene, Ian, et al. "The Young Offenders Act: The Alberta Youth Court Experience in the First Year." *Canadian Journal of Family Law* 5 (1986).

Griffiths, Curt T., John F. Klein, and Simon N. Verdun-Jones. *Criminal Justice in Canada: An Introductory Text.* Toronto: Butterworths, 1980.

Griffiths, Curt T., and Simon N. Verdun-Jones. *Canadian Criminal Justice*. Toronto and Vancouver: Butterworths, 1989.

Gruhl, John, et al. "Women as Policymakers: The Case of Trial Judges." *American Journal of Political Science* 25 (1981).

Hall, Melinda Gann, and Paul Brace. "Order in the Courts: A Neo-Institutional Approach to Judicial Consensus." *Western Political Quarterly* 42 (1989).

Haney, Craig. "Psychology and Legal Change: On the Limits of a Factual Jurisprudence." *Law and Human Behavior* 4 (1980).

Hatherly, Mary E. "The Chilling Effect of Section 96 on Dispute Resolution." *University of New Brunswick Law Journal* 37 (1988).

Heard, Andrew D. *Canadian Constitutional Conventions: The Marriage of Law and Politics*. Toronto: Oxford University Press, 1991.

———. "The Charter in the Supreme Court of Canada: The Importance of Which Judges Hear an Appeal." *Canadian Journal of Political Science* 24 (1991).

Heiner, Ronald A. "Imperfect Decisions and the Law: On the Evolution of Legal Precedents and Rules." *Journal of Legal Studies* 15 (1986).

Henderson, Thomas, and Cornelius M. Kerwin. "The Changing Character of Court Organization." *Justice System Journal* 7 (1982).

Hodder-Williams, Richard. *The Politics of the U.S. Supreme Court*. London: George Allen and Unwin, 1980.

Hogg, Peter. *Constitutional Law of Canada*. 3rd ed. Toronto: Carswell, 1992.

Holland, Kenneth M. "The Courts in the United States." In *Political Role of Law Courts in Modern Democracies,* edited by Jerold A. Waltman and Kenneth M. Holland. London: Macmillan, 1988.

Howard, J. Woodford. "Litigation Flow in Three U.S. Courts of Appeals." *Law and Society Review* 8 (1973).

———. "Role Perceptions and Behavior in Three U.S. Courts of Appeals." *Journal of Politics* 39 (1977).

Johnson, Charles A., and Bradley C. Canon. *Judicial Policies: Implementation and Impact*. Washington DC: CQ Press, 1984.

Kagan, et al. "The Evolution of State Supreme Courts." *Michigan Law Review* 76 (1978).

Katsch, M. Ethan *The Electronic Media and the Transformation of Law*. New York and Oxford: Oxford University Press, 1989.

Kearney, Richard, and Reginald S. Sheehan. "Supreme Court Decisionmaking: The Impact of Court Composition on State and Local Governments." *Journal of Politics* 54 (1992).

Kerans, Roger P. "A Review of Standards of Review." Paper presented at National Judicial Institute Canadian Appellate Court Seminar, Quebec City, April 1993.

Kerwin, Cornelius M., et al. "Adjudicatory Processes and the Organization of Trial Courts." *Judicature* 70 (1986).

Kornhauser, Lewis A., and Lawrence G. Sager. "Unpacking the Court." *Yale Law Journal* 96 (1986–87).

Kramer, Daniel C. "Courts, Legislatures and Social Reform: A Comparative Study." *Comparative Politics* 3 (1972).

Krislov, Samuel. "Theoretical Perspectives on Case Load Studies: A Critique and a Beginning." In *Empirical Theories about Courts,* edited by Keith O. Boyum and Lynn Mather. New York and London: Longman, 1983.

Kritzer, Herbert M. "Fee Arrangements and Fee Shifting: Lessons from the Experience in Ontario." *Law and Contemporary Problems* 47 (1984).

Kritzer, Herbert M., et al. "The Aftermath of Injury: Cultural Factors in Compensation Seeking in Canada and the United States." *Law and Society Review* 25 (1991). 499.

————. "The Impact of Fee Arrangement on Lawyer Effort." *Law and Society Review* 19 (1985).

Lachapelle, Guy, et al. *The Quebec Democracy: Structures, Processes and Policies.* Toronto: McGraw-Hill Ryerson, 1993.

Lafon, Jacqueline Lucienne. "The Judicial Career in France: Theory and Practice under the Fifth Republic." *Judicature* 75 (1991).

Landes, William M., and Richard A. Posner. "Legal Precedent: A Theoretical and Empirical Analysis." *Journal of Law and Economics* 19 (1976).

Lawrence, Susan E. "Justice, Democracy, Litigation and Political Participation." *Social Science Quarterly* 72 (1991).

————. "Participation through Mobilization of the Law: Institutions Providing Indigents with Access to the Civil Courts." *Polity* 23 (1991).

Lawlor, Reed C. "Personal Stare Decisis." *Southern California Law Review* 41 (1968).

Lewis, Philip S.C. "Comparison and Change in the Study of Legal Professions." In *Lawyers in Society: Volume III, Comparative Theories,* edited by Richard L. Abel and Philip S.C. Lewis.

Berkeley, Los Angeles, and London: University of California Press, 1988.

L'Heureux-Dubé, Claire. "The Length and Plurality of Supreme Court of Canada Decisions." *Alberta Law Review* 28 (1990).

Little Bear, Leroy. "Dispute Settlement among the Naidanac." In *Canadian Perspectives in Legal Theory,* edited by Richard F. Devlin. Toronto: Emond Montgomery, 1991.

Lyon, Noel. "Is Amendment of s.96 Really Necessary?" *University of New Brunswick Law Review* 36 (1987).

McConkie, Stanford S. "Decision-making in State Supreme Courts: A Look inside the Conference Room." *Judicature* 59 (1976).

McConnell, W.H. *Commentary on the British North America Act.* Toronto: Macmillan, 1977.

McCormick, Peter. "Caseload and Output of the Manitoba Court of Appeal 1990." *Manitoba Law Review* 21 (1992).

———. "Do Provincial Inferior Courts Deliver Inferior Justice?" *Windsor Yearbook of Access to Justice* 13 (1993).

———. "Judicial Councils for Provincial Judges in Canada." *Windsor Yearbook of Access to Justice* 6 (1986).

———. "Party Capability Theory and Appellate Success in the Supreme Court of Canada, 1949–1992." *Canadian Journal of Political Science* 26 (1993).

McCormick, Peter, and Twyla Job. "Do Women Judges Make a Difference?" *Canadian Journal of Law and Society* 8 (1993).

McCormick, Peter (with W.D. Griffiths). "Canadian Courts of Appeal: A Comparison of Procedures 1993." Paper presented at National Judicial Institute, Canadian Appellate Court Seminar, Montreal, April 1993.

McCormick, Peter, and Ian Greene, *Judges and Judging: Inside the Canadian Judicial System.* Toronto: James Lorimer and Co., 1990.

———. "The Provincial Judicial Setting." Paper presented at Canadian Political Science Association Annual Meeting (Learned Societies), Guelph, Ontario, June 1984.

McEvoy, John. "The Constitutionality of Canada's Youth Court under the *Young Offenders Act.*" *McGill Law Journal* 32 (1986).

———. "Courts of Criminal Jurisdiction and Section 96: An Overdue Evaluation." *University of New Brunswick Law Journal* 36 (1987).

———. "The Division of Powers and the Reference Power: Is There a Right to Refuse?" *Supreme Court Law Review* 10 (1988).

McIntosh, Wayne. "A State Court's Clientele: Exploring the Strategy of Trial Litigation." *Law and Society Review* 19 (1985).

————. "Courts and Socioeconomic Change." In *The American Courts: A Critical Assessment,* edited by John B. Gates and Charles A. Johnson. Washington, DC: CQ Press, 1991.

————. "150 Years of Litigation and Dispute Settlement: A Court Tale." *Law and Society Review* 15 (1981).

McIntosh, Wayne. "Private Use of a Public Forum: A Long Range View of the Dispute Processing Role of Courts." *American Political Science Review* 77 (1983).

Mandel, Michael. *The Charter of Rights and the Legalization of Politics in Canada.* Toronto: Wall and Thompson, 1989.

Mander, Jerry. *Four Arguments for the Elimination of Television.* New York: Quill, 1978.

Manfredi, Christopher. *Judicial Power and the Charter: Canada and the Paradox of Liberal Constitutionalism.* Toronto: McClelland and Stewart, 1993.

Marvell, Thomas B. "State Appellate Court Responses to Caseload Growth." *Judicature* 72 (1989).

Masse, Claude. "Chronique de Droit Civil Québécois: Session 1988–89." *Supreme Court Law Review* 1 (2nd series) (1991).

Mather, Lynn, and Barbara Yngvesson. "Language, Audience and the Transformation of Disputes." *Law and Society Review* 15 (1980).

Mefford, Dwain. "Case-Based Reasoning, Legal Reasoning and the Study of Politics." *Political Behavior* 12 (1990).

Menkel-Meadow, Carrie. "The Comparative Sociology of Women Lawyers: The 'Feminization' of the Legal Profession." *Osgoode Hall Law Journal* 24 (1986).

Merry, Sally Engle, and Susan S. Silbey. "What Do Plaintiffs Want? Reexamining the Concept of Dispute." *Justice System Journal* 9 (1984).

Merryman, Henry. "Towards a Theory of Citations: An Empirical Study of the Citation Practices of the California Supreme Court in 1950, 1960 and 1970." *Southern California Law Review* 50 (1977).

Millar, Perry S., and Carl Baar, *Judicial Administration in Canada.* Kingston and Montreal: McGill-Queen's University Press, 1981.

Monahan, Patrick. *Politics and the Constitution: The Charter, Federalism and the Supreme Court of Canada.* Toronto, New York, and London: Carswell/Methuen, 1987.

Monture, Patricia A. "Reflecting on Flint Woman." In *Canadian Perspectives in Legal Theory,* edited by Richard F. Devlin. Toronto: Emond Montgomery, 1991.

Moore, Robert J. "Reflections of Canadians on the Law and the Legal System: Legal Research Institute Survey of Respondents in Montreal, Toronto and Winnipeg." In *Law in a Cynical Society,* edited by Dale Gibson and Janet K. Baldwin. Calgary and Vancouver: Carswell, 1985.

Morrow, W.G. "The Last Case." *Alberta Law Review* 16 (1978).

Morton, F.L. *Morgentaler v. Borowski: Abortion, the Charter and the Courts.* Toronto: McClelland and Stewart, 1992.

Morton, F.L., and Rainer Knopf. "Does the Charter Mandate 'One Person, One Vote'?" *Alberta Law Review* 30 (1992).

Morton, F.L., et al. "The Supreme Court of Canada's First One Hundred Charter of Rights Decisions, 1982–1989." *Osgoode Hall Law Journal* 30 (1992).

Mullan, David. "The Uncertain Constitutional Position of Canada's Administrative Appeal Tribunals." *Ottawa Law Review* 14 (1982).

Neely, Richard. *How the Courts Govern America.* New Haven and London: Yale University Press, 1981.

———. *Why Courts Don't Work.* New York: McGraw-Hill, 1983.

Oaks, D. H. "Studying the Exclusionary Rule in Search and Seizure." *University of Chicago Law Review* 37 (1970).

Olson, Walter K. *The Litigation Explosion: What Happened When America Unleashed the Lawsuit.* New York: Truman Talley Books/Dutton, 1991.

Palmer, Jan. "An Econometric Analysis of the U.S. Supreme Court's Certiorari Decisions." *Public Choice* 39 (1982).

Pannick, David *Judges.* Oxford and New York: Oxford University Press, 1988.

Posner, Richard A. *The Problems of Jurisprudence.* Cambridge, MA, and London: Harvard University Press, 1990.

Postman, Neil. *Technopoly: The Surrender of Culture to Technology.* New York: Knopf, 1992.

Rabkin, Jeremy. *Judicial Compulsions: How Public Law Distorts Public Policy.* New York: Basic Books, 1989.

Radamaker, Dallis. "The Courts in France." In *Political Role of Law Courts in Modern Democracies,* edited by Jerold A. Waltman and Kenneth M. Holland. London: Macmillan, 1988.

Ratushny, Edward. "Judicial Appointments: The Lang Legacy." In *The Canadian Judiciary,* edited by Allen M. Linden. Toronto: Osgoode Hall Law School, 1976.

————. "What Are Administrative Tribunals? Pursuit of Uniformity in Diversity." *Canadian Public Administration* 30 (1987).

Rosenberg, Gerald N. *The Hollow Hope: Can Courts Bring About Social Change?* Chicago and London: The University of Chicago Press, 1991.

Russell, Peter H. "Bold Statescraft, Questionable Jurisprudence." In *And No One Cheered: Federalism, Democracy and The Constitution Act,* edited by Keith Banting and Richard Simeon. Toronto: Methuen, 1983.

————. "Constitutional Law/Judicial Independence/Whether a Provincial Commission of Inquiry can Require Judges to Explain How and Why They Made Certain Decisions: *MacKeigan v. Hickman.*" *Canadian Bar Review* 69 (1991).

————. "Judicial Power in Canada's Political Culture." In *Courts and Trials: A Multi-disciplinary Approach,* edited by M.L. Friedland. Toronto: University of Toronto Press, 1975.

————. *The Judiciary in Canada: The Third Branch of Government.* Toronto: McGraw-Hill Ryerson, 1987.

————. "The Political Role of the Supreme Court in Its First Century." *Canadian Bar Review* 53 (1975).

Russell, Peter H., and Jacob S. Ziegel. "Federal Judicial Appointments: An Appraisal of the First Mulroney Government's Appointments and the New Judiciary Advisory Committees." *University of Toronto Law Journal* 41 (1991).

Salhany, Justice Roger. "Ethnic Bias in the Courts." Paper presented at National Judicial Institute, 1993 Canadian Appellate Court Seminar, Montreal, April 1993.

Sarat, Austin. "Studying American Legal Culture: An Assessment of Survey Evidence." *Law and Society Review* 11 (1977).

Schattschneider, E.E. *The Semisovereign People.* Hinsdale, IL: Dryden, 1975.

Schauer, Frederick. "Easy Cases." *Southern California Law Review* 58 (1985).

————. "Precedent." *Stanford Law Review* 39 (1987).

Scheingold, Stuart A. *The Politics of Rights: Lawyers, Public Policy and Political Change.* New Haven and London: Yale University Press, 1974.

Schiff, Stanley A. *Evidence in the Litigation Process.* 2 vols. Toronto: Carswell, 1978.

Shapiro, Martin. *Courts: A Comparative and Political Analysis.* Chicago and London: University of Chicago Press, 1981.

———. *The Supreme Court and Administrative Agencies.* New York: Free Press, 1968.

Shapiro, Martin, and Alec Stone. "The New Constitutional Politics of Europe." *Comparative Political Studies* 26 (1994).

Sheehan, Reginald S. "Governmental Litigants, Underdogs and Civil Liberties: A Reassessment of a Trend in Supreme Court Decision-making." *Western Political Quarterly* 45 (1992).

Shklar, Judith N. *Legalism: Law, Morals and Political Trials.* Cambridge, MA, and London: Harvard University Press, 1964 and 1986.

Silbey, Susan. "Making Sense of Lower Courts." *Justice System Journal* 6 (1981).

Simpson, Jeffrey. *Spoils of Power: The Politics of Patronage.* Toronto: Collins, 1988.

Snell, James G., and Frederick Vaughan, *The Supreme Court of Canada: History of the Institution.* Toronto: University of Toronto Press, 1985.

Songer, Donald R., and Reginald S. Sheehan. "Supreme Court Impact on Compliance and Outcomes: *Miranda* and *New York Times* in the United States Courts of Appeals." *Western Political Quarterly* 43 (1990).

Songer, Donald, and Reginald Sheehan. "Who Wins on Appeal? Upperdogs and Underdogs in the United States Courts of Appeals." *American Journal of Political Science* 36 (1992).

Sopinka, John. "Intervention." *The Advocate* 46 (1988).

Sopinka, John, et al. *The Law of Evidence in Canada.* Toronto: Butterworths, 1992.

Spohn, Cassia. "Decision Making in Sexual Assault Cases: Do Black and Female Judges Make a Difference?" *Women and Criminal Justice* 2 (1990).

———. "The Sentencing Decisions of Black and White Judges: Expected and Unexpected Similarities." *Law and Society Review* 24 (1990).

Stager, David A.A., and Harry W. Arthurs. *Lawyers in Canada.* Toronto, Buffalo, and London: University of Toronto Press, 1990.

Stern, F.M. "Remedies for Appellate Overload." *Judicature* 72 (1988).

Stookey, John A. "Trials and Tribulations: Crises, Litigation and Legal Change." *Law and Society Review* 24 (1990).

Strayer, Barry L. *The Canadian Constitution and the Courts: The Function and Scope of Judicial Review*. Toronto and Vancouver: Butterworths, 1988.

Supreme Court of Canada. *Statistics 1992*. Bulletin of Proceedings/Special Edition. 5 May 1993.

Szelenyi, Ivan, and Bill Martin. "The Legal Profession and the Rise and Fall of the New Class." In *Lawyers in Society: Volume III, Comparative Theories*, edited by Richard L. Abel and Philip S.C. Lewis. Berkeley, Los Angeles, and London: University of California Press, 1988.

Taggart, Michael. "Should Canadian Judges Be Legally Required to Give Reasoned Decisions in Civil Cases?" *University of Toronto Law Journal* 33 (1983).

Tate, Neil. "Explaining the Decision-Making of the Canadian Supreme Court 1949–1985: Extending the Personal Attributes Model across Nations." *Journal of Politics* 51 (1989).

Terrell, Timothy P. "Flatlaw: An Essay on the Dimensions of Legal Reasoning and the Development of Fundamental Normative Principles." *California Law Review* 72 (1984).

Tomasi, Timothy B., and Jess A. Velona. "All the President's Men: A Study of Ronald Reagan's Appointments to the U.S. Courts of Appeals." *Columbia Law Review* 87 (1987).

Uhlman, Thomas M. "Black Elite Decision Making: The Case of Trial Judges." *American Journal of Political Science* 22 (1978).

Ulmer, S. Sidney. "Governmental Litigants, Underdogs and Civil Liberties in the Supreme Court: 1903–1968 Terms." *Journal of Politics* 47 (1985).

Van Caenegem, R.C. *Judges, Legislators and Professors: Chapters in European Legal History*. Cambridge and New York: Cambridge University Press, 1987.

VanKoppen, Peter, and Jan TenKate. "Individual Differences in Judicial Behavior: Personal Characteristics and Private Law." *Law and Society Review* 18 (1984).

Vaughan, Frederick. "Critics of the Judicial Committee of the Privy Council: The New Orthodoxy and an Alternative Explanation." *Canadian Journal of Political Science* 19 (1986).

Vidmar, Neil. "The Small Claims Court: A Reconceptualization of Disputes and an Empirical Investigation." *Law and Society Review* 18 (1984).

Vines, Kenneth. "The Role of Circuit Courts of Appeals in the Federal Judicial Process: A Case Study." *Midwest Journal of Political Science* 7 (1963).

Walker, Thomas G., and Deborah J. Barrow. "The Diversification of the Federal Bench: Policy and Process Implications." *Journal of Politics* 47 (1985).

Wanner, Craig. "The Public Ordering of Private Relations: Part One, Initiating Civil Cases in Urban Trial Courts." *Law and Society* 8 (1974).

Wanner, Craig. "The Public Ordering of Private Relations: Part Two, Winning Civil Cases." *Law and Society* 9 (1975).

Wasby, Stephen L. *The Impact of the United States Supreme Court: Some Perspectives.* Homewood, IL: Dorsey Press, 1970.

———. "Toward Impact Theory: An Inventory of Hypotheses." In *The Impact of Supreme Court Decisions,* edited by T.L. Becker and M. Feely. New York: Oxford University Press, 1973.

———. *The Supreme Court in the Federal Judicial System.* 3rd ed. Chicago: Nelson-Hall, 1988.

Weiler, J.H.H. "A Quiet Revolution: The European Court of Justice and Its Interlocutors." *Comparative Political Studies* 26 (1994).

Weiler, Paul. *In the Last Resort: A Critical Study of the Supreme Court of Canada.* Toronto: Carswell, 1974.

———. "Legal Values and Judicial Decision-making." *Canadian Bar Review* 48 (1970).

———. "Two Models of Judicial Decision-making." *Canadian Bar Review* 46 (1968).

Welch, Karen. "No Room at the Top: Interest Group Interveners and Charter Litigation." *University of Toronto Faculty of Law Review* 43 (1985).

Wexler, Stephen. "Discretion: The Unacknowledged Side of Law." *University of Toronto Law Journal* 25 (1975).

———. "Non-judicial Decision-making." *Osgoode Hall Law Journal* 13 (1975).

Wheat, David. "Disposition of Civil Law Appeals by the Supreme Court of Canada." *Supreme Court Law Review* 1 (1980).

Wheeler, Stanton, et al. "Do the 'Haves' Come Out Ahead? Winning and Losing in State Supreme Courts, 1870–1970." *Law and Society Review* 21 (1987).

Wilson, Madame Justice Bertha. "Will Women Judges Really Make a Difference?" *Osgoode Hall Law Journal* 28 (1990).

Wold, John T. "Going through the Motions: The Monotony of Appellate Court Decisionmaking." *Judicature* 62 (1978–79).

Wold, John T., and Gregory A. Caldeira. "Perceptions of 'Routine' Decision-making in Five California Courts of Appeal." *Polity* 13 (1980–81).

Zemans, Frances Kahn. "Legal Mobilization: The Neglected Role of the Law in the Political System." *American Political Science Review* 77 (1983).

Zimmer, Warren K. "The Appeal Process." In *From Crime To Punishment,* edited by Joel E. Pink and David Perrier. Toronto: Carswell, 1988.

List of Cases

A.-G. Canada v. A.-G. Ontario [Labour Conventions] 1937 [A.C.] 326

A.-G. Canada v. Mossop [1993] 1 S.C.R. 801

A.-G. Ontario v. Winner (1954) A.C. 541

A.-G. Quebec v. Grondin [1983] 2 S.C.R. 364

Baker v. Carrd (1962) 369 U.S. 186

Borowski v. A.-G. Canada [Borowski #1] [1987] 39 D.L.R. (4th) 731

Borowski v. Can. [Borowski #2] [1989] 1 S.C.R. 342

Brown v. Board of Education (1954) 374 U.S. 483

Carter v. A.-G. Saskatchewan [1991] 2 S.C.R. 158

Dixon v. A.-G. British Columbia (1989) 59 D.L.R. (4th) 247 (B.C.S.C.)

Entinck v. Carrington [1765] 95 E.R. 807 [K.B.]

MacKay v. Manitoba [1989] 2 S.C.R. 357

MacKeigan v. Hickman [1989] 2 S.C.R. 796

McEvoy v. A.-G. New Brunswick [1983] S.C.R. 704

Moysa v. Alberta (1989) 60 D.L.R. (4th) 1

Patriation Reference [Re Resolution to Amend the Constitution] [1981] 1 S.C.R. 753

Pelech v. Pelech [1987] 1 S.C.R. 801

R. v. Askov [1990] 2 S.C.R. 1199

R. v. Big M Drug Mart [1985] 2 S.C.R. 295

R. v. Lavallée [1989] 1 S.C.R. 852

R. v. Lippé [1990] 2 S.C.R. 114

R. v. Morgentaler [Morgentaler #1] [1976] 1 S.C.R. 616

R. v. Morgentaler [Morgentaler #2] [1988] 1 S.C.R. 30

R. v. Morin [1992] 1 S.C.R. 771

R. v. Oakes [1986] 1 S.C.R. 103

R. v. Therens [1985] 1 S.C.R. 613

Re Residential Tenancies Act [1981] S.C.R. 714

Reynolds v. Sims (1964) 377 U.S. 533

Roncarelli v. Duplessis [1959] S.C.R. 121
Russell v. The Queen (1882) 7 App.Cas. 829
RWDSU v. Saskatchewan [1987] 1 S.C.R. 460
Sobeys Stores v. Yeomans [1989] 1 S.C.R. 238
Tremblay v. Daigle [1989] 2 S.C.R. 530
Valente v. R. [1985] 2 S.C.R. 673

Index